MAKING

BETTER

EXPANDING INFORMATION
TECHNOLOGY RESEARCH TO
MEET SOCIETY'S NEEDS

Committee on Information Technology Research
in a Competitive World

Computer Science and Telecommunications Board

Commission on Physical Sciences, Mathematics, and Applications

National Research Council

NATIONAL ACADEMY PRESS
Washington, D.C.

NATIONAL ACADEMY PRESS • 2101 Constitution Avenue, NW • Washington, DC 20418

NOTICE: The project that is the subject of this report was approved by the Governing Board of the National Research Council, whose members are drawn from the councils of the National Academy of Sciences, the National Academy of Engineering, and the Institute of Medicine. The members of the committee responsible for the report were chosen for their special competences and with regard for appropriate balance.

Support for this project was provided by the National Science Foundation under Sponsor Award Number ANI-9616857. Any opinions, findings, conclusions, or recommendations expressed in this material are those of the authors and do not necessarily reflect the views of the sponsor.

Library of Congress Cataloging-in-Publication Data

Making IT better : expanding information technology research to meet society's needs.
    p. cm.
ISBN 0-309-06991-2
1. Information technology. 2. Information technology—Social aspects. I. Title.
T58.5. M35 2000
303.48'33--dc21

                         00-009738

Making IT Better: Expanding Information Technology Research to Meet Society's Needs is available from the National Academy Press, 2101 Constitution Avenue, NW, Box 285, Washington, DC 20055 (1-800-624-6242 or 202-334-3313 in the Washington metropolitan area; Internet: http://www.nap.edu).

Copyright 2000 by the National Academy of Sciences. All rights reserved.

Printed in the United States of America

THE NATIONAL ACADEMIES

National Academy of Sciences
National Academy of Engineering
Institute of Medicine
National Research Council

The **National Academy of Sciences** is a private, nonprofit, self-perpetuating society of distinguished scholars engaged in scientific and engineering research, dedicated to the furtherance of science and technology and to their use for the general welfare. Upon the authority of the charter granted to it by the Congress in 1863, the Academy has a mandate that requires it to advise the federal government on scientific and technical matters. Dr. Bruce M. Alberts is president of the National Academy of Sciences.

The **National Academy of Engineering** was established in 1964, under the charter of the National Academy of Sciences, as a parallel organization of outstanding engineers. It is autonomous in its administration and in the selection of its members, sharing with the National Academy of Sciences the responsibility for advising the federal government. The National Academy of Engineering also sponsors engineering programs aimed at meeting national needs, encourages education and research, and recognizes the superior achievements of engineers. Dr. William A. Wulf is president of the National Academy of Engineering.

The **Institute of Medicine** was established in 1970 by the National Academy of Sciences to secure the services of eminent members of appropriate professions in the examination of policy matters pertaining to the health of the public. The Institute acts under the responsibility given to the National Academy of Sciences by its congressional charter to be an adviser to the federal government and, upon its own initiative, to identify issues of medical care, research, and education. Dr. Kenneth I. Shine is president of the Institute of Medicine.

The **National Research Council** was organized by the National Academy of Sciences in 1916 to associate the broad community of science and technology with the Academy's purposes of furthering knowledge and advising the federal government. Functioning in accordance with general policies determined by the Academy, the Council has become the principal operating agency of both the National Academy of Sciences and the National Academy of Engineering in providing services to the government, the public, and the scientific and engineering communities. The Council is administered jointly by both Academies and the Institute of Medicine. Dr. Bruce M. Alberts and Dr. William A. Wulf are chairman and vice chairman, respectively, of the National Research Council.

COMMITTEE ON INFORMATION TECHNOLOGY RESEARCH IN A COMPETITIVE WORLD

SAMUEL H. FULLER, Analog Devices, Inc., *Co-chair*
DAVID G. MESSERSCHMITT, University of California at Berkeley, *Co-chair*
PAUL BARAN, Com21, Inc.
LINDA COHEN, University of California at Irvine
JOHN A. COPELAND, Georgia Institute of Technology
ALBERT M. ERISMAN, The Boeing Company
DANIEL T. LING, Microsoft Corporation
ROBERT L. MARTIN, Lucent Technologies
JOEL MOSES, Massachusetts Institute of Technology
NORINE E. NOONAN, U.S. Environmental Protection Agency
    (formerly of the Florida Institute of Technology)
DAVID A. PATTERSON, University of California at Berkeley
STEWART PERSONICK, Drexel University (formerly of Bellcore)
ROBERT SPROULL, Sun Microsystems Laboratories
MARK WEISER,* Xerox Palo Alto Research Center
PATRICK WINDHAM, Windham Consulting
IRVING WLADAWSKY-BERGER, IBM Corporation

Staff

JERRY R. SHEEHAN, Senior Program Officer (Study Director)
LISA L. SHUM, Project Assistant (through August 1998)
D.C. DRAKE, Project Assistant (after August 1999)

---

*Deceased.

COMPUTER SCIENCE AND TELECOMMUNICATIONS BOARD

DAVID D. CLARK, Massachusetts Institute of Technology, *Chair*
JAMES CHIDDIX, Time Warner Cable
JOHN M. CIOFFI, Stanford University
ELAINE COHEN, University of Utah
W. BRUCE CROFT, University of Massachusetts at Amherst
SUSAN L. GRAHAM, University of California at Berkeley
JUDITH HEMPEL, University of California at San Francisco
JEFFREY M. JAFFE, Lucent Technologies Incorporated
ANNA KARLIN, University of Washington
BUTLER W. LAMPSON, Microsoft Corporation
EDWARD D. LAZOWSKA, University of Washington
DAVID LIDDLE, U.S. Venture Partners
TOM M. MITCHELL, WhizBang! Labs, Inc.
DONALD NORMAN, UNext.com
RAYMOND OZZIE, Groove Networks
DAVID A. PATTERSON, University of California at Berkeley
CHARLES SIMONYI, Microsoft Corporation
BURTON SMITH, Tera Computer Company
TERRY SMITH, University of California at Santa Barbara
LEE SPROULL, New York University

Staff

MARJORY S. BLUMENTHAL, Director
HERBERT S. LIN, Senior Scientist
JERRY R. SHEEHAN, Senior Program Officer
ALAN S. INOUYE, Program Officer
JON EISENBERG, Program Officer
GAIL PRITCHARD, Program Officer
JANET D. BRISCOE, Office Manager
DANIEL LLATA, Project Assistant
SUZANNE OSSA, Project Assistant
MICKELLE RODGERS RODRIGUEZ, Senior Project Assistant
D.C. DRAKE, Project Assistant
MARGARET MARSH, Project Assistant
BRANDYE WILLIAMS, Office Assistant

COMMISSION ON PHYSICAL SCIENCES, MATHEMATICS, AND APPLICATIONS

PETER M. BANKS, Veridian ERIM International, Inc., *Co-chair*
W. CARL LINEBERGER, University of Colorado, *Co-chair*
WILLIAM F. BALLHAUS, JR., Lockheed Martin Corporation
SHIRLEY CHIANG, University of California at Davis
MARSHALL H. COHEN, California Institute of Technology
RONALD G. DOUGLAS, Texas A&M University
SAMUEL H. FULLER, Analog Devices, Inc.
JERRY P. GOLLUB, Haverford College
MICHAEL F. GOODCHILD, University of California at Santa Barbara
MARTHA P. HAYNES, Cornell University
WESLEY T. HUNTRESS, JR., Carnegie Institution
CAROL M. JANTZEN, Westinghouse Savannah River Company
PAUL G. KAMINSKI, Technovation, Inc.
KENNETH H. KELLER, University of Minnesota
JOHN R. KREICK, Sanders, a Lockheed Martin Company (retired)
MARSHA I. LESTER, University of Pennsylvania
DUSA M. McDUFF, State University of New York at Stony Brook
JANET NORWOOD, Former Commissioner, U.S. Bureau of Labor Statistics
M. ELISABETH PATÉ-CORNELL, Stanford University
NICHOLAS P. SAMIOS, Brookhaven National Laboratory
ROBERT J. SPINRAD, Xerox PARC (retired)

MYRON F. UMAN, Acting Executive Director

This book is dedicated to the memory of Mark Weiser, whose untimely death in April 1999 prevented him from seeing the report's completion, but whose ideas, energy, and enthusiasm live on in its pages.

Preface

The United States enjoys an enviable position in the Information Age. The nation's information technology (IT) industry is thriving, and virtually every facet of society has been influenced by it. Indeed, IT is transforming a large—and growing—portion of the nation's economic and personal activities. As a result, IT-related issues are of interest to a widening circle of users, not just the vendors of IT products and services. These obvious trends do not, however, ensure continued progress in IT and its applications because they do not indicate whether sufficient investments are being made in IT research.

As previous reports by the Computer Science and Telecommunications Board (CSTB) of the National Research Council demonstrate,[1] the nation's leadership in the development and application of IT derives in large part from an effective program of research that has been conducted and managed jointly by industry, universities, and government since the end of World War II. Today's IT systems continue to draw on the knowledge base constructed by research conducted over the past five decades.

---

[1] The role of federal research funding in the innovation process has been examined in two CSTB reports: Computer Science and Telecommunications Board, National Research Council. 1995. *Evolving the High Performance Computing and Communications Initiative to Support the Nation's Information Infrastructure*. National Academy Press, Washington, D.C.; Computer Science and Telecommunications Board, National Research Council. 1999. *Funding a Revolution: Government Support for Computing Research*. National Academy Press, Washington, D.C.

Continued leadership and innovation in IT—and the continued flow of societal benefits that derive from such leadership—depend on suitable investments in IT research today and in the future. A critical examination is needed to define the kinds of research investment needed for the early twenty-first century, a time when IT will play a much more prominent role than it did in the second half of the twentieth century, when most of today's IT capabilities and expectations were built.

THE COMMITTEE AND ITS CHARGE

To improve understanding of these issues and help guide future endeavors, the National Science Foundation (NSF) asked CSTB to conduct a study of IT research that would examine ongoing trends in industry and academic research, determine the possible effects of those trends on the well-being of the nation's IT industry and the nation as a whole, and explore options for strengthening the research base, if necessary. Of particular interest is support for research that advances our fundamental understanding of capabilities, architectural designs, and principles that can have a pervasive influence on innovation throughout the IT industry (called "fundamental research" in this report) rather than advancing a single product, process, or service (called "applied research" in this report).[2] Is the nation investing sufficient resources in the types of research that will ensure its capability to innovate in the future, or have research investments become more narrowly targeted to near-term efforts? Representative issues include the following:[3]

- *Trends in IT research and development spending.* What trends in computing and communications industry research and development (R&D) spending can be documented, and at what level of detail? How has support for fundamental and more targeted research programs shifted? Is the overall level of effort sufficient?
- *The scope of IT research.* Are the scope and scale of computing and communications R&D changing? Is IT research sufficiently broad to

---

[2] The federal government tends to classify research as either "basic" or "applied." There is some correspondence between these terms and the terminology used in this report, as described in greater detail in Chapter 1.

[3] The original concept for the study also included attention to international issues, in particular, the relative position of U.S. research efforts in IT compared with those of other countries. As the project unfolded, issues of international competitiveness became less of a motivational factor. The growth of the Internet and U.S. IT industries led to a perception that the greatest threats to the nation's IT base were not external, but internal—the lack of fundamental understanding of large-scale systems and their broad range of societal applications.

address new challenges resulting from the convergence of computing and communications? Are government, universities, and industry well organized to conduct research across disciplinary boundaries?

- *Changes in private-sector support for research.* How do major technology market trends, such as the growing emphasis on and pervasiveness of network-based systems, affect private sector R&D investments? How do computing and communications companies of different sizes and types make R&D decisions, and how have the decision processes and outcomes been changing?
- *Mechanisms for strengthening IT research.* What are some promising approaches to filling in gaps in the research portfolio and/or sustaining the flow of R&D? Is the government investment adequate? What types of institutional approaches might be the focus of experimentation? What factors, structures, and mechanisms enable success in research collaborations?

To conduct the study, CSTB assembled a committee of 16 members with expertise in the IT industry, IT research, applications of IT in government and industry, the organization of IT research, and federal support for research. Members were drawn from both industry and academia and brought with them technical expertise in computing, communications, software, and devices. Several committee members had experience with federal research programs and backgrounds in economics and public policy.

The committee met five times between July 1997 and August 1998 to plan its course of action, solicit testimony from relevant experts, deliberate over its findings, and draft its final report. It continued its work by electronic communications throughout 1999 and into the beginning of 2000. During the course of the project, the committee heard from researchers and research managers in industry and universities and from directors of government agencies involved in funding computing research. It met with engineers involved in the development and deployment of sophisticated information systems for clients in a range of fields. The committee also gathered available statistics on IT research investments in the public and private sectors. These data have a number of limitations (as described in this report) so they could not by themselves provide definitive insight into trends in IT research. Accordingly, the committee supplemented the data with information provided by its members and by those who briefed the committee. This range of input was used to develop the conclusions and recommendations contained in the report. The unusually long time it took the committee to do its work reflects the challenges involved in integrating diverse inputs and perspectives and in shaping a contribution to the rapidly evolving national debate about IT and IT research.

During the committee's working period, a number of important developments took place that were factored into the committee's conclusions. Most notably, an advisory committee authorized by the High Performance Computing and Communications Act of 1991 and encouraged by earlier CSTB reports was finally established in 1997, albeit in a form tailored to suit the times: the President's Information Technology Advisory Committee (PITAC). The CSTB study committee and PITAC shared one common member (Irving Wladawsky-Berger), but the work of the two committees proceeded independently, preserving the CSTB committee's ability to offer its own perspective and comment on PITAC's work. The CSTB committee reviewed the interim and final reports from PITAC, as well as information on the Clinton Administration's Information Technology Research initiative (originally constituted as Information Technology for the Twenty-First Century, or IT^2) and ongoing federal programs, ensuring that the present report would be relevant to the evolving environment for federal support of IT research. Similarities between the main conclusions of this report and the PITAC report, which were arrived at independently, reflect a degree of consensus within the field regarding the research base for IT.

Although it attempted to complement the work of PITAC, the CSTB committee differentiated itself by (1) concentrating on two specific areas that it deemed to be of great importance to the nation and also insufficiently addressed by ongoing IT research initiatives and (2) relating its substantive research recommendations to an assessment of trends and supportive mechanisms for IT research. Rather than compete with PITAC or duplicate its work, the committee monitored the reception given to PITAC's recommendations and attempted to address questions that were raised about their rationale. The resulting report is a vehicle for maintaining the momentum imparted by PITAC—which itself drew on the evolution of thinking and programs throughout the 1990s—and for furthering the realignment of IT research to which PITAC and others have contributed. It draws on the work of other CSTB committees, which have looked in great detail at a number of specific components of the IT research arena and developed recommendations for IT research (both its substance and process) related to those components. Finally, the committee strove to present its conclusions in a form consistent with its intention to target the report at a broad, high-level audience, including policymakers, research managers in government and industry, corporate executives, and the research community.

ACKNOWLEDGMENTS

As with any project of this magnitude, thanks are due to the many individuals who contributed to the work of the committee. First, thanks are due to the members of the committee itself, who volunteered consid-érable time during the course of the study to attend meetings, engage in e-mail and telephone discussions, draft sections of the report, and respond to comments from external reviewers. Although they shared a common interest in IT research, committee members brought to the table a wide-ranging set of perspectives, concerns, and vocabularies that took time and effort to blend into a common view. Their overwhelming consensus on the main themes of this report is a testament to the importance of these themes to the field.

Beyond the committee, numerous persons provided valuable infor-mation through briefings to committee meetings. These presenters include John Best (IBM Almaden Research Center); Joel S. Birnbaum (Hewlett-Packard Co.); Timothy F. Bresnahan (Stanford University); Joseph K. Carter (Andersen Consulting); Vinton G. Cerf (MCI WorldCom); Ashok K. Chandra (IBM Almaden Research Center); Melvyn Ciment (then with NSF, now with the Potomac Institute); James A. Desveaux (UCLA); Fred Fath (Boeing Shared Services Group); Jim Gray (Microsoft Corporation); Anoop Gupta (Microsoft Corporation); Peter Hart (Ricoh); Juris Hartmanis (then with the NSF, now at Cornell University); John L. Hennessy (Stanford University); John Jankowski (NSF); Don E. Kash (George Mason University); Chuck Larson (Industrial Research Institute); Edward A. Lee (University of California at Berkeley); David Liddle (then with Interval Research, now with U.S. Venture Partners); Larry Lynn (then director of the Defense Advanced Research Projects Agency (DARPA)); Peter G. Neumann (SRI International); Greg Papadopoulos (Sun Microsystems); Richard Pledereder (Sybase, Inc.); Robert W. Rycroft (George Mason University); David Tennenhouse (then with DARPA, now with Intel Corpo-ration); and Gilbert Weigand (then with the Department of Energy).

Others also provided valuable assistance to the committee behind the scenes. Raymond Wolfe at the NSF provided detailed statistics on indus-try R&D spending and answered numerous questions about the data. Elinor Champion, Andrew Hildreth, Nelson Lim, Janet Shapiro, Mary Streitwieser, and Ron Taylor at the Census Bureau helped committee members and staff navigate the process of accessing detailed data on corporate R&D spending. Hoyle Curtis provided information on research expenditures at Hewlett-Packard Co. Jed Gordon, an undergraduate in the Science, Technology, and Society program at the Massachusetts Insti-tute of Technology, worked with the CSTB during the summers of 1997, 1998, and 1999, collecting and analyzing corporate expenditures on R&D, writing summaries of his investigations, and conducting a wide range of related research and writing assignments. As she has done so many times in the past, Laura Ost, a free-lance editor, provided invaluable assistance in preparing the final manuscript under incredibly tight deadlines.

Theresa Fisher and Claudette Baylor-Fleming of the National Research Council's Space Studies Board assisted with the final preparation of this report. Marjory Blumenthal, director of the CSTB, provided critical commentary, advice, and writing in the final stages of the project to help bring the project to a successful conclusion.

Finally, thanks are due to Aubrey Bush at the NSF, whose interest and vision gave impetus to the project and who provided ongoing encouragement during the course of the study. The committee and staff are thankful for his continued patience and support throughout the duration of this project.

Samuel H. Fuller and David G. Messerschmitt
Co-chairs
Committee on Information Technology
Research in a Competitive World

Acknowledgment of Reviewers

This report was reviewed by individuals chosen for their diverse perspectives and technical expertise, in accordance with procedures approved by the NRC's Report Review Committee. The purpose of this independent review is to provide candid and critical comments that will assist the authors and the NRC in making the published report as sound as possible and to ensure that the report meets institutional standards for objectivity, evidence, and responsiveness to the study charge. The contents of the review comments and draft manuscript remain confidential to protect the integrity of the deliberative process. The committee wishes to thank the following individuals for their participation in the review of this report:

Duane Adams, Carnegie Mellon University,
John Armstrong, IBM Corporation (retired),
Robert Epstein, Sybase, Inc.,
Kenneth Flamm, University of Texas at Austin,
Peter Freeman, Georgia Institute of Technology,
Robert Frosch, Harvard University,
Paul Gray, Massachusetts Institute of Technology,
Juris Hartmanis, Cornell University,
John Hopcroft, Cornell University,
John King, University of Michigan,
Robert Lucky, Telcordia Technologies,
Thomas Malone, MIT Sloan School of Management,
Linda Sanford, IBM Corporation,

Marvin Sirbu, Carnegie Mellon University, and
Keith Uncapher, Corporation for National Research Initiatives.

Although the individuals listed above provided many constructive comments and suggestions, responsibility for the final content of this report rests solely with the authoring committee and the NRC.

Contents

Executive Summary

The United States—indeed much of the world—is in the midst of a great transformation wrought by information technology (IT). Fueled by continuing advances in computing and networking capabilities, IT has moved out of the laboratories and back rooms of large organizations and now touches people everywhere. The indicators are almost pedestrian: computing and communications devices have entered the mass market, and the language of the Internet has become part of the business and popular vernacular. These changes are often considered to be the outcomes of technology development—the second half of the familiar term "research and development" (R&D)—whose role is to create specific IT systems and products. What is sometimes overlooked is the critical role of the first half of the R&D process: the research that uncovers underlying principles, fundamental knowledge, and key concepts that fuel the development of numerous products, processes, and services. Research has been an important enabler of IT innovations—from the graphical user interface to the Internet itself—and it will continue to enable the more capable systems of the future, the forms of which have yet to be determined. It has another role as well: in universities especially, it serves to educate and to build a knowledgeable IT workforce.

The future of IT, and of the society it increasingly powers, depends on continued investments in research. Despite the incredible progress made over the past five decades, IT is anything but a mature, stable technology. Revolutionary new technologies based on quantum physics, molecular chemistry, and biological processes are being examined as replacements for or complements to the silicon-based chips that perform basic computing functions. Computing and communications capabilities are being embedded in a widening range of existing and novel devices, presaging an age of ubiquitous or pervasive computing, when IT is absorbed almost invisibly into the world around us. IT systems are being deployed to support countless tasks, from monitoring the health of patients with chronic diseases to controlling the flight paths of aircraft to analyzing mountains of data for private corporations and government agencies. Yet, the potential of IT will not be harnessed to meet society's needs automatically; it is not simply a matter of producing IT products and distributing them more widely. Research is needed to enable progress along all these fronts and to ensure that IT systems can operate dependably and reliably, meeting the needs of society and complementing the capabilities of their users. The question becomes, Can the nation's research establishment generate the advances that will enable tomorrow's IT systems? Are the right kinds of research being conducted? Is there sufficient funding for the needed research? And are the existing structures for funding and conducting research appropriate to the challenges IT researchers must address?

This report by the Committee on Information Technology Research in a Competitive World, convened by the Computer Science and Telecommunications Board (CSTB) of the National Research Council, attempts to answer these questions. It examines the overall funding levels for IT research from industry and government, the scope of ongoing research efforts, and the structures and mechanisms that support research. It advances the argument that the nation's needs for IT systems have changed in ways that demand a much broader agenda for such research— one that includes more explicit support for research on large-scale IT systems and the social applications they support (see Box ES.1)—and mechanisms for funding and conducting research that are better attuned to this broadened agenda. The report was written with an awareness of the legacy of reports about IT research and recognizes that some of the research it covers is not new. What distinguishes this report is that it considers the big picture emerging from research programs that have been cataloged and recommended in other reports and uses this perspective to assess the sufficiency of today's research efforts. The report recognizes that long-standing problems cannot be solved instantly, and it acknowledges the institutional, cultural, and resource factors that will make the recommended changes difficult to achieve. But after lengthy analysis and deliberation, the authoring committee concluded, with conviction, that a reorientation of IT research is vital to the well-being of the technology base.

BOX ES.1
Defining Large-Scale Systems and
Social Applications of IT

Large-scale systems are IT systems that contain many (thousands, millions, billions, or trillions or more) interacting hardware and software components. They tend to be heterogeneous—in that they are composed of many different types of components—and highly complex because the interactions among the components are numerous, varied, and complicated. They also tend to span multiple organizations (or elements of organizations) and have changing configurations. Over time, the largest IT systems have become ever larger and more complex, and, at any given point in time, systems of a certain scale and complexity are not feasible or economical to design with existing methodologies.

Social applications of IT serve groups of people in shared activities. The most straightforward of these applications improve the effectiveness of geographically dispersed groups of people who are collaborating on some task in a shared context. More sophisticated applications may support the operations of a business or the functioning of an entire economy; systems for e-commerce are an example. Characteristic of social applications of IT is the embedding of IT into a large organizational or social system to form a "sociotechnical" system in which people and technology interact to achieve a common purpose—even if that purpose is not obviously social, such as efficient operation of a manufacturing line (which is a conjunction of technological automation and human workers) or rapid and decisive battlefield management (which is a conjunction of command-and-control technology and the judgment and expertise of commanders). Social applications of IT—especially those supporting organizational and societal missions—tend to be large-scale and complex, mixing technical and nontechnical design and operational elements and involving often-difficult social and policy issues such as those related to privacy and access.

TOWARD AN EXPANDED RESEARCH AGENDA

Overall, the nation's IT research base appears to be thriving. Federal funding for IT research rose steadily throughout the 1990s, from approximately $1.4 billion in 1990 to $2.0 billion in 1998 (the most recent year for which consistent data are available),[1] and the Clinton Administration's budget for fiscal year 2001 proposes to increase funding for IT R&D by $1 billion above 1999 levels. Industrial support for R&D also appears to be increasing dramatically. The combined R&D expenditures of companies in the six industry sectors most closely associated with IT totaled $52 billion in 1998, of which approximately $14 billion was classified as research.[2] These figures compare to $39 billion and $8.5 billion, respectively, in 1995.[3] Over the past decade, a number of large IT firms, including Microsoft Corporation, Motorola, Inc., and Intel Corporation, have established central research laboratories, signaling their increased commitment to long-term research.

Nevertheless, current investments in IT research are insufficient to support an important expansion of the IT research agenda. Work needs to continue in ongoing areas of research, but society's growing reliance on IT also demands greater attention to problems associated with the design, deployment, and operation of large-scale systems and social applications. The proliferation of the Internet has greatly accelerated the deployment of large-scale IT systems to serve a variety of personal, social, and business needs. Yet large-scale system efforts in both government and industry are often characterized by cost overruns, development failures, and operational problems, ranging from limited adaptability to breakdowns of various types.[4] As more and more people, activities, and organizations come to depend on such systems—that is, as the systems become critical societal infrastructures—their impact, and the cost to society of their failure, grow. But the necessity of addressing systems problems is only one of the reasons for renewing and reorienting the focus on fundamental research. There is also the promise of much greater societal good from IT systems, a promise hinted at by the systems that have already been successfully deployed and used and by the connectedness achieved through the Internet and the exuberant experimentation with new types of businesses, services, and social and nonprofit activity it has fostered. This is a future that can be attained only with significant improvements in the science and technology base.

Research is needed on the science and engineering issues associated with large-scale systems, to devise ways to make IT systems better—more scalable, flexible, predictable, and reliable (see Box ES.2). Work is also needed to better understand the technical and nontechnical issues that arise when such systems are integrated into social applications. Social applications of IT are expected to motivate technical research that will develop new capabilities to satisfy a growing set of societal needs, and they will demand that technological needs be considered in the social and organizational context in which they will be applied. Such work is by its very nature interdisciplinary, demanding insight into both the technical capabilities of IT and the ways in which people engage or are affected by IT systems in a variety of operational settings. It requires computer science and engineering, but it also requires economists and other social scientists and business-school researchers who understand how IT systems are selected, used, and integrated into organizational processes (see Box ES.3). Such work also benefits from practical perspectives—the knowledge of people working in systems development and end-user organizations—to ground thinking about systems in the contexts of their development, deployment, and use.

BOX ES.2
What Makes Large-Scale IT Systems So Difficult to Design, Build, and Operate?

- *Large number of components*—Large IT systems can contain thousands of processors and hundreds of thousands or even millions of lines of software. Research is needed to understand how to build systems that can scale gracefully and add capacity as needed without needing overall redesign.
- *Deep interactions among components*—Components of large IT systems interact with each other in a variety of ways, some of which may not have been anticipated by the designers. A single misbehaving router can flood the Internet with traffic that will bring down thousands of local hosts and cause traffic to be rerouted worldwide. Research is needed to provide better analytical techniques for modeling system performance and building systems with more comprehensible structures.
- *Unintended and unanticipated consequences of changes or additions to the systems*—For instance, upgrading the memory in a personal computer can lead to timing mismatches that cause memory failures that in turn lead to loss of application data, even if the memory chips are themselves perfectly functional. In this case it is the system that fails to work, even though all its components work. Research is needed to uncover techniques or architectures that provide greater flexibility.
- *Emergent behaviors*—Systems sometimes exhibit surprising behaviors that arise from unanticipated interactions among components. These behaviors are "emergent" in that they are unspecified by any individual component and are the unanticipated product of the system as a whole. Research is needed to find techniques for better analyzing system behavior.
- *Constantly changing needs of the users*—Many large systems are long-lived, meaning they must be modified while preserving some of their own capabilities and within the constraints of the performance of individual components. Development cycles can be so long that requirements change before systems are even deployed. Research is needed to develop ways of building extendable systems that can accommodate change.
- *Independently designed components*—Today's large-scale IT systems are not typically designed from the top down but often are assembled from off-the-shelf components. These components have not been customized to work in the larger system and must rely on standard interfaces and, often, customized software. Modern IT systems are essentially assembled in each home or office. As a result, they are notoriously difficult to maintain and subject to frequent, unexplained breakdowns. Research could help to develop architectural approaches that can accommodate heterogeneity and to extend the principles of modularity to larger scales than have been attempted to date.
- *Large numbers of individuals involved in design and operation*—When browsing the Internet, a user may interact with thousands of computers and hundreds of different software components, all designed by independent teams of designers. For that browsing to work, all of these designs must work sufficiently

continued

BOX ES.2 Continued

well without anyone doing the integrating or anyone handling complaints if they fail to work as a whole. Research is needed on ways to prevent failures in one part of a system from affecting the system as a whole in ways evident to a user.

• *Large numbers of users*—Large IT systems must be able to support large numbers of users, and they must be able to scale up gracefully as the number of users grows. This is seldom the case today. Changes in scale lead to new, unforeseen problems that no company could have anticipated given the state of the art in understanding these systems. Research is needed to find ways of extending the scale of systems easily, without taking them out of operation.

• *Large number of independent requirements*—For instance, a typical computer is built and manufactured without any knowledge of whether it will be used for word processing, scientific simulation, or game playing. It must be good at all of them. Many large-scale systems must also serve a variety of functions. New approaches may be able to provide universal computing capabilities without penalties in performance compared with dedicated devices.

• *Embedding within a larger social and business system context*—Large-scale IT systems tend to form just one element of larger sociotechnical systems that consist of people, organizations, and other technologies. The most effective applications of IT in such systems are not those that merely automate existing processes, but those that enable a transformation of processes that cannot be comprehended without a significant understanding of social and organizational dynamics. Research is needed on the relationships among organizations, people, and technology.

• *Usability*—Engineering that addresses the human factors and social factors of IT systems is paramount. As IT systems serve more users and are used to perform a larger number of functions, they must be made easier to use. They will increasingly be operated by novices rather than experts in IT design and operation. Research is needed to develop techniques for making systems easier to use.

Neither large-scale systems nor social applications of IT are adequately addressed by the IT research community today. Most IT research is directed toward the *components* of IT systems: the microprocessors, computers, and networking technologies that are assembled into large systems, as well as the software that enables the components to work together.[5] This research nurtures the essence of IT, and continued work is needed in all these areas. But component research needs to be viewed as part of a much larger portfolio, in which it is complemented by research aimed directly at improving large-scale systems and the social applications of IT. The last of these includes some work (such as computer-supported cooperative work and human-computer interaction) traditionally viewed as within the purview of computer science. Research in all

BOX ES.3
Research on the Social Applications of Information Technology

Research on the social applications of information technology (IT) combines work in technical disciplines, such as computing and communications, with research in the social sciences to understand how people, organizations, and IT systems can be combined to most effectively perform a set of tasks. Such research can address a range of issues related to IT systems, as demonstrated by the examples below (more detailed discussion is contained in Chapters 3 and 4):

- *Novel activities and shifts in organizational, economic, and social structures*— What will people do (at work, in school, at play, in government, and so on) when computers can see and hear better than they can? How will activities and organizations change when robotic technology is widespread and cheap? How will individual and organizational activities change when surveillance via IT becomes effectively universal? New technologies will affect all kinds of people in many ways, and they hold particular promise for those with special situations or capabilities, because they will give them broader access to social and economic activities.

- *Electronic communities*—How can IT systems be best designed to facilitate the communication and coordination of groups of people working toward a common goal? Progress requires an understanding of the sociology and dynamics of groups of users, as well as of the tasks they wish to perform. Psychologists and sociologists could offer insight for the conceptualization and refinement of these social applications, and technologists could mold their technological aspects.

- *Electronic commerce*—How can buyers and sellers be best brought together to conduct business transactions on the Internet? What kinds of security technologies will provide adequate assurances of the identities of both parties and protect the confidentiality of their transactions without imposing unnecessary burdens on either? How will electronic commerce affect the competitive advantage of firms, their business strategies, and the structure of industries (e.g., their horizontal and vertical linkages)? Such work requires the insight of economists, organizational theorists, business strategists, and psychologists who understand consumer behavior, as well as of technologists.

- *Critical infrastructures*—How can IT be better embedded into the nation's transportation, energy, financial, telecommunications, and other infrastructures to make them more efficient and effective without making them less reliable or more prone to human error? For example, how can an air traffic control system be designed to provide controllers with sufficient information to make critical decisions without overwhelming them with data? Such work requires the insight of cognitive psychologists and experts in air traffic control, as well as of technologists.

- *Complexity*—How can the benefits of IT be brought to the citizenry without the exploding complexity characteristic of professional uses of IT? Although networks, computers, and software can be assembled and configured by professionals to support the mission-critical computing needs of large organizations, the techniques that make this possible are inadequate for information appliances designed for the home, car, or individual. Research is needed to simplify and automate system configuration, change, and repair. Such research will require insight from technologists, cognitive psychologists, and those skilled in user interface design.

three areas—components, systems, and social applications—will make IT systems better able to meet society's needs, just as in the medical domain work is needed in biology, physiology, clinical medicine, and epidemiology to make the nation's population healthier.

Research on large-scale systems and the social applications of IT will require new modes of funding and performing research that can bring together a broad set of IT researchers, end users, system integrators, and social scientists to enhance the understanding of operational systems. Research in these areas demands that researchers have access to operational large-scale systems or to testbeds that can mimic the performance of much larger systems. It requires additional funding to support sizable projects that allow multiple investigators to experiment with large IT systems and develop suitable testbeds and simulations for evaluating new approaches and that engage an unusually diverse range of parties. Research by individual investigators will not, by itself, suffice to make progress on these difficult problems.

Today, most IT research fails to incorporate the diversity of perspectives needed to ensure advances on large-scale systems and social applications. Within industry, it is conducted largely by vendors of IT components: companies like IBM, Microsoft, and Lucent Technologies. Few of the companies that are engaged in providing IT services, in integrating large-scale systems (e.g., Andersen Consulting, EDS, or Lockheed Martin), or in developing enterprise software (e.g., Oracle, SAP, PeopleSoft) have significant research programs.[6] Nor do end-user organizations (e.g., users in banking, commerce, education, health care, and manufacturing) tend to support research on IT, despite their increasing reliance on IT and their stake in the way IT systems are molded. Likewise, there is little academic research on large-scale systems or social applications. Within the IT sector, systems research has tended to focus on improving the performance and lowering the costs of IT systems rather than on improving their reliability, flexibility, or scalability (although systems research is slated to receive more attention in new funding programs). Social applications present an even greater opportunity and have the potential to leverage research in human-computer interaction, using it to better understand how IT can support the work of individuals, groups, and organizations. Success in this area hinges on interdisciplinary research, which is already being carried out on a small scale.

One reason more work has not been undertaken in these areas is lack of sufficient funding. More fundamentally, the problems evident today did not reach critical proportions until recently. There has been no crisis to motivate the research community or to compel a broader set of companies to fund research, no compelling set of visions to inspire broad-based interest. From a practical perspective, conducting the types of research advocated here is difficult. Significant cultural gaps exist between researchers in different disciplines and between IT researchers and the end users of IT systems. These groups tend to have different sets of motivations, interests, and even perspectives on what constitutes research.[7] But if IT is to meet society's growing needs, then the challenges of collaborative research will have to be overcome. Luckily, a few seeds have been planted that, if nurtured, may sprout and blossom in ways that can support and encourage a larger, more diverse range of efforts. Government, industry, and universities need to ensure that this happens. This report provides guidance that they can follow in doing so.

RECOMMENDATIONS

Now is the time to adjust and expand the IT research portfolio, both to overcome problems that have become urgent and to better meet society's needs. Doing so will require efforts on many fronts. Increased funding will be needed to extend the scope of IT research more fully into large-scale systems and social applications. At the same time, existing mechanisms for funding IT research will have to be strengthened to ensure that fundamental research continues to be supported in a way that will prove most productive for the IT industry and, ultimately, the nation. New mechanisms will be needed to fund and conduct research on large-scale systems and social applications of IT—the nature of which differs from that of traditional components research. In many cases, mechanisms for research on large-scale systems and social applications can build on existing programs and initiatives, expanding their scale and scope.

Changes like these have been suggested before. The less-than-satisfactory outlook today simply reflects insufficient follow-through on those earlier suggestions. All of the relevant recommendations made by CSTB committees, past and present, draw on the expertise of the IT research community and other relevant experts; engaging the community effectively requires listening to its advice. The committee's recommendations in each of these areas are presented below, organized according to the group that would carry them out, and elaborated on in Chapter 5.

Recommendations for Government

Recommendation 1. **The federal government should continue to boost funding levels for fundamental information technology research, commensurate with the growing scope of research challenges.**

The first step toward strengthening the nation's IT research base is to ensure that sufficient investments are made in IT research. Increased federal funding for such research is necessary to support continued growth in existing component-oriented research (e.g., microprocessors, computing systems, networking equipment, and software) while expanding the research base to look at the problems of large-scale systems and the social applications of IT, to help the nation harness IT's potential for a range of public and private-sector missions. Although it is not possible to specify precisely how much additional funding is needed, the committee believes that the increases proposed in recent years by the President's Information Technology Advisory Committee ($1 billion over 5 years) and the Clinton Administration ($1 billion between 1999 and 2001) are the right order of magnitude and would allow the IT research community to grow larger while providing adequate resources for each investigator.

Funding increases need to be aimed primarily at fundamental research, not applied research. Not only is such work important to the long-term evolution of the field, but it would also shift some of the responsibility from industry, which faces a number of strong disincentives to investment in fundamental, long-term research. The results of such work cannot be anticipated and their most important implications often lie far in the future, even if some benefits can be gained more immediately. As experience demonstrates—and economic theory supports—companies that make fundamental breakthroughs often have difficulty capturing the benefits of these advances while preventing competitors from doing so. Hence, they tend to underinvest in such research.[8] Only the largest, most profitable, and most dominant IT firms tend to be able to invest in long-term research (in part because they are better positioned to capture its benefits), and even this source of funding has been in short supply. Increasing competition, which can erode the market share of leading firms in an industry, and the need to introduce new products and services rapidly into the marketplace have forced even the most forward-thinking companies to shift more of their resources to applied research efforts. The federal government is much better able to provide sustained funding for research with long-term potential, but it, too, has increased funding for applied research more quickly than funding for fundamental research in recent years. IT researchers corroborate this trend, noting that federally funded projects have become more focused on near-term objectives and demonstrations of capability—precisely the same types of things that industry is likely to do—rather than on fundamental advances in the technology. As shown in earlier CSTB reports, federal funding for fundamental research laid the groundwork for many of today's common commercial innovations, from graphical user interfaces and relational databases to computer graphics and even the Internet itself (CSTB, 1995, 1999).

The need for it has not diminished. Although the IT industry has grown and is highly profitable, the barriers to investments in long-term research persist, and the government continues to have a role to play.

Recommendation 2. **The National Science Foundation and the Defense Advanced Research Projects Agency should establish significant programs of fundamental research in large-scale information technology systems.**

The National Science Foundation (NSF) and the Defense Advanced Research Projects Agency (DARPA) each have a number of efforts under way that address aspects of large-scale systems. As yet, these efforts have not been integrated into a larger programmatic thrust that attempts to gain a more fundamental understanding of large-scale systems (as opposed to pursuing development of specific applications). The NSF and DARPA should exercise the leadership they have demonstrated in the past and create more comprehensive, cohesive programs in this area that would allow a vibrant research community to coalesce around the problems of large-scale systems. The programs run by the organizations should complement one another and should together have the following characteristics:

- Support both theoretical and experimental work;
- Offer awards in a variety of sizes (small, medium, and large) to support individual investigators, small teams of researchers, and larger collaborations;
- Investigate a range of approaches to large-scale systems problems, such as improved software design methodologies, system architecture, reusable code, and biological and economic models (see Chapter 3);
- Attempt to address the full scope of large-scale systems issues, including scalability, heterogeneity, trustworthiness, flexibility, and predictability;[9] and
- Give academic researchers some form of access to large-scale systems for studying and demonstrating new approaches.

Given the wide circle of agencies interested in and involved with IT research and the even wider circle coming to depend on large-scale IT systems, the NSF and DARPA should attempt to involve in their research other federal agencies, such as the Department of Health and Human Services and the Federal Aviation Administration, that operate large-scale IT systems and would benefit from advances in their design. Such involvement could provide a means for researchers to gain access to operational systems for analytical and experimental purposes.

Recommendation 3. **Federal agencies should increase support for interdisciplinary work on social applications of information technology that draws on the expertise of researchers from IT and other disciplines and includes end users of IT systems.**

Research on the social applications of IT demands the perspectives of IT researchers, researchers in other academic disciplines, and end users of IT systems who are familiar with the particular challenges faced and the viability of different solutions. A number of programs are in place, such as the Digital Government program, the Digital Libraries Initiative, and the NSF's Computing and Social System program, that combine these perspectives and apply them to problem areas, but an initiative is needed that has a larger scale and scope and that possesses the following characteristics:

• Support provided through a variety of research mechanisms, including single-investigator grants, small teams of researchers, and larger research centers that bring together researchers from several disciplines and different industries for an extended period of interaction;

• Explicit participation in the research process of end users and systems integrators who understand the problems faced in using large-scale systems and social applications;

• Participation of the federal agencies that are major users of IT systems and that invest considerable resources in the development of IT systems (such as the Internal Revenue Service, the Social Security Administration, and the Federal Aviation Administration), not just the traditional funders of IT research;

• Access to large systems or testbeds so that researchers can gain insight into operational problems and appreciate the relationships between an IT system and the larger social or organizational context in which it operates; and

• Management and oversight by traditional funders of IT research to ensure that the work retains a research focus and does not become linked too closely to development efforts at particular end-user organizations.

The NSF has already allocated some funding for IT research centers focusing on social, economic, and workforce issues associated with IT. These centers could make valuable contributions to research and education in this area if they incorporate end-user perspectives as well as the perspectives of disciplines such as business, law, economics, and other social sciences. They should also be sure to complement their attention to the effects of IT on society and the economy with parallel efforts to develop the scientific and engineering knowledge needed to improve the design of IT systems. Additional effort will be needed to review proposals for interdisciplinary work related to IT and for assuring its quality. Quality controls are especially important in fields with growing research budgets, and interdisciplinary research can be especially difficult to evaluate. Review and evaluation processes will need to reflect the full range of perspectives involved in the research.

Recommendation 4. **The Bureau of the Census should work with the National Science Foundation to develop more effective procedures for classifying data on federal and industry investments in information technology R&D that better account for the dynamic nature of the industry.**

Before they can make better decisions on IT research, policy makers need better data on current expenditures by the federal government and industry on such research. Existing data fluctuate from year to year, largely because of reclassifications of companies among sectors. These reclassifications occur as a result of changes within the individual companies (e.g., new lines of business, mergers, outsourcing of production) as well as the rules for the classification process itself, which are based on the composition of the payrolls of individual firms. The result is inconsistent data that make it difficult to discern trends, even very general ones. The NSF and the Census Bureau need to develop ways to collect and disseminate more-consistent data describing past, present, and future investments in IT R&D. Additional efforts will be needed to develop more consistent time-series data for the IT industries in particular and to develop robust procedures for classifying firms within industrial sectors.

Recommendations for Universities

Recommendation 5. **Universities should take steps to increase the ability of faculty members and students to participate in interdisciplinary research related to information technology and research on large-scale systems.**

Universities have the potential to make significant strides in large-scale systems and social applications research because they have all the key ingredients: researchers in a broad range of related areas, from computer science and electrical engineering to business, law, economics, and other social sciences. They are also able to complement this research with educational initiatives that can teach students about large-scale systems and social applications, thereby helping create a future workforce capable of researching, developing, and using them. For the most part, universities are not currently set up properly to make progress on these issues. With some degree of change, they could contribute to the research base at the same time as they educate students and imbue them with an appreciation of the issues. Because getting diverse researchers to work together has never been easy, incentives must be provided and barriers to collaboration removed. The availability of funding for work on large-scale IT systems and the social applications of IT would motivate academic researchers to pursue the sorts of interdisciplinary research needed to make progress in these fields, but additional efforts will also be needed to create a more suitable environment for interdisciplinary research and one that ensures the quality of such research.

The first step should be to ensure that hiring, reviewing, and tenure processes are aligned to suit the interdisciplinary nature of the research that this report recommends and to ensure its quality. This can be accomplished through a variety of mechanisms, including the creation of interdisciplinary schools or departments that have their own hiring and promotion processes[10] or the establishment of guidelines for evaluating faculty in traditional academic departments who pursue interdisciplinary work. The sharing of information should be encouraged between university researchers (both faculty and students) and their counterparts in industry, especially in companies that urgently need to resolve problems of large-scale systems and social applications of IT. The purpose of industry involvement should not be to facilitate the commercialization of university research (although this is a welcome outcome) but to provide researchers with the knowledge they will need to make progress in large-scale systems and social applications. In particular, universities should work with industry to establish more internship opportunities for students and sabbatical opportunities for faculty, especially in end-user organizations that do not have established programs aimed at technologists. Although such activities may take students away from their faculty supervisors for a time, the committee believes the experience will ultimately prove valuable to the work that these students perform at the university. Universities should also bring industry leaders into the classroom and the research lab.

Recommendation 6. **Senior faculty members should take the lead in pioneering research on large-scale systems and social applications of information technology.**

Even though they may have innovative ideas, junior faculty members are at a distinct disadvantage when they set off in new research directions that are not considered part of the intellectual core of their disciplines. Concerns about tenure can limit their willingness to work on topics such as large-scale systems and social applications of IT that do not fall neatly within established research areas. Senior faculty members, by contrast, sometimes seek a refreshing change in emphasis. They should be encouraged to establish interdisciplinary research projects, to attract funding and people to them, and to articulate a vision for such work. Their involvement would help legitimize these areas of inquiry and provide an umbrella under which junior faculty could join them, bringing new ideas and insights.

Recommendations for Industry

Recommendation 7. **Organizations that are significant end users of information technology systems should actively seek opportunities to engage in IT research.**

Large end-user organizations in industries ranging from banking to health care to manufacturing face significant challenges in designing, developing, and operating the IT systems on which they rely and in whose development they invest large sums of money. Ideally, they too should support IT research that would address problems of large-scale systems and the social applications of IT. These organizations could benefit handsomely from research in these areas. They also have knowledge of the application and its operation (as well as its failures) that will prove vital in these areas of research. Involving end users in IT research will not be easy, because few have much interest in research, let alone experience in conducting or managing it, and the benefits of such engagement may not be immediately apparent to them. Nevertheless, the time is right to overcome these obstacles and experiment with ways to bring end users more effectively into the research process. As a first step, end-user representatives should be engaged to serve on advisory boards to IT research programs, labs, or academic departments. Over time, they should become more directly involved, and some end-user organizations could even fund research for groups or centers whose capabilities match their needs. Recent research support by leading financial services firms shows it is possible to meaningfully engage end-user organizations, albeit on a limited scale.

Recommendation 8. **Information technology companies with established R&D organizations should develop mechanisms for engaging end users more actively in the research process.**

To help end users become better engaged in IT research, IT companies with a tradition of research (as opposed to development) should develop mechanisms for involving end users more extensively in interdisciplinary and large-scale systems-related work. Such IT companies have track records in research and an interest in better understanding customer needs. Companies such as IBM Corporation and Microsoft Corporation have demonstrated the utility of working more closely with customers and researchers from different disciplines. Other companies may be able to build on these examples and develop other mechanisms for achieving similar results.

A FINAL WORD

The committee believes that these recommendations will strengthen the nation's IT research base sufficiently to help meet society's growing need for, and dependence on, IT systems. By strengthening the existing mechanisms for IT research and experimenting with new mechanisms to expand IT research into large-scale systems and social applications of IT, the nation will be able to ease its transition to an information economy. A strong research base will provide the industry and the nation with the knowledge resources needed to harness IT for the common good.

REFERENCES

Arrow, Kenneth. 1962. "Economic Welfare and the Allocation of Resources for Invention," in Richard Nelson, ed., *The Rate and Direction of Innovative Activity*. Princeton University Press, Princeton, N.J.

Barr, Avron, and Shirley Tessler. 1998. "How Will the Software Talent Shortage End?" *American Programmer* 11(1). Available online at <http://www.cutter.com/itjournal/itjtoc.htm#jan98>.

Campbell, Donald T. 1969. "Ethnocentrism of Disciplines and the Fish-Scale Model of Omniscience," pp. 328-348 in Muzafer Sherif and Carolyn W. Sherif, eds., *Interdisciplinary Relationships in the Social Sciences*. Aldine Publishing Co., Chicago.

Computer Science and Telecommunications Board (CSTB), National Research Council. 1995. *Evolving the High Performance Computing and Communications Initiative to Support the Nation's Information Infrastructure*. National Academy Press, Washington, D.C.

Computer Science and Telecommunications Board (CSTB), National Research Council. 1999. *Funding a Revolution: Government Support for Computing Research*. National Academy Press, Washington, D.C.

Gibbs, W.W. 1994. "Software's Chronic Crisis," *Scientific American* (September):86-95.

Johnson, Jim. 1999. "Turning Chaos into Success," *Software Magazine*, December. Available online at <http://www.softwaremag.com/archives/1999dec/Success.html>.

Jones, C. 1996. *Applied Software Measurement*. McGraw-Hill, New York.

Nelson, Richard. 1959. "The Simple Economics of Basic Research," *Journal of Political Economy* 67(2):297-306.

Standish Group International, Inc. 1995. *The Chaos*. Available online at <http://www.standishgroup.com/chaos.html>.

NOTES

1. These figures represent combined federal obligations for research (basic and applied) in computer science and electrical engineering, the two academic disciplines most closely associated with information technology (IT). Some work in electrical engineering, such as research on power systems, is not applicable to IT, and some work in other disciplines is applicable but is not captured in these statistics.

2. These sectors, as defined by the Standard Industrial Classification (SIC) system, are SIC 357, office, computing, and accounting machines; SIC 366, communications equipment; SIC 367, electronic components (including semiconductor devices); SIC 48, communications (services); SIC 504, professional and commercial equipment and supplies; and SIC 737, computer and data processing services (including prepackaged software, custom programming, systems integration, and other services).

3. As described in greater detail in Chapter 2, federal statistics on IT industries' R&D investment are not compiled in a consistent manner from year to year because of the frequent reclassification of firms from one IT sector to another as well as into and out of the IT industries. The aggregate figures used in this report account for reclassifications among IT sectors but not into or out of the IT industry.

4. It is estimated that between 70 and 80 percent of all major system development efforts are never completed, are late, or overrun cost projections by a wide margin. Estimates of failure rates in large-scale system development efforts are contained in several studies. See Johnson (1999), Standish Group (1995), Gibbs (1994), Jones (1996), and Barr and Tessler (1998).

5. This definition of a component is much broader than the definition typically used in the research community.

6. The most notable exception to this general rule is IBM, which derives a significant portion of its revenues from IT-related services and systems work and which maintains a substantial research program. About one-quarter of the work conducted by IBM Research supports its systems and services businesses.

7. A discussion of the long-standing challenges inherent in interdisciplinary work in the social sciences can be found in Campbell (1969).

8. Most notably, Xerox failed to capture much of the benefit of its pioneering work in personal computing. IBM's work in relational databases and reduced-instruction-set computing seeded not only its own product development efforts but also those of numerous competitors. Economics provides a theoretical verification of this phenomenon. See CSTB (1999), Nelson (1959), and Arrow (1962).

9. See Chapter 3 for a more in-depth discussion of each of these topics.

10. In recent years, a number of universities have created interdisciplinary schools that examine issues at the intersection of IT, business, and the social sciences. Examples include the School of Information Management and Systems at the University of California at Berkeley and the School of Information at the University of Michigan. Carnegie Mellon University and the Massachusetts Institute of Technology also have a number of interdisciplinary departments and divisions in this general area. Chapter 4 contains a more complete list of such programs.

1

Introduction

"May your wildest dreams come true" is an old adage brought to mind by the phenomenal advances in computing and communications technology and their deployment in a widening array of business, government, commercial, and social applications. The underlying industrial base for computing and communications—the information technology (IT) industries—has grown rapidly, creating jobs, improving the standard of living, and fueling the nation's transition to an information economy. Since 1992, firms that produce computers, semiconductors, software, and communications equipment and provide computing and communications services have contributed one-third of the nation's economic growth, and in 1998 they employed 5.2 million workers at wages 85 percent higher than the private-sector average (U.S. Department of Commerce, 2000). Companies throughout the economy are using IT to compete in global markets, and IT promises to transform the way people work, play, live, and learn. The nation's dependence on the vitality of the technology base for IT was underscored in the late 1990s by such voices as the chairman of the Federal Reserve, the director of the National Science Foundation, and the President of the United States. This technology base and tomorrow's information economy depend, in turn, on continued research on IT.

The role of research in driving innovation and social transformations is often difficult to see. The seemingly endless introduction of new goods and services by entrepreneurs and established corporations obscures the fundamental science and engineering bases underlying innovation. It

18

also creates the appearance of a self-sustaining process. If businesses are growing and new products are proliferating, why should national leaders be concerned about IT research? This question remains central to contemporary political debate about federal budgets for IT research, despite recent increases in funding. The difficulty of explaining and justifying federal IT research spending influenced the evolution and eventual transformation of the first large federal IT research initiative, the High Performance Computing and Communications Initiative (HPCCI);[1] it enlarged the scope of the President's Information Technology Advisory Committee (PITAC) and the associated federal proposals for new and larger research programs, notably the 1999 Information Technology for the Twenty-First Century (IT^2) initiative, and shaped the reports that came out of them;[2] and it continues to color the annual budget debates about the level and distribution of IT research funds.

An enduring lack of understanding of the nature of both IT research and industrial innovation in IT makes debates about federal programs in this area unusually contentious. Experts from industry and academia, individually and as participants in groups such as Computer Science and Telecommunications Board (CSTB) committees, PITAC, and professional organizations, have asserted publicly that both government and industry are underinvesting in IT research—especially fundamental research. Calls for increased funding have met with skepticism from those who are critical of the rationale for increased funding, uncertain about the nature of IT research (which is apparently less comprehensible than, for example, classical scientific research) and who question why it should be expensive (a concern that reflects a limited understanding of software research). Unless these criticisms and questions can be answered, technological progress may be stymied by a lack of needed research funding.

The nation's increasing reliance on IT demands a reexamination of the IT research base. Both the substance of the research and how it is carried out are at issue. As for substance, the potential is mounting for problems to arise and for opportunities to be lost as a result of deficiencies in the technologies already being distributed quickly and widely into the economy. Society is becoming dependent on information systems that are fragile, and companies striving to be competitive in the short term sacrifice opportunities for IT innovations that depend on sustained or less-constrained exploration, raising questions about long-term prospects. Research is needed to address a host of new problems—many arising as a consequence of interactions among a large and growing number of individual components—as well as long-standing problems that are becoming more prominent and, once a technology is in use, more difficult to manage.

Procedurally, the situation challenges the confederation of government, industry, and academia that drives IT research. The give-and-take among these parties was healthy for several decades, as is clear from today's commercial and societal successes with IT, but recently it has become weaker. In addition, industry has faced increasing pressures to streamline research and development (R&D) as a result of waves of structural change in the IT industries in the 1980s and 1990s.[3] These conditions discourage investments of time and money in research, instead favoring the creative exploitation of existing science and technology in the guise of new products. Today's IT industry is thriving because it is leveraging a rich base of historical investments in research (see Box 1.1); emblematic of the practice is the now-familiar story of the Internet's roots in government-sponsored academic research (see CSTB, 1999a). But where, today, is the base for a thriving industry tomorrow?

This report examines the approaches to sustaining IT research, including institutional support mechanisms for the nation's IT research base. The definition of IT research is broad, encompassing work that advances computing and communications technologies as well as systems that combine those technologies to serve a range of social needs. The report does not attempt to develop a detailed research agenda (that information can be gleaned from other CSTB reports and assorted government documents). Rather, it addresses four main topics:

1. *Levels of funding for IT research*—Are government and industrial sponsors providing sufficient funding for research to keep up with the fast pace of innovation and the explosive growth of the IT marketplace?

2. *The scope of IT research*—Is the scope broad enough to address the range of challenges to IT systems as they are increasingly integrated into business, societal, and government applications?

3. *The constituencies supporting IT research*—Is the base of organizations supporting IT research broad enough to ensure sufficient financial and intellectual contributions needed to advance the field?

4. *Mechanisms for supporting research*—Are existing structures for funding and conducting IT research adequate to address future challenges? Are new mechanisms needed?

This report offers recommendations in each of these areas, with the objective of ensuring that the investments in IT research will propel the nation through the Information Age.

WHY FOCUS ON INFORMATION TECHNOLOGY?

Few in the IT industry—or elsewhere—foresaw the dramatic progress in IT that has occurred over the last few decades. Fewer still can read a

BOX 1.1
Research and Innovation in IT: A Historical Perspective

Many of the information technologies commonly used today have roots in research conducted decades ago. That research was often supported by a combination of government agencies and private firms. Federal funding for computing research began in earnest immediately following World War II and supported the development of many of the nation's earliest computers. Beginning in the late 1960s, federal support for long-term fundamental research created a growing knowledge base for exploitation by innovators and entrepreneurs. Industry also funded such research and brought the new technologies to the marketplace. The following list presents some of the better-known examples of current technologies that leverage historical investments in research:

- *The Internet*—The seeds of today's Internet were planted by the Defense Advanced Research Projects Agency (DARPA) in the late 1960s, when it began to develop the ARPANET, a packet-switched network used to connect its computing researchers. This work sparked the development of the basic communications protocols used for the Internet as well as electronic mail.
- *Graphical User Interfaces*—Work sponsored by DARPA in the late 1960s led to development of the computer mouse and its use as part of a graphical user interface. The technology was later incorporated into the Xerox Corporation's Alto computer and then into Apple Computer's MacIntosh. It has since become the standard interface for personal computers.
- *Computer graphics*—Work on computer graphics dates back to Project Whirlwind in the late 1940s and its successor, the U.S. Air Force air defense system SAGE, which used interactive graphics consoles and displays. Algorithms for rendering graphical images (in three dimensions) on a computer screen were first developed during the 1960s, with many advances emerging from DARPA-funded work at the University of Utah.
- *Speech recognition*—Today's speech-recognition programs build on decades of research in artificial intelligence and speech recognition sponsored by both industry and government. AT&T and IBM Corporation maintained programs in the field, as did DARPA, which seeded early work in hidden Markov models on which the first commercial products were based.
- *Reduced-instruction-set computing (RISC)*—Many of today's fastest computer workstations rely on RISC, a technology pioneered by IBM in the 1970s and further developed by researchers with funding from DARPA's Very Large Scale Integrated Circuit Program, which ran until the early 1980s.
- *Relational databases*—The relational databases sold by companies like IBM, Informix, Oracle, and Sybase are the products of research first conducted at IBM in the 1970s. Simultaneously, relational databases were pursued by researchers at the University of California at Berkeley with funding from the National Science Foundation. Today's products still rely on the relational model developed by those early projects.

SOURCE: Computer Science and Telecommunications Board (1999a).

newspaper today without coming across comments, articles, or special sections that remark on trends in IT and their social and economic impacts. Dramatic advances in computer processing speeds, communications bandwidth, and storage capacities are almost clichés. A popular yardstick is Moore's law: for the last 40 years, computing capability per dollar has doubled every 18 to 24 months, equivalent to a 100-fold improvement every 10 to 13 years, reflected in both rapidly increasing performance and declining price. These performance gains, the associated development of software applications, and falling prices for IT relative to its capabilities have propelled IT into new markets. For instance, controllers are now embedded within products such as cellular telephones and automobile transmissions, and complex information systems are used to manage air traffic, book air travel reservations, and process electronic commerce transactions. Research has borne fruit in a cumulative manner, transforming the IT baseline. The early emphasis on computation, combined with the advent, later on, of mass storage devices, focused attention on the capture, storage, and retrieval of massive amounts of data. Likewise, early developments in networking led to ever more sophisticated communications and to distributed processing. With each advance came a dramatic expansion in the uses of computing. The expansion in the use of communications has been more recent; the combined progress in each field has stimulated applications of increasing scope and sophistication.

To a technologist, IT is being applied to increasingly complex systems, thanks to past advances in microprocessors, algorithms, packet networking, memory, and information storage and retrieval. To a layperson, IT is becoming infrastructure, an enabler of more and more of what people do, even in situations in which the use of a "computer" is neither obvious nor intentional. The Internet, because of its pervasiveness and intrinsic ability to connect many elements, epitomizes these advances, as does the proliferation of personal computers for applications such as electronic banking and home shopping and the now-routine use of cellular telephones, especially those capable of Internet access. All of this is happening because decades of research led to proven concepts and technologies, lowering risks enough to enable commercialization.

The lesson of the recent growth of the Internet, and the World Wide Web that rides atop it, is that technical success can generate new challenges: in short, IT is neither stable nor static. What will tomorrow's Web be like? No one knows for sure, but today's research and experimentation hint at advances in the design and implementation of virtual reality systems, which enable telepresence and other blends of real and virtual environments; advances in integrating computing and biology that enable novel approaches to computation, such as through molecular or chemical processes; leaps in the capacity to collect, store, and retrieve both previously generated and new information; and capabilities surpassing those of humans for seeing, hearing, and speaking (see Box 1.2). The integration of such specific advances into applications and systems that are more complex than today's state of the art can only be speculated on. What is not speculation is the fact that today's society depends greatly on IT, and tomorrow's will do so even more. The Internet of today is a beginning, not an end point: it may be thought of as infrastructure, but it is far from offering the stability and predictability associated with the traditional infrastructures of the physical world.

WHAT IS INFORMATION TECHNOLOGY RESEARCH?

The Many Faces of Information Technology Research

IT research takes many forms. It consists of both theoretical and experimental work, and it combines elements of science and engineering. Some IT research lays out principles or constraints that apply to all computing and communications systems; examples include theorems that show the limitations of computation (what can and cannot be computed by a digital computer within a reasonable time) or the fundamental limits on capacities of communications channels. Other research investigates different classes of IT systems, such as user interfaces, the Web, or electronic mail (e-mail). Still other research deals with issues of broad applicability driven by specific needs. For example, today's high-level programming languages (such as Java and C) were made possible by research that uncovered techniques for converting the high-level statements into machine code for execution on a computer. The design of the languages themselves is a research topic: how best to capture a programmer's intentions in a way that can be converted to efficient machine code. Efforts to solve this problem, as is often the case in IT research, will require invention and design as well as the classical scientific techniques of analysis and measurement. The same is true of efforts to develop specific and practical modulation and coding algorithms that approach the fundamental limits of communication on some channels. The rise of digital communication, associated with computer technology, has led to the irreversible melding of what were once the separate fields of communications and computers, with data forming an increasing share of what is being transmitted over the digitally modulated fiber-optic cables spanning the nation and the world.

Experimental work plays an important role in IT research. One modality of research is the design experiment, in which a new technique is proposed, a provisional design is posited, and a research prototype is built in order to evaluate the strengths and weaknesses of the design.

BOX 1.2
Some Research Goals for Information Technology

Despite the incredible progress made in information technology over the past 50 years, the field is far from mature. A number of compelling goals will drive research. The following is just a partial list of possible research goals articulated by Jim Gray, a leading IT researcher and recipient of the Turing Award, the top prize in computer science. They are envisioned as well-defined goals that can stimulate considerable research.

- *Scalability*—Devise a software and hardware architecture that scales up by a factor of a million. In other words, an application's storage and processing capacity would have to be able to automatically grow by a factor of a million, doing jobs faster or doing a million jobs in the same time, just by adding more resources.
- *Turing test*—Build a computer that wins the "imitation game" at least 30 percent of the time. In a blind contest, the computer should be able to behave convincingly like a human 30 percent of the time.
- *Speech-to-text*—Build a device that can hear as well as a native speaker.
- *Text-to-speech*—Build a device that can speak as well as a native speaker.
- *See as well as a person*—Build a device that can recognize objects and behavior.
- *Personal memex*—Build a system that can record everything a person sees and hears and quickly retrieve any item on request.
- *World memex*—Build a system that given a text corpus can answer questions about the text and summarize the text as precisely and quickly as a human expert in that field. Do the same for music, images, art, and cinema.
- *Telepresence*—Build a system that can simulate being some other place retrospectively as an observer (Teleobserver: hear and see as well as actually be there, and as well as a participant), and simulate being some other place as a participant (Telepresent: interact with others and with the environment as though actually there).
- *Trouble-free systems*—Build a system used by millions of people each day and yet administered and managed by a single part-time person.
- *Secure system*—Assure that the system in the preceding goal services only authorized users, that service cannot be denied by unauthorized users, and that information cannot be stolen (and prove it).
- *Always up*—Build a system that is unavailable for less than 1 second per hundred years (and prove it).
- *Automatic programmer*—Devise a specification language or user interface that (a) makes it easy for people to express designs (1,000 times easier), (b) computers can compile, and (c) can describe all applications (is complete). The system should reason about the applications, asking questions about exception cases and incomplete specifications, but it should not be onerous to use.

SOURCE: Gray (1999).

Although much of the effect of a design can be anticipated using analytic techniques, many of its subtle aspects are uncovered only when the prototype is studied. Some of the most important strides in IT have been made through such experimental research. Time-sharing, for example, evolved in a series of experimental systems that explored different parts of the technology. How are a computer's resources to be shared among several customers? How do we ensure equitable sharing of resources? How do we insulate each user's program from the programs of others? What resources should be shared as a convenience to the customers (e.g., computer files)? How can the system be designed so it's easy to write computer programs that can be time-shared? What kinds of commands does a user need to learn to operate the system? Although some of these trade-offs may succumb to analysis, others—notably those involving the user's evaluation and preferences—can be evaluated only through experiment.

Ideas for IT research can be gleaned both from the research community itself and from applications of IT systems. The Web, initiated by physicists to support collaboration among researchers, illustrates how people who use IT can be the source of important innovations. The Web was not invented from scratch; rather, it integrated developments in information retrieval, networking, and software that had been accumulating over decades in many segments of the IT research community (Schatz, 1997; Schatz and Hardin, 1994). It also reflects a fundamental body of technology that is conducive to innovation and change (CSTB, 1994). Thus, it advanced the integration of computing, communications, and information. The Web also embodies the need for additional science and technology to accommodate the burgeoning scale and diversity of IT users and uses: it became a catalyst for the Internet by enhancing the ease of use and usefulness of the Internet, it has grown and evolved far beyond the expectations of its inventors, and it has stimulated new lines of research aimed at improving and better using the Internet in numerous arenas, from education to crisis management.

Progress in IT can come from research in many different disciplines. For example, work on the physics of silicon can be considered IT research if it is driven by problems related to computer chips; the work of electrical engineers is considered IT research if it focuses on communications or semiconductor devices; anthropologists and other social scientists studying the uses of new technology can be doing IT research if their work informs the development and deployment of new IT applications; and computer scientists and computer engineers address a widening range of issues, from generating fundamental principles for the behavior of information in systems to developing new concepts for systems. Thus, IT research combines science and engineering, even though the popular— and even professional—association of IT with systems leads many people to concentrate on the engineering aspects. Fine distinctions between the science and engineering aspects may be unproductive: computer science is special because of how it combines the two, and the evolution of both is key to the well-being of IT research. Because of its emphasis on IT systems in the service of society, this report emphasizes the engineering perspective, but takes an even broader view of the field that includes the interaction between IT systems and their end users.[4]

A Classification of Information Technology Research

Distinguishing different types of research is problematic and politicized; it feeds enduring science policy debates that can seem to confuse the issues, but it remains important for diagnosing what needs to be done and how that might differ from what is being done. A variety of terms have been used to distinguish between different types of scientific and technological research. The most widely used distinction is between basic and applied research. In this classification, which is used by federal statistical agencies, basic research is defined as work motivated by a desire to better understand fundamental aspects of phenomena without specific applications in mind; it is often called curiosity-driven research. Applied research is defined as work performed to gain the understanding needed to meet a particular need; it is often called problem-oriented research. Although useful in some respects, this distinction tends to place utility and understanding at the extremes of a one-dimensional research spectrum.

Another, more useful classification, developed by Donald Stokes, overcomes these limitations by explicitly separating the usefulness of research results from the degree to which the research seeks fundamental understanding (Stokes, 1997). It classifies research along two dimensions: whether use is considered, and whether or not the research pursues fundamental understanding (Figure 1.1). Stokes distinguishes four types of research: (1) pure basic research performed with the goal of fundamental understanding, without any thought of practical use (exemplified by Niels Bohr's research on atomic structure); (2) use-inspired basic research that pursues fundamental understanding but is motivated by a particular question or application (exemplified by Louis Pasteur's research on the biological bases of fermentation and disease, and by the fundamental work done for the Manhattan Project); (3) pure applied research that is motivated by use but does not seek fundamental understanding (exemplified by Thomas Alva Edison's inventive work); and (4) applied research that is not motivated by a particular application (such as the development of taxonomies for birds and plants, or Tycho Brahe's work to document the position of the planets, which later informed Kepler's developments of laws about planetary motion). In contrast to the basic/applied research

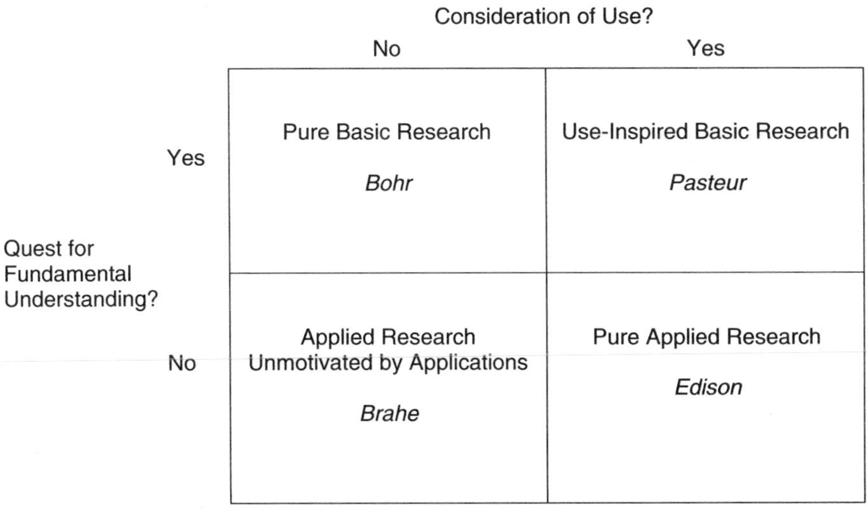

Consideration of Use?

	No	Yes
Yes	Pure Basic Research *Bohr*	Use-Inspired Basic Research *Pasteur*
No	Applied Research Unmotivated by Applications *Brahe*	Pure Applied Research *Edison*

Quest for Fundamental Understanding?

FIGURE 1.1 Stokes' quadrant model of research. SOURCE: Stokes (1997).

dichotomy, this taxonomy explicitly recognizes the category of research that is simultaneously inspired by use and seeks fundamental knowledge. This category of research—"Pasteur's quadrant" in Stokes' formulation—is especially important in IT.

A considerable amount of basic IT has been developed as a result of Pasteur-style research that focuses on understanding the fundamental principles of information representation and behavior, addresses widespread and enduring problems, and yields broad capabilities rather than a specific product or system (e.g., better ways to specify, build, and maintain software of all sorts). Operating systems stem from research into how multiple tasks can share a single computer. Communications and networking research seeks better ways to overcome constraints on communication, such as the nature ("quality") of service needed for delivering real-time video or audio. Today's reduced-instruction-set computing (RISC) microprocessors are based on research that showed how to increase performance by optimizing the speed of the processor instructions that are used most frequently in actual computer programs. Speech recognition and machine vision technologies have matured through research into the machine collection of information from the physical world and its interpretation, which has to be quick and accurate to be useful.

Pasteur-style research in IT sometimes aims at solving new problems that arise in older areas. The Internet satisfied an older research goal of carrying many types of data traffic over a single network, and it generates new research problems associated with multimedia (including audio and video), congestion control, quality of service, and new communication paradigms such as broadcast and multicast. In wireless communications, rapidly increasing demands for service stimulate research into smart antenna systems and multiuser detection to achieve dramatic increases in capacity. More generally, IT researchers are still struggling to find the best ways to tell computers what to do—that is, to write correct software efficiently. They are also still struggling to find the best hardware designs that can scale up to many thousands of processors harnessed to a single computation. These are difficult research problems that endure.

Pasteur-style research tends to have long time horizons. It involves a cycle in which novel designs are worked out, implemented, and evaluated in use. The cycle is often long because each individual stage may require that new techniques be developed. For example, new programming language designs require developing techniques for translating programs into machine language. Implementations of the language have to be complete, robust, and widely available before widespread use begins; evaluation requires that a number of programmers learn the new language, apply it to a range of systems, and accumulate evidence about the value of the language; only some languages will survive these processes. Previous reports on retrospective assessments of IT have demonstrated how much of IT research has yielded results that became evident only after periods of time measurable in decades, a reality that may seem counterintuitive—the new cliché of "Internet time" has not erased the inherent lags in creating and leveraging new scientific and engineering knowledge (see CSTB, 1995, 1999a). A long-term perspective also fosters recognition of the key role of unexpected research results, which lay the foundations for new technologies, products, and entire industries.

In the IT sector, applied research differs from Pasteur-style research only in degree: the focus is sufficiently narrow that results usually apply only to specific applications, products, or systems. Applied IT research tends to be short term, with clear paths to the transfer of research results into production. In one example from industry, a research project investigated how to obtain maximum data rates from a specific disk drive attached to a specific computer that was to be used to transmit digital video data over a network in real time. Unlike conventional disk-driver software, which sacrifices performance to ensure that there are no errors in the data read from the disk, this application emphasized speed above all else. This investigation was (arguably) research because it was not known beforehand what data rates could be achieved or how best to control the disk drive. But the research targeted a particular product, and the results were unlikely to apply to a broad class of settings.

Sometimes, what is intended to be applied research achieves far-reaching results more characteristic of Pasteur-style research. For example, researchers at Carnegie Mellon University who were investigating ways to improve scheduling on a particular factory shop floor devised a new type of optimization algorithm, called constrained optimization, that was able to solve more complex problems than could previous algorithms. The new algorithm went far beyond solving a shop-floor problem: it had applications in many other domains. In fact, its use for optimizing the assignment of payload to transport aircraft during Operation Desert Storm saved millions of dollars in transportation costs. This result epitomizes the benefits that can emerge from research on specific problems that also attempts to arrive at broad-based solutions.

Both basic and applied research differ from development. Development exploits the knowledge generated by research into scientific and technological phenomena, creating specific goods, processes, or services. In general, Internet start-ups, electronic commerce (e-commerce) technology, and the growing variety of information appliances are creatures of development. Although useful knowledge is often created in the process of developing new goods and services (as well as in manufacturing and selling them) and development generates new questions for research to address, research has the primary aim of creating scientific and technical knowledge, and in the process it serves to train people, who go on to generate (and apply) more knowledge. Unless the research base is replenished, development—and innovation—will eventually slow. The distinction between research and development and the relationship of one to the other are often obscured by glib references to R&D; tallies of industrial investment in R&D, which tends to favor development, can produce large numbers without, however, yielding research value. Part of the misunderstanding lies in the available data, part in interpretation of the data.

THE CHANGING ENVIRONMENT FOR INFORMATION TECHNOLOGY RESEARCH

The 1990s witnessed the rise of a new environment for IT research investments. The structure of the IT industry has changed, and the nature of IT applications has greatly expanded. A review of the changes that have taken place underscores why now is an appropriate time to examine the structures and mechanisms used to fund and conduct research, to ensure that they will help the nation reach its IT-related objectives.

Changing Industrial Structure

The IT industry appears to be growing faster than the research base that has supported it, raising questions about the future in an arena where ideas and talent, or intellectual capital, are the most critical assets. Most obvious is the influx of smaller firms that leverage fundamental research undertaken in universities (and elsewhere). Also obvious is the relative decline of several large U.S. industrial laboratories as sources of IT research. Players present in the early 1990s, such as Digital Equipment Corporation, Control Data Corporation, Cray Research, and even Apple Computer, are no longer contributing to the research base. Enduring players, such as IBM Corporation and AT&T, have reorganized and now focus their research more narrowly than they did in the 1970s and 1980s. Newer companies, such as Microsoft Corporation, and foreign corporations, such as NEC and Mitsubishi, launched U.S. research laboratories in the late 1980s and 1990s; the impact of these new efforts remains to be seen—what is known is that they have attracted leading researchers from academia.[5] Industrial research relevant to IT has grown, both in absolute terms and as a share of all such research, but that growth is dwarfed by the IT industry's growth. In this environment, any research investment can have great leverage and influence developments across a broad spectrum of industry and society.

Why does change in the IT industry matter? One might expect, after all, that as an industry matures, R&D spending would decline as a proportion of revenues; such a decline could also come from expanding sales of a stable product—one for which the R&D has been more or less completed. An industry whose history is measured in decades cannot, however, be called mature. Indeed, the evidence of the 1990s points to rejuvenation rather than senescence—the rapid growth of the Internet and its associated business activity, for example, are new phenomena, and that activity will shape yet other phenomena through cumulative experimentation with the network-based interactions of people and systems. Information technology is neither mature nor stable, and the structure and competitive conduct of the industry continue to change.

Measuring the IT research effort is difficult; the most common yardstick is funding. Several factors contribute to concerns about the sufficiency of IT research funding. First, attempts to reduce federal budget deficits and trim defense spending (which historically supported a significant portion of computing and electrical engineering research) constrained federal funding for university research in the early 1990s, affecting career decisions and research output in ways that are beginning to have an impact now. Efforts to enhance accountability in federal government operations and spending also led to increasing support for near-term, mission-oriented research by federal agencies, at the expense of more fundamental long-term research.[6] Yet, as the Congressional Budget Office (CBO) observed, federal funding for long-term research "may have a disproportionately large effect on the direction that information technology takes in the long run" (Webre, 1999). Indeed many argue that the true value of the early research investments in IT by agencies such as the Defense Advanced Research Projects Agency (DARPA) and the National Science Foundation (NSF) has been support for the creation of technologies and capabilities not known before (CSTB, 1999a). External validation of these claims may be gauged not only from industry growth, which lags research investments, but also in flows of venture capital funds, which, according to the CBO, "raise the efficiency of existing R&D by raising the rate at which ideas developed in the laboratory are brought to market" (Webre, 1999). Realizing the future potential of IT therefore depends on continued federal support for fundamental research.

Second, the private sector also faces growing disincentives to investing in long-term research. Increased competition has forced many blue-chip firms to restructure their IT research and development programs to concentrate on problems with greater market relevance. The most obvious examples are the reduction in, and reorientation of, research and development investments by historical industry leaders IBM and AT&T. At the same time, a broader move toward a more horizontal, layered industry structure has resulted in the transfer of research and development to the suppliers of IT components, whether microprocessors, disk drives, or software. The associated specialization may militate against sufficient progress in systems research, which unifies efforts across the IT industries (see Box 1.3 for a description of component research vs. systems research). At the same time, new entrants into the marketplace, and the new mix of products, feature players without a research history. New software enterprises and Web-based ventures can be started with a few highly talented people and a little capital. The venture capital industry is ready and willing to provide the additional funding needed if the start-up appears to be on its way to success.

Third, Moore's law has the effect of driving IT companies to offer the very latest technology continually. To do otherwise would mean losing out to competitors. There is an unusually high obsolescence factor driven by the rapid advances in IT. Any company attempting to offer 2-year-old versions of its systems would, in effect, be offering technology only half as cost-effective as the latest technology allows. In other words, the penalty for being late to market is to lag the performance of more rapidly developed competitive products. Abbreviated product development cycles accelerate the pace of research—if researchers can produce tangible results faster, then products can change faster. If research is done at all, it

---

BOX 1.3
Components, Systems, and Applications

Even in fields traditionally associated with information technology (IT), the methods and subjects of research can vary. These problems can be viewed on three levels:

• Components are individual elements of computing and communications systems that have specific interfaces and functions. They include hardware and software.
• Systems are amalgams of many interacting components that are combined to perform a particular set of functions, however broadly those functions may be defined. Systems must maintain their performance guarantees under widely varying and unknown external (and internal) conditions.
• Applications are components and systems that are embedded in a larger environmental or organizational context to solve particular problems, such as air traffic control or electronic commerce. They provide value to end-users, whether the end user is an individual or an organization.

The distinction between components, systems, and applications is not absolute but depends on the perspective from which they are viewed. A personal computer (PC), for example, may be considered an application by a microprocessor designer, a system by a PC designer, and a component by a network designer. As IT has become more integral to everyday life and work, the set of research problems associated with systems and applications has grown. These problems result from success in building components, such as the PC and the Internet, which have in turn created opportunities for new systems and applications.

---

is often impossible to follow the traditional open research model, with results broadly available for review. As suggested earlier in this chapter, research investments that are coupled more closely to market objectives tend to refine and exploit existing knowledge rather than lay the groundwork for the more radical innovations upon which the industry's future success will surely rely. The shortcomings of this mode of operation are obvious in the areas of security—where, for example, the cycle of iterative product release, public announcement of product flaws, and product fixes has become the norm (CSTB, 1999b)—and of usability, where, for example, the lack of time for studying how real people with differing abilities use systems and what they need and want from the systems continues to constrain ease of use (CSTB, 1997). The situation is compounded by long-standing difficulties in improving productivity in the development of quality software; progress in software engineering continues to be elusive (CSTB, 1999b).

Expanding Applications of Information Technology

The second major change affecting IT research is the expanding role of IT systems in a number of important social applications of IT that support groups of people performing tasks related to government, industry, business, and commerce and in which the technology and larger organizational or social processes are inseparable. It is no exaggeration to say that, today, virtually every facet of government, industry, and commerce is touched by IT, and some depend heavily on it. Many crucial organizational and societal systems operate at a scale and complexity that would simply not be feasible without the assistance of IT. These applications tend to implemented in large-scale systems—IT systems that contain many hardware and software components that interact with each other in complex ways. Many social applications of IT are characterized by the deep interrelationship of the IT with nontechnological elements, such as people, workers, groups of people, students, and organizations of workers. For example, data storage has become a foundation of organizational processes that involve people and material as well as data. Networking has integrated computing into many human interactions, supporting group activities and collaboration: for example, collaboration on the design of a complex vehicle by manufacturers, suppliers, and major customers who share in the development and modification of plans and specifications or the enhancement of retail product and pricing strategies and customer service by capturing information about customer buying behavior.

Newfound applications of IT represent a significant step forward in the evolution of computing, much of which has been shaped by the needs of and conditions in the scientific and engineering communities.[7] The runaway success of the Internet has vastly expanded the range and sophistication of applications, making the issues surrounding large-scale system design, which were for a long time open issues, more critical and immediate. For example, growing numbers of IT applications are spanning different organizations and administrative domains, incorporating not only multiple users but also multiple organizations (with different preferences, procedures, capabilities, and so on) into a single application. As a result, it is becoming much less appropriate to design applications with the assumption that they will be implemented, deployed, operated, and maintained in a coordinated fashion under central control.[8]

Increasing complexity and sophistication are predictable trends. They are standard phenomena in technologically advanced industries, in which productivity gains, fundamental innovations, and difficult, if less fundamental, research problems continue for many years.[9] A corollary is the generation of research problems, discussed in the subsequent chapters, that arise from technical complexity. New IT systems are especially complex because of their large size, the number of interacting components, and their intimate involvement with people who are themselves complex components. The performance of these cannot be fully modeled, so it is difficult to understand how they work before they are put to actual use. Their intended applications and design continue to evolve, and they are increasingly embedded in real-world systems. This situation stands in contrast to the large-scale systems of the past, such as the telephone system, which, because it was so regulated and standardized, did not have to address heterogeneity to the same degree as do today's large-scale IT systems.

The shortcomings in the current state of technology supporting social applications of IT are painfully evident. Engineers are building IT systems that venture beyond the state of knowledge, much as designers of the Tacoma Narrows bridge ventured too far into lightweight suspension bridge design.[10] Today's news reports of system outages in electronic trading, Internet access, and telephony signal that users expect IT systems to have characteristics of reliability and availability that parallel those of physical infrastructures, such as roads, bridges, and power supplies. Aggravating the situation is the distribution of the underlying computing and networking infrastructure across multiple organizations, with components designed by multiple equipment and software vendors. A low level of coordination is possible, but the virtual distributed computing infrastructure cannot be designed or even "tuned" in the same way as earlier generations of computing infrastructure were, when everything was typically under the control of a single organization and its hand-picked vendors. As a result, today's infrastructure forms a rather shaky substrate for the distributed social applications of IT that depend on it.

One manifestation of this reality is vulnerability to various security threats, unpredictable emergent behaviors, and breakdowns. It is difficult to predict or control the performance of large-scale systems or the environment in which they operate. Challenges include constant change in both functional requirements and regulatory constraints, as well as in the underlying infrastructure itself, all of which have the effect of compounding the vulnerability and performance issues. The responses to these challenges are generally ad hoc and not based on any fundamental understanding that could inspire confidence in the methodologies and outcomes. Indeed, the many shortcomings and even failures of past efforts suggest that confidence would not be justified.

Many system problems have been evident for decades, but the broadening deployment of IT and growing dependence on it mean that the payoff from finally resolving them will be greater than ever. Enduring difficulties include achieving parallelism in systems, reusing system components, enhancing ease of use and trustworthiness, and supporting a larger scale. Some other difficulties are becoming more compelling: for example, achieving adaptability (the ability to evolve over time) or maintaining availability of use in the face of predictable and unpredictable problems.[11] The need for progress on these problems has become acute.[12] Major users of large-scale systems, networks, and applications are severely limited in their ability to develop new IT systems by high development costs, uncertain outcomes, and the need to maintain existing operations even though a new system could reduce operational costs, speed product innovation, and improve the services they provide to their customers.

The problems associated with large-scale systems are much the same as those associated with the large, monolithic systems created by organizations like the Federal Aviation Administration (FAA), the Internal Revenue Service (IRS), and large private companies. They could become characteristics of systems used for health care, education, manufacturing, and other social applications that have become widespread.[13] The continued development of computing systems embedded in other devices and systems promises to exacerbate these problems. Microprocessors are being incorporated into an increasing array of devices, from automobile transmissions and coffeemakers to a range of electronic measuring devices, such as thermostats, pollution detectors, cameras, microphones, and medical devices (*Business Week Online*, 1999b). They are also entering a range of information appliances that can be used for playing music, reading electronic books, sending and reading e-mail, and browsing the Web. Such devices are expected to become more numerous than stand-alone computers and will be able to share information across the Internet and other information infrastructures. Some believe that, within 10 years, discrete microprocessors will be knitted together into ad hoc distributed computers whose terminals are laptops, cell phones, or handheld devices.

In considering the social applications of IT, two distinct but related categories of research are relevant. The first is systems research, which has long been pursued in the computing community but takes on added significance in light of the broadening range of functions supported by large-scale systems. In fact, the definition of systems research has changed. In the past, it meant primarily computer architecture, operating systems, and related computer science subjects. Research in these subjects continues, driven by the need for highly scalable systems, around-the-clock availability, and the like. However, the greatest impact of systems and opportunities for them transcend the technology per se: they lie in the social applications of IT. There is a huge demand for research in e-commerce systems and technologies, content management and analysis, community and collaboration systems, and so forth. There is a broad spectrum of social applications of IT, ranging from those that serve primarily a single user operating in a larger context (as in home banking applications that are used by a single user but connect into the bank's financial system) through those that serve groups of users in a time-limited activity, through those that serve the needs of organizations, through those that serve groups of organizations (in commerce or tax collection, for example), to those that serve individual users interacting with groups of organizations (as in online shopping). Systems research will aim at new levels of automation and integration of activities within and among organizations. It will couple IT more closely than ever to complex social and business processes, making IT more truly an information infrastructure. But such coupling also complicates the pursuit of success.

The second category of research focuses on IT embedded in a social context. This research addresses the technology itself, asking how IT can be changed to provide greater benefits to users and end-user organizations through social applications. This perspective is the opposite of the more conventional perspective on the impact of technology, which emphasizes how people must change to accommodate IT: the question is how technology can be changed to accommodate people and organizations.

One characteristic of IT is its extreme malleability. At the level of software and applications, there are few physical limits to be concerned about, and the inherent flexibility of the technology enables it to adjust rather unconstrainedly to application needs, at least in theory. There are, however, serious obstacles to carrying out such adjustments. These include the practical difficulties of changing existing approaches and infrastructure, known by economists as "path-dependent effects" and "lock-in." But even if these economic obstacles could be overcome, there is simply a lack of fundamental understanding of how the technology could be made to better serve the social applications of IT. Furthermore, there are serious gaps in the methodologies for translating contextual application requirements into concrete architectures and specifications for a software implementation (as well as gaps in methods for modifying the context to take maximum advantage of IT). The implication is that trial and error is inevitable, as are false starts and dead ends.

Technical and organizational factors are intertwined, adding to the scientific and engineering challenges. For example, despite its leveraging of work on constrained optimization in the Gulf War, cited above, the United States experienced notable logistical failures in that war: some 40 percent of the sea containers that arrived dockside at the Saudi disembarkation points had to be physically opened and inspected for want of documentation of their contents and its disposition, and it took at least twice as long as the Department of Defense's worst-case projections to mobilize the necessary warfighting materiel in Saudi Arabia and other key points and nearly four times as long to get all that materiel to where it was supposed to go. These represent failures in information systems and reflect underinvestments in areas such as sealift, containerization, and logistics, none of which is as intriguing as, say, smart bombs. They underscore the importance of human and organizational factors in harnessing IT and demonstrate why more research needs to be done on the blend of factors. Although in practice IT has always been shaped by the environment in which it is used, IT research needs to focus more on the overall system and the operational context in which such systems will be used.

To date, IT research has not emphasized systems and applications to nearly the extent called for by the virtual explosion of sophisticated social applications of IT as a result of the Internet. This is not to say there has been a complete void. Indeed, there has been a substantial effort, but it appears to have been inadequate when weighed against the significant challenges and tremendous opportunities. There is a critical need for more fundamental understanding, given the rapidly expanding deployment of applications that support organizational missions and the interaction of many entities (such as businesses, universities, and government) as well as of society in general. This is an area in which opportunities abound for substantial advances in technology, with the goal of making applications much more effective and improving their development, administration, operation, and maintenance in terms of effectiveness, reliability, trustworthiness, and cost.

IMPLICATIONS FOR INFORMATION TECHNOLOGY RESEARCH

The challenges posed by large-scale IT systems and the social applications of IT can be addressed effectively only if the IT research base is expanded. Past research in IT has tended to focus on areas such as the following:

- Fundamental understanding of the limitations on computation and communications;
- Underlying technologies (such as integrated circuits), design techniques and tools (such as compilers), components (such as microprocessors), and computer systems (such as parallel and networked computers); and
- Applications and usability for isolated users, improvements in the human-computer interface, and applications that serve an isolated user.

This technology base must be carried forward; continuing substantial progress will be needed to support and maintain the progress in larger domains. As the importance of networking increases, research in associated challenges (such as distributed file systems and transaction and multicast protocols) is expanding. A number of engaging social applications (such as e-mail, newsgroups, chat rooms, multiplayer games, and remote learning) have emerged from the research community. As is true for other relatively immature suites of technologies, much of the research was begun in academia, and large segments of both the research agenda and its commercial applications have migrated to industry.

Past research in technology emphasized underlying technologies and components, in part because these were necessary ingredients for getting started and in part because it was challenging to obtain the functionality and performance required of even the most basic applications. Today, the challenge is almost the reverse. In the wake of several decades of exponential advances in the capabilities of both electronics and fiber optics, it can be argued that the technologies are beginning to outstrip society's understanding of how to use them effectively. Increasingly, the challenge can be stated as follows: Wonderful technologies are now in our grasp; how can they be put to good use? This is not to minimize either the importance or the challenges of advancing the core technologies, because such advances are critical to progress in applications built on these technologies. Rather, the point is that the existing research agenda needs to accommodate a major push into the uses of technology.

The idea of an expanded IT research agenda is not entirely new. A study committee convened by CSTB in the early 1990s observed both that intellectually substantive and challenging computing problems can and do arise in the context of problem domains outside computer science and engineering per se and that computing research can be framed within the discipline's own intellectual traditions in a manner that is directly applicable to other problem domains (CSTB, 1992). The committee viewed computing research as an engine of progress and conceptual change in other problem domains, even as these domains contribute to the identification of new areas of inquiry within computer science and engineering. Its recommendations sought to sustain the core effort in computer science and engineering (similar to "components" research as defined in this report) while simultaneously broadening the field to explore intellectual opportunities available at the intersection of computer science and engineering and other problem domains (see Box 1.4). Efforts over the past decade have shown both the virtue and the difficulty of including more application-inspired work under the umbrella of IT research, but the need for such work continues to outstrip efforts to produce it.

As the emphasis shifts from applications serving solitary users and single departments to those serving large groups of users, entire enterprises, and critical societal infrastructures, the issues related to this embedding become more interesting and challenging. In particular, research is needed in two areas in addition to IT components: (1) the technical

BOX 1.4
Echoes of CSTB's *Computing the Future*

In the early 1990s, the CSTB Committee to Assess the Scope and Direction of Computer Science and Technology was charged to assess how best to organize the conduct of research and teaching in computer science and engineering (CS&E) in the future. In considering appropriate responses, the committee formulated a set of priorities, the first two of which are relevant to this report:

Priority 1—Sustain the core effort in CS&E, i.e., the effort that creates the theoretical and experimental science base on which computing applications build. This core effort has been deep, rich, and intellectually productive and has been indispensable for its impact on practice in the last couple of decades.
Priority 2—Broaden the field. Given the solid CS&E core and the many intellectual opportunities available at the intersection of CS&E and other problem domains, the committee believes that academic CS&E is well positioned to broaden its self-concept. Such broadening will also result in new insights with wide applicability, thereby enriching the core. Furthermore, given the pressing economic and social needs of the nation and the changing environment for industry and academia, the committee believes academic CS&E *must* broaden its self-concept or risk becoming increasingly irrelevant to computing practice.

These priorities led the committee to offer a set of recommendations that, while linked to particular programs of the time, have continued relevance today and foreshadow the recommendations made in Chapter 5 of this report.

Recommendation 1—The High Performance Computing and Communications (HPCC) Program should be fully supported throughout the planned 5-year program. The HPCC program is of utmost importance for three reasons. The first is that high-performance computing and communications are essential to the nation's future economic strength and competitiveness, especially in light of the growing need and demand for ever more advanced computing tools in all sectors of society. The second reason is that the program is framed in the context of scientific and engineering grand challenges. Thus the program is a strong signal to the CS&E [computer science and engineering] community that good CS&E research can flourish in an application context and that the demand for interdisciplinary and applications-oriented CS&E research is on the rise. And finally, a fully funded HPCC Program will have a major impact on relieving the funding stress affecting the academic CS&E community. . . .
Recommendation 2—The federal government should initiate an effort to support interdisciplinary and applications-oriented CS&E research in academia that is related to the missions of the mission-oriented federal agencies and departments that are not now major participants in the HPCC [High Performance Computing and Communications] Program. Collectively, this effort would cost an additional $100 million per fiscal year in steady state above amounts currently planned. Many federal agencies are not currently participating in the HPCC Program, despite the utility of computing to their missions, and they should be brought into the program. Those agencies that support substantial research efforts, though not in CS&E, should support interdisciplinary CS&E research, i.e., CS&E research undertaken jointly with research in other fields. Problems in these other fields often include an

continued

BOX 1.4 Continued

important computational component whose effectiveness could be enhanced substantially by the active involvement of researchers working at the cutting edge of CS&E research. Those agencies that do not now support substantial research efforts of any kind, i.e., operationally oriented agencies, should consider supporting applications-oriented CS&E research because of the potential that the efficiency of their operations would be substantially improved by some research advance that could deliver a better technology for their purposes. Such research could also have considerable "spin-off" benefit to the private sector as well.

Recommendation 3—Academic CS&E should broaden its research horizons, embracing as legitimate and cogent not just research in core areas (where it has been and continues to be strong) but also research in problem domains that derive from nonroutine computer applications in other fields and areas or from technology-transfer activities. The academic CS&E community should regard as scholarship any activity that results in significant new knowledge and demonstrable intellectual achievement, without regard for whether that activity is related to a particular application or whether it falls into the traditional categories of basic research, applied research, or development. Chapter 5 describes appropriate actions to implement this recommendation.

Recommendation 4—Universities should support CS&E as a laboratory discipline (i.e., one with both theoretical and experimental components). CS&E departments need adequate research and teaching laboratory space, staff support (e.g., technicians, programmers, staff scientists); funding for hardware and software acquisition, maintenance, and upgrade (especially important on systems that retain their cutting edge for just a few years); and network connections. New faculty should be capitalized at levels comparable to those in other scientific or engineering disciplines.

SOURCE: Excerpts from Computer Science and Telecommunications Board (1992), pp. 5-8.

challenges, such as trustworthiness, scalability, and location transparency, associated with large-scale systems and (2) challenges that surround the molding of embedded IT within its application context, that is, within the social applications of IT. The second challenge can be considered only partly a technical one, arising as it does from the context of IT. These are difficult problems to characterize, let alone solve.

An analogy to the health sciences may be helpful in understanding the relationship between the more traditional components-oriented research and the additional work that is needed on large-scale systems and on the social applications of IT. One way to classify the health sciences is to divide them into three related and overlapping sets of disciplines, each with its own research base:

- The biological sciences, which examines the basic scientific processes that underlie much of the progress in medicine;
- Physiology, anatomy, and pathology, which focus on understanding how biological systems, such as organisms composed of interacting organs, work and how their components can be manipulated to provide medical benefits; and
- Clinical medicine and epidemiology. The former focuses on treating human diseases, drawing on the other disciplines but also working closely and empirically with patients; the latter focuses on the relationship between environments and health.

Pursuing this analogy, the component- and technology-oriented research that has so far dominated IT research is similar to research in the biological sciences: it develops the basic understanding and techniques that are invaluable in constructing working systems. Research related to large-scale systems that use IT is analogous to physiology: it attempts to understand the interactions among components and the development of systems. Interdisciplinary research involving the social sciences, business, and law, in collaboration with technologists and addressing many of the social and organizational challenges posed by the social applications of IT, is analogous to medicine and epidemiology. This research is focused on applications and is justified by the direct impact it can have on them and society as a whole.

As this report argues, research in components, systems, and applications is needed to ensure the development of fundamental understanding that will allow IT systems to evolve to meet society's growing needs. This is not research directed at finding a more effective way to use IT in a narrow application domain; rather, it is research directed at revolutionizing the understanding of how distributed computing environments with decentralized design and operations can offer predictable, reproducible performance and capability and controlled vulnerability. It is also directed at revolutionizing the ability to accommodate rapid change in both the context and requirements of the infrastructure and applications. It is directed at fundamentally revamping methodologies for capturing application requirements and transforming them into working applications. It is directed at revolutionizing the organizational processes and group dynamics that form the application context in ways that can most effectively leverage IT. This is long-term research that is extremely challenging.

IMPLICATIONS FOR THE RESEARCH ENTERPRISE

The trends in IT suggest that the nation needs to reinvent IT research and develop new structures to support, conduct, and manage it. The history of U.S. support for IT research established enduring principles for research policy: support for long-term fundamental research; support for the development of large systems that bring together researchers from different disciplines and institutions to work on common problems; and work that builds on innovations pioneered in industrial laboratories (CSTB, 1999a).

As IT permeates many more real-world applications, additional constituencies need to be brought into the research process as both funders and performers of IT research. This is necessary not only to broaden the funding base to include those who directly benefit from the fruits of the research, but also to obtain input and guidance. An understanding of business practices and processes is needed to support the evolution of e-commerce; insight from the social sciences is needed to build IT systems that are truly user-friendly and that help people work better together. No one truly understands where new applications such as e-commerce, electronic publishing, or electronic collaboration are headed, but business development and research together can promote their arrival at desirable destinations.

Many challenges will require the participation and insight of the end user and the service provider communities. They have a large stake in seeing these problems addressed, and they stand to benefit most directly from the solutions. Similarly, systems integrators would benefit from an improved understanding of systems and applications because they would become more competitive in the marketplace and be better able to meet their estimates of project cost and time. Unlike vendors of component technologies, systems integrators and end users deal with entire information systems and therefore have unique perspectives on the problems encountered in developing systems and the feasibility of proposed solutions. Many of the end-user organizations, however, have no tradition of conducting IT research—or technological research of any kind, in fact—and they are not necessarily capable of doing so effectively; they depend on vendors for their technology. Even so, their involvement in the research process is critical. Vendors of equipment and software have neither the requisite experience and expertise nor the financial incentives to invest heavily in research on the challenges facing end-user organizations, especially the challenges associated with the social applications of IT.[14] Of course, they listen to their customers as they refine their products and strategies, but those interactions are superficial compared with the demands of the new systems and applications. Finding suitable mechanisms for the participation of end users and service providers, and engaging them productively, will be a big challenge for the future of IT research.

Past attempts at public-private partnerships, as in the emerging arena of critical infrastructure protection, show it is not so easy to get the public and private sectors to interact for the purpose of improving the research base and implementation of systems: the federal government has a responsibility to address the public interest in critical infrastructure, whereas the private sector owns and develops that infrastructure, and conflicting objectives and time horizons have confounded joint exploration. As a user of IT, the government could play an important role. Whereas historically it had limited and often separate programs to support research and acquire systems for its own use, the government is now becoming a consumer of IT on a very large scale. Just as IT and the widespread access to it provided by the Web have enabled businesses to reinvent themselves, IT could dramatically improve operations and reduce the costs of applications in public health, air traffic control, and social security; government agencies, like private-sector organizations, are turning increasingly to commercial, off-the-shelf technology.

Universities will play a critical role in expanding the IT research agenda. The university setting continues to be the most hospitable for higher-risk research projects in which the outcomes are very uncertain. Universities can play an important role in establishing new research programs for large-scale systems and social applications, assuming that they can overcome long-standing institutional and cultural barriers to the needed cross-disciplinary research. Preserving the university as a base for research and the education that goes with it would ensure a workforce capable of designing, developing, and operating increasingly sophisticated IT systems. A booming IT marketplace and the lure of large salaries in industry heighten the impact of federal funding decisions on the individual decisions that shape the university environment: as the key funders of university research, federal programs send important signals to faculty and students.

The current concerns in IT differ from the competitiveness concerns of the 1980s: the all-pervasiveness of IT in everyday life raises new questions of how to get from here to there—how to realize the exciting possibilities, not merely how to get there first. A vital and relevant IT research program is more important than ever, given the complexity of the issues at hand and the need to provide solid underpinnings for the rapidly changing IT marketplace.

ORGANIZATION OF THIS REPORT

The remainder of this report elaborates on the themes introduced in this chapter. Chapter 2 examines trends in support for IT research by government, industry, and universities. It reviews statistics on funding for R&D and describes the linkages between existing funding patterns and the trends outlined above. Chapter 3 examines challenges in large-scale systems research that are not new but that have taken on renewed importance as social applications of computing and communications emerge. It identifies existing shortfalls in the research community's understanding of large-scale systems and suggests avenues for further investigation. Chapter 4 examines IT systems that are embedded in a social context, outlining the research problems that result from the integration of IT into a range of social applications and discussing the value of interdisciplinary research in this area. It identifies areas in which interdisciplinary research drawing on the social sciences is needed to complement the strictly technical research being conducted by IT researchers; outlines different mechanisms for pursuing an expanded IT research agenda that considers systems and applications as well as components; and discusses ways in which government, industry, and universities need to alter their organization and management of IT research to ensure that mechanisms exist for conducting the kinds of research that will be needed for the future. Chapter 5 presents the committee's recommendations for strengthening the resource base in IT. It outlines actions that government, universities, and industry should take to advance a broader research agenda for IT.

BIBLIOGRAPHY

Buderi, Robert. 1998. "Bell Labs Is Dead: Long Live Bell Labs," *Technology Review* 101(5):50-57.

Business Week Online. 1999a. "Q&A: An Internet Pioneer Moves Toward Nomadic Computing," August 30.

Business Week Online. 1999b. "The Earth Will Don an Electronic Skin," August 30.

Carey, John. 1997. "What Price Science?" *Business Week,* May 26. Available online at <www.businessweek.com/1997/21/b3528136.htm>.

Committee for Economic Development (CED). 1998. *America's Basic Research: Prosperity Through Discovery.* Committee for Economic Development, New York.

Computer Science and Telecommunications Board (CSTB), National Research Council. 1992. *Computing the Future.* National Academy Press, Washington, D.C.

Computer Science and Telecommunications Board (CSTB), National Research Council. 1994. *Realizing the Information Future: The Internet and Beyond.* National Academy Press, Washington, D.C.

Computer Science and Telecommunications Board (CSTB), National Research Council. 1995. *Evolving the High-Performance Computing and Communications Initiative to Support the Nation's Information Infrastructure.* National Academy Press, Washington, D.C.

Computer Science and Telecommunications Board (CSTB), National Research Council. 1997. *More Than Screen Deep*. National Academy Press, Washington, D.C.

Computer Science and Telecommunications Board (CSTB), National Research Council. 1999a. *Funding a Revolution: Government Support for Computing Research*. National Academy Press, Washington, D.C.

Computer Science and Telecommunications Board (CSTB), National Research Council 1999b. *Trust in Cyberspace*. National Academy Press, Washington, D.C.

Council on Competitiveness. 1996. *Endless Frontier, Limited Resources: U.S. R&D Policy for Competitiveness*. Council on Competitiveness, Washington, D.C., April.

Council on Competitiveness. 1998. *Going Global: The New Shape of American Innovation*. Council on Competitiveness, Washington, D.C., September.

Critical Infrastructure Assurance Office (CIAO). 2000a. *Defending America's Cyberspace: National Plan for Information Systems Protection, Version 1.0, An Invitation to a Dialogue*. The White House, Washington, D.C., January. Available online at <http://www.ciao.gov/National_Plan/national_plan%20_final.pdf>.

Critical Infrastructure Assurance Office (CIAO). 2000b. Practices for Securing Critical Information Assets. CIAO, Washington, D.C., January. Available online at <http://www.ciao.gov/CIAO_Document_Library/Practices_For_Securing_Critical_Information_Assets.pdf>.

David, Paul. 1990. "The Dynamo and the Computer: An Historical Perspective on the Modern Productivity Paradox," *The American Economic Review* 80(2):355-361, May.

Gray, Jim. 1999. *What's Next: A Dozen Information-Technology Research Goals*. Technical report MS-TR-99-50, Microsoft Research, Redmond, Washington, June. Available online at HtmlResAnchor http://www.research.microsoft.com/~Gray/.

Leibovich, Mark. 1999. "Microsoft Skims Off Academia's Best for Research Center," *Washington Post*, April 5, p. A1.

President's Commission on Critical Infrastructure Protection (PCCIP). 1997. *Critical Foundations: Protecting America's Infrastructures*, Washington, D.C., October. Available online at <http://www.ciao.gov/CIAO_Document_Library/PCCIP_Report.pdf>.

President's Information Technology Advisory Committee (PITAC). 1999. *Information Technology Research: Investing in Our Future*. National Coordination Office for Computing, Information, and Communications, Arlington, Va., February. Available online at <http://www.ccic.gov/ac/report/>.

Schatz, Bruce R. 1997. "Information Retrieval in Digital Libraries: Bringing Search to the Net," *Science* 275(5298):327-334, January 17.

Schatz, Bruce R., and Joseph B. Hardin. 1994. "NCSA Mosaic and the World Wide Web: Global hypermedia protocols for the Internet," *Science* 265(5174):895-901, August 12.

Stokes, Donald E. 1997. *Pasteur's Quadrant: Basic Science and Technological Innovation*. Brookings Institution Press, Washington, D.C.

Uchitelle, Louis. 1996. "Basic Research Is Losing Out As Companies Stress Results," *New York Times*, pp. A1 and D6, October 8.

U.S. Department of Commerce, Economics and Statistics Administration. 2000. *Digital Economy 2000*. U.S. Department of Commerce, Washington, D.C., June.

Webre, Philip. 1999. "Current Investments in Innovation," Congressional Budget Office, Washington, D.C., April.

Ziegler, Bart. 1997. "Lab Experiment: Gerstner Slashed R&D by $1 Billion: For IBM, It May Be a Good Thing, Latest Breakthrough Shows," *Wall Street Journal*, October 6, p. A1.

NOTES

1. For a discussion of the influence that debates over federal research policy had on the High Performance Computing and Communications Initiative (HPCCI), see CSTB (1995).

2. The recommendations of PITAC regarding federal funding for IT research can be found in PITAC (1999). Additional information on the Clinton Administration's IT[2] initiative is available online at <http://www.ccic.gov/it2/>.

3. Numerous press accounts from the mid- and late 1990s reported on the reorientation of research labs in the IT industry and resulting concerns about long-term, fundamental research. See, for example, Uchitelle (1996), Carey (1997), Ziegler (1997), and Buderi (1998).

4. A new CSTB study on the fundamentals of computer science will emphasize the science aspects, including the interaction of computer science with other sciences. Additional information on this project is available on the CSTB Web site at <www.cstb.org>.

5. Microsoft, in particular, has been noted for tapping top academic talent for its research lab. See Leibovich (1999).

6. The Government Performance and Results Act of 1993, for example, called for explicit attempts to measure the results of government programs, including research programs. The act therefore added to the pressure for near-term and mission-oriented work.

7. In scientific computing, IT is used to model, emulate, and simulate various scientific and technical processes. Scientific computing has received considerable attention from the IT research community from the earliest days, for several reasons. First, IT researchers are technically oriented and can appreciate and understand the issues related to scientific computing. Second, scientific computing has been critical to the scientific and engineering enterprise and to major government programs such as nuclear energy and weapons and the military and so has been admirably supported by the government. Scientific computing continues to be important to the future of computing, science, many fields of engineering, and the military enterprise and should not be deemphasized.

Because it has been strongly supported by funding agencies and the research community, scientific computing is an inspirational example of the interrelationship and synergy between application and technology. Scientific computing applications have been a major driver of high-performance computing technologies and parallel programming techniques. In turn, scientific computing has influenced engineering and science, providing not only substantial benefits but also approaches to problem solving—such as the characteristics of numerical algorithms that yield to parallelism. The very methodologies of science have been substantially affected in ways that make scientific progress more rapid as well as cost effective. Scientific computing has benefited greatly from its long-term association with the research environment.

Scientific computing also demonstrates the importance of long-term and fundamental research on technology in application contexts. There are fundamental gaps in understanding and unexploited opportunities that can be addressed by taking a long-term perspective, one that is not generally pursued by industrial organizations with their more short-term profit motivation. Much of the benefit of research outcomes will accrue not to individual private firms but to industry, government, and society in general. The government is a major user and developer of scientific computing applications and, in many ways, its challenges are much greater than those of the private sector. If government-funded research in any facet of technology is justified, then surely research in the more effective application of technology to the needs of government and its citizens is even more strongly justified.

8. As recalled recently by Leonard Kleinrock: "In the early days of ARPA [the Advanced Research Projects Agency], even when we had only three machines, we were able to uncover logical errors in the routing protocol, or the flow-control protocol, that would cause network failures. Those errors are hard to detect ahead of time, especially as the systems get more complex. It's easy to detect the cause of a massive crash or degradation. But complex systems have latent failure modes that we have not yet excited. There is always potential for deadlocks, crashes, degradations, errant behavior. . . . As systems get more complex, they crash in incredible and glorious ways. What you want to have is a self-

repairing mode [so that if] one part fails, other parts continue to function" *(Business Week Online*, 1999a).

9. A considerable economics literature exists on the increasing complexity of technologies as they evolve over time. See, for example, David (1990).

10. The first Tacoma Narrows suspension bridge, near the city of Tacoma, Washington, collapsed as a result of wind-induced vibrations on November 7, 1940, just 4 months after it was opened to traffic. The collapse was attributed to the bridge's structure, which caught the wind instead of letting it pass through. A windstorm caused the bridge to undergo a series of undulations, which were caught on film before its collapse, earning the bridge the nickname "Galloping Gertie." Video footage of the bridge's collapse is available online at <http://mecad.uta.edu/~bpwang/me5311/1999/lecture1/intro25.htm>.

11. This material derives from a set of briefing slides entitled "Computer Systems Research: Past and Present" prepared by Butler Lampson from Microsoft Research. The slides are available online at <http://www.research.microsoft.com/lampson/Slides/ComputerSystemsResearchAbstract.htm>.

12. As evidence of the recognition that issues of security and reliability have received in the policy community, President Clinton signed Presidential Decision Directive 63 on May 22, 1998, which calls for a national effort to ensure the security of critical information infrastructures, such as the telephone system and electric power grid. The directive also established the Critical Infrastructure Assurance Office (CIAO), which was charged with integrating the plans of various industry sectors into a national plan for infrastructure assurance and with coordinating an analysis of the federal government's own dependence on critical infrastructures. Its work to date is captured in CIAO (2000a,b). It builds on the efforts of its predecessor, the President's Commission on Critical Infrastructure Protection, which was established in July 1996 as the first national effort to address vulnerabilities of infrastructure in the information age. See PCCIP (1997).

13. The 1999 PITAC report outlines nine areas that could be dramatically transformed by information technology. It describes specific transformations in communications, processing information, teaching and learning, the provision of health care, the conduct of commerce, the way people work, the design and manufacture of goods, the conduct of research, and government operations. The full potential of these and similar applications cannot be achieved without a much better fundamental understanding of the applications themselves, the supporting IT, and the relationship between the two. A great deal of research needs to be done to gain this understanding.

14. As noted in a previous CSTB study (CSTB, 1997), most of the people involved in the design and implementation of IT systems are sophisticated users of computing and communications devices. They do not, in general, understand the ways in which IT is used in different applications, nor the more limited technical prowess of the average end user. As a result, it is difficult for researchers and system designers to know what will be easy and gratifying for many of their ultimate customers.

2

Resources for Information Technology Research

The resources needed for research include funding and human capital, which are interrelated. Increases in funding for information technology (IT) research can enable industrial and university laboratories to hire more researchers, increase the number of graduate students trained in the nation's research universities, and allow the purchase of more IT hardware, software, and services to support those people. Similarly, increasing the size of the research workforce demands additional financial resources for salaries and technical infrastructure. But numbers alone do not tell the whole story. Equally important are the types of work supported and the types of organizations that fund or undertake the research. Vendors of computing and communications products, systems integrators, and end users all have different perspectives on the IT challenges that need to be addressed, and these perspectives combine with those of government funders of research and the researchers themselves to influence the scale and scope of the research agenda.

This chapter reviews trends in the nation's overall investment in IT research. The first section provides a framework for evaluating trends by explaining the importance of diversity in research portfolios, a theme carried forward through the chapter. The next two sections examine levels of government and industry funding for IT research, concentrating on the years 1987 to 1998. Distinctions are made, when possible, among funding sources (e.g., specific federal agencies, vendors, or users of IT components) and the types of research supported (e.g., component advances vs. system integration issues). The last section of the chapter reviews trends in academic IT research, which receives much of the government and industrial support.

A credible discussion of research resources presupposes the existence of data: unfortunately, the present discussion is limited by the nature and quality of available statistics on IT research expenditures, as well as by lags between the time conditions are measured and the time they are reported. Despite extensive efforts by the National Science Foundation (NSF) and the Bureau of the Census, federal statistics on industrial and federally funded research remain difficult to track over time because some individual firms have been reclassified into different industry sectors and survey methodologies have been revised. Private sources of information, whether corporate reports or statistics from industry associations, typically do not distinguish expenditures on basic research from those on technology development (or applied research). Further complicating matters, neither federal nor private statistics speak to IT as a whole. Rather, they refer to academic disciplines (e.g., computer science and electrical engineering) or industry classifications (e.g., office and computing equipment and computing and data processing services). Some of the categories are being updated, but it is too soon to assess the impact of those changes. As computing and communications technologies converge and IT is infused into a growing number of products and services, assessing the size and needs of IT research will become even more difficult.

Because of the limitations in the available data sets, this chapter does not attempt a definitive assessment. Instead, it presents and analyzes a mosaic of available statistics to elucidate the dominant themes in support for research. In some cases, funding for combined expenditures on research and development (R&D) is used as a proxy for research; in others, the distinctions in federal data between basic and applied research are used to gain some insight, however limited, into the overall investments in these areas.

DIVERSITY IN THE RESEARCH BASE

The payoff of any research, especially fundamental research, is inherently uncertain. Research managers cannot predict which projects will prove successful or produce the greatest benefit to their organizations, industry, or society as a whole. Accordingly, savvy research managers seek to invest in a range of diverse research programs as a strategy for ensuring that at least a fraction of the overall portfolio will pay off—preferably enough to justify the entire investment. The concept of preparing for the unpredictable by investing in diverse activities that pursue a spread of the best possible ideas is known as "portfolio management" in financial markets, which rely on this concept to manage risk.

Diversity within a research or financial portfolio plays much the same role as does genetic diversity in a species. A living organism carries a small amount of genetic material in addition to the genes that are essential for function. In a static environment, this genetic diversity imposes a cost beyond that carried by a species whose members are genetically identical and specifically tuned to exploit the environment. However, in times of a change or competition from other species, genetic diversity enables a species to adapt to the new environment using its extra resources. Similarly, diversity in the research base ensures that a nation's innovations will continue in the face of unforeseen changes in the technical, business, or societal landscape.[1] Diverse approaches will thus be available when changing conditions require new solutions quickly.

No one can fully predict future needs. The need for high-speed packet switching could not have been predicted 25 years ago, yet it is the heart of the Internet today. The need for ultralow-power microprocessors was largely unexplored 20 years ago, whereas today it is a critical underpinning in the growing area of portable and handheld computing. The economic payoffs of specific investments are likewise difficult to predict. Coding theory and digital signal processing were important research areas 40 years ago because of their applications in telephony and military radio. There was no way to know, however, that this research would have such enormous importance for consumer cellular telephones and Internet multimedia conferencing, which have hundreds of millions of users.

Lack of diversity in the IT research base can result from several factors. First, inbreeding can dilute the effectiveness of a research area as the same small community keeps funding and peer reviewing its members' projects. Or a research area can become too focused on a single approach that in retrospect turns out to have been unproductive. This can happen in a vigorous industry when firms adopt common approaches in their products, implying to researchers that even a successful new idea could not be introduced into practice. For example, radical new ideas for microprocessor designs might seem futile, because a tiny number of designs dominate today's market and the cost of market entry is enormous. However, low-power designs, crafted for the battery-powered portable devices that are sure to increase in number, might offer an opportunity for a very different approach.

Second, there can be a lack of funding for certain types of research—resulting in an absence of understanding of some technology that might suddenly become important to the field. This can happen when innovation moves ahead of research and new products and services are developed without sufficient intellectual underpinnings. Arguably, some of the problems inherent in large-scale systems fall into this category (as discussed further in Chapter 4).

Third, research can reflect, to too great a degree, the objectives of the funders rather than the ideas of researchers. Although narrowly defined project goals can sometimes drive research that has serendipitous outcomes, they typically undermine diversity. This prospect fueled debate within the IT research community in the 1990s, when the High Performance Computing and Communications Initiative focused attention on the nature of research program definition and its impacts. Of course, it can be difficult to quantify the opportunity cost, which, at best, may be measurable only in retrospect.

FEDERAL SUPPORT FOR INFORMATION TECHNOLOGY RESEARCH

The federal government has been a strong supporter of IT research since World War II. Some of this research is conducted in federal laboratories, such as those supported by the Department of Energy (DOE) and the Department of Defense (DOD), but the greatest impact may have come from federally funded research carried out in university and industrial laboratories (CSTB, 1999). Over the past 50 years, this research has contributed to a wide range of important developments, including interactive time-shared computing, computer graphics, artificial intelligence, relational databases, and internetworking (CSTB, 1995, 1999).[2] These technologies laid the foundation for new firms and new industries that have made substantial contributions to the nation's economic and social development. The context for decisions about new IT research continues to change—the industrial context seems particularly uncertain as this report is written—but broad lessons can be extracted from history to inform future decision making.

As noted in earlier reports by the Computer Science and Telecommunications Board (CSTB, 1995, 1999), federal support for IT research has been most effective when (1) directed toward fundamental research with long-term payoffs, (2) used to support experimental prototypes that pushed the technological frontier and created communities of researchers that crossed institutional boundaries, and (3) expanded on research pursued in industry laboratories. Such investments not only generated new technical ideas and knowledge that subsequently were incorporated into new products, processes, and services, but also—especially in the case of university research—trained generations of researchers who went on to lead the IT revolution. Continued federal support for projects that complement industry-funded research in these ways will help maintain the strength of the IT sector. Federal agencies also need to continue to look forward, supporting computing and communications research in areas that are likely to grow in importance.

The following sections examine trends in federal funding between 1990 and 1998, the relative contributions of particular agencies, the operating styles of major federal agencies, and the characteristics of some large IT research programs. That period was chosen because it constitutes the most recent period for which consistent statistics are available. Other sections draw on data for 1999 and 2000.

Trends in Federal Funding

Trends in federal support for IT research over the past decade can be gleaned from data on funds obligated for research in computer science and electrical engineering, the two academic disciplines most closely associated with IT. Computer science encompasses the study of the theory of computing; the design, development, and application of computing devices; information science and systems; programming languages; and systems analysis—all topics that are directly applicable to IT. Electrical engineering includes the study of electronic devices and communication systems, which is directly relevant to IT, as well as the study of electric power systems, which is not. The sum of research expenditures for computer science and electrical engineering is an imperfect, but reasonable, proxy for IT research. Although it overstates federal expenditures by including work on electric power, this overstatement is offset by uncounted research in other academic disciplines relevant to IT, such as mathematics and cognitive science (important for understanding human-computer interaction).

The data indicate that federal funding for IT research has, in general, been strong over the past decade. Combined federal funding for computer science and electrical engineering grew from $1.4 billion to $2 billion in constant dollars between 1990 and 1998—a 40 percent increase in real terms (Figure 2.1).[3] However, federal funding for IT research remained virtually unchanged in real terms between 1993 and 1997, when the Internet and the World Wide Web began to exert a significant influence on the nation's economic and social structure, and when combined sales of IT goods and services were growing at an annual rate of more than 10 percent in real terms.[4] In other words, the explosion in IT applications throughout industry, government, and society was not matched by a commensurate increase in federal research support for the field—even as those applications began pushing beyond the knowledge limits of the underlying technology and began opening up new research opportunities.

Despite the gains in funding for IT as a whole, federal support for research in electrical engineering appears to have declined between 1990

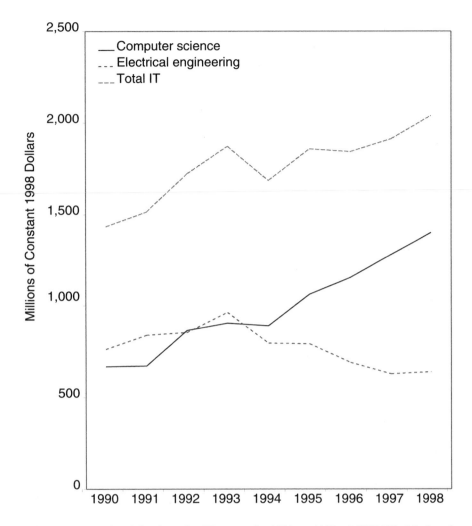

FIGURE 2.1 Federal funding for IT research, 1990 to 1998. SOURCE: National Science Foundation (2000a).

and 1998. The data suggest a 16 percent drop in real terms, from $764 million to $639 million in constant dollars (Figure 2.2). Most of the cuts were in the applied research budget, effectively boosting the share of funds devoted to basic research from 23 percent to 34 percent of total research spending in electrical engineering. However, support for basic research did not grow appreciably until 1998. Reductions in total research

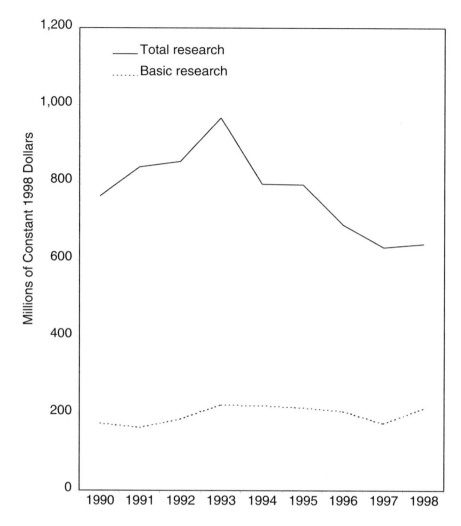

FIGURE 2.2 Federal obligations for research in electrical engineering, 1990 to 1998.
SOURCE: National Science Foundation (2000a).

in electrical engineering appear to be due almost entirely to cutbacks in support from the DOD, which accounted for as much as 84 percent of the nation's total research funding for the field during this time period. This observation suggests that a significant portion of the cutbacks was directed toward those areas of electrical engineering that are directly related to IT, but sufficiently detailed data are not available to confirm this statement. Nor can available statistics reveal whether apparent reductions in funding for electrical engineering resulted from the reclassification of some research from electrical engineering to computer science.

In computer science, combined federal expenditures for basic and applied research (also referred to as "total research") more than doubled in real terms between 1990 and 1998, growing from $671 million to $1.4 billion in constant 1998 dollars (Figure 2.3). Here, however, funding for applied research grew more quickly than that for basic research. Although

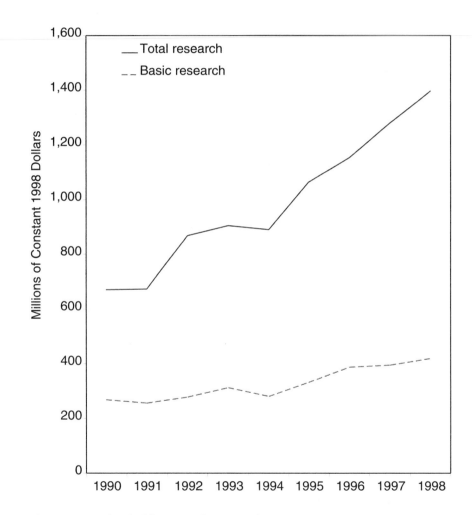

FIGURE 2.3 Federal obligations for research in computer science, 1990 to 1998. SOURCE: National Science Foundation (2000a).

spending on basic research increased from $269 million to $419 million during the 8-year period, its share of total federal funding for computer science research fell from 40 percent to 30 percent. Statistics on basic versus applied research must be used with caution because distinctions between the two categories are notoriously difficult to make and may only reflect differences in accounting methods. Nevertheless, the data correlate with the testimony to this committee (and others) by IT researchers—especially university researchers—who perceive a decided shift in federal funding away from fundamental research and toward more applied projects with narrower scopes of inquiry, additional project milestones, mandatory system demonstrations, and interim deliverables. This trend has an upside and a downside: it may enhance the accountability of government agencies and help document the benefits of public investments (objectives set forth by the Government Performance and Results Act), but IT researchers report that it hampers their ability to conduct long-term research with inherently uncertain outcomes. At risk is the type of work that has been the cornerstone of federally funded IT research for decades.

Sources of Federal Support

Despite growth in the number of agencies listed as supporting IT research, federal funding remains concentrated in a handful of agencies. As recently as 1998, 88 percent of all federal funds for computer science research were distributed by just three federal agencies: the Department of Defense (DOD), the Department of Energy (DOE), and the National Science Foundation (NSF). The DOD alone contributed 40 percent of the total, with much of its funding coming from the Defense Advanced Research Projects Agency (DARPA) (see Table 2.1). A similar proportion of all funding for basic research in computer science came from the same three agencies, with the NSF alone contributing 62 percent of the total in 1998. This funding pattern continues a historical trend: as far back as 1976 (the earliest date for which consistent data are available), these three agencies contributed 91 percent of federal funding for computer science research, with the DOD alone contributing 68 percent.

Although the DOD has driven many important IT innovations in the past 50 years, the field's reliance on this one agency makes IT research support especially sensitive to fluctuations and directions in defense spending—and to repeated calls for research to be more relevant to defense missions. Defense budgets declined significantly in the post-Cold War environment, with total defense R&D declining 24 percent in real terms from its high in 1989 to 1999.[5] Although DOD funding for computer science research grew 32 percent in real terms between 1990 and

TABLE 2.1 Federal Funding for Computer Science Research by Agency, 1998

Agency	Total Research		Basic Research	
	Millions of Dollars	Percent of Total	Millions of Dollars	Percent of Total
Department of Defense	562	40	85	20
Department of Energy	396	28	22	5
National Science Foundation	267	19	258	62
Department of Health and Human Services	66	5	35	8
Department of Commerce	58	4	1	0
National Aeronautics and Space Administration	26	2	17	4
Other	25	2	1	0
Total	1,399	100	419	100

SOURCE: National Science Foundation (2000a).

1998, it varied from year to year, declining in real terms in 1991, 1994, and 1996. Steep increases in spending by NSF and DOE during those years more than compensated for fluctuating military funding, but increases in computer science spending were not matched in spending for electrical engineering. The DOD funding for electrical engineering research dropped 20 percent in real terms between 1990 and 1998, driving the decline in total federal funding for the field.

The concentration of federal IT research funding within three organizations may have other limiting effects, not only on technology but also, perhaps, on the performance of government operations. Several agencies, including the Department of Health and Human Services (DHHS), the Social Security Administration, the Federal Aviation Administration, and the Internal Revenue Service, find their missions increasingly reliant on capable IT systems, which figure not only in internal processes (e.g., determinations and tracking of Social Security benefits) but also, increasingly, in the conduct of external activities for which they have some responsibility and in the very fabric of their relationships with external parties, from entities in regulated industries to individual citizens. The potential benefits to government agencies from IT are such that special federal efforts have been mounted to pursue them, including the Digital Government program described in Chapter 4. This level of attention and effort distinguishes IT from other types of infrastructure, such as transportation, on which agencies also depend.

Achieving the benefits of IT within agencies has been more difficult than articulating their promise. The difficulties these agencies have experienced with systems modernization over the past decade (see Chapter 3) suggest that adequate solutions to their IT needs are not available and cannot be developed within existing time and budget constraints. The problems are related mostly to the large scale of the systems and applications—a common issue that might have the best chance of being resolved if the agencies supported the relevant IT research. Yet the agencies are not mounting significant IT research programs, nor have they rushed to support the exploratory Digital Government program launched by the NSF to couple IT researchers to agencies with IT challenges—an initiative that could stretch the state of the art. Surely, support for IT research from federal agencies other than DOD, DOE, and NSF has increased as a percentage of total federal support since 1990, but the fraction remains small. Only 12 percent of total IT research funding and 13 percent of basic research support came from other agencies in 1998—and most of that was provided by science-based agencies such as DHHS and the National Aeronautics and Space Administration (NASA), which have long histories of attention to IT. Few other agencies have established IT research programs, and without the impetus of their resources and problem definitions, technical progress on these problems will probably be a matter of chance.

Styles of Federal Support

Federal agencies support IT research in different ways that tend to be suited to different types of problems. The most notable distinction is that between the research management styles of DARPA and the NSF. Research at DARPA has always emphasized the design and engineering aspects of IT, and building and experimenting with research prototypes are an essential aspect of that research.[6] Such experimental work requires continuity—more funding per investigator and longer projects than are necessary for theoretical or paper studies (CSTB, 1994). DARPA's program managers assemble and oversee research portfolios within particular thematic areas. Researchers themselves play an indirect role in setting the objectives of the program through their interactions with program managers, and some DARPA programs specifically allow investigator-initiated proposals within the research theme of the program. Program managers are technically savvy—usually researchers on leave from university or industry—and know both the field and its researchers well. They work with research leaders and military leaders to develop long-term objectives that are both tractable for the research community and valuable to the DOD, balancing near-term military needs against longer-term fundamental research that will advance the field. Program managers often devise ways for researchers from different organizations to work together on common problems or to bring new expertise or disciplines to bear on a problem.

The NSF, by contrast, relies much more heavily on peer review to allocate its IT research funding. Proposals are submitted by principal investigators, reviewed by several research peers, and acted on by a program manager. As a result, ideas are derived from the research community without the programmatic framework characteristic of a DARPA-funded effort. At the same time, most research proposals are for individual-investigator research. Grants are typically small, on the order of $90,000 per year, and include support for graduate research assistants. More than 10 years ago, the Computing and Information Science and Engineering (CISE) directorate within the NSF began to address experimental research with grants that could support modest-sized research teams for several years, something that had not been possible within conventional grant programs. Recently, this approach has been extended from hardware to software systems experiments. In partnership with DARPA, the DHHS's National Library of Medicine, NASA, and others, CISE supports the Digital Libraries Initiative (DLI), characterized by research themes focused more on an application vision than is typical of traditional computer-science research programs, which support subdisciplines such as programming languages, operating systems, and artificial intelligence. In keeping with a trend throughout the NSF, CISE is sponsoring more inter-disciplinary work, engaging more social scientists (e.g., in support of better user interfaces or better systems to support group interaction) and researchers in the natural sciences to work in collaboration with computer scientists and engineers.

In addition, CISE sponsors a variety of efforts designed to provide IT infrastructure to support NSF's broader mission, namely, the support of scientific research. The most notable examples originated with the super-computer centers established in the mid-1980s. Now called Partnerships for Advanced Computational Infrastructure (PACI), two facilities with high-performance computers are linked nationwide to groups of academic and industrial partners to constitute a "distributed metacomputing environment," featuring large-scale computing and visualization techniques to address scientific questions in many disciplines.[7] Other efforts aim at improving networking infrastructure for the scientific community, leveraging the multiagency Next Generation Internet (NGI) initiative. These activities routinely provoke comments from IT researchers who fear that these efforts will be counted as programs that contribute to IT research, when in fact their purpose is to provide IT systems for other scientists to use in their research. They are, for the most part, infrastructure programs, not research programs. The DLI, as well as some of the larger activities likely to emerge from the Information Technology Research initiative (see below), are different from PACI and the infrastructure component of the NGI because of their more balanced integration of application objectives with IT research.

Federal Information Technology Research Programs

The majority of recent federal funding for IT research has been provided under the umbrella of the High Performance Computing and Communications Initiative (HPCCI), which involved 10 federal agencies and offices and had a total budget of over $800 million in 1999 (Table 2.2). This initiative pursues research in several areas, primarily high-end computing and large-scale networking. High-end computing research includes work components and architectures for high-speed computers (i.e., computers capable of 10^{15} operations per second); software for operating them and supporting various applications (e.g., scientific visualization, weather prediction, biomedical research); and theoretical computer

TABLE 2.2 Federal Funding for High Performance Computing and Communications by Agency, FY99 (millions of dollars)

Agency	High-End Computing	Large-Scale Networking	Other[a]	Total
National Science Foundation	224.7	72.0	4.3	301
DARPA	48.0	82.2	10.4	141
Department of Energy	91.9	33.9	0	126
National Institutes of Health	27.1	67.9	8	103
National Aeronautics and Space Administration	71.4	20.6	0.6	93
National Security Agency	24.0	3.0		27
National Institute of Standards and Technology	3.5	5.2	4.3	13
National Oceanic and Atmospheric Administration	8.8	2.7		12
Agency for Health Care Policy and Research	0	3.1	4.9	8
Environmental Protection Agency	4.2			4
Total	503.6	290.6	32.5	828

[a]This category includes funding for high-confidence systems; human-centered systems; and education, training, and human resources.

SOURCE: National Science and Technology Council (1999b).

science. Research in large-scale networking involves attempts to develop and deploy innovative technologies for high-speed networking and to experiment with applications that can take advantage of these networks. The NGI initiative falls into this category.[8] Smaller amounts of funding are allocated to the development of high-confidence systems that have predictably high levels of availability and security; human-centered systems that enhance interactions between computers and users; and education, training, and human resources.

Other federal programs are aimed at more specific needs of federal agencies and contribute to the research base in different ways. For example, the DOE spent $484 million in 1999 on its Accelerated Strategic Computing Initiative (ASCI), which is intended to develop technologies that will enable the agency to simulate the performance of nuclear weapons without testing them (in compliance with the Comprehensive Test Ban Treaty). Through this program, the DOE is establishing centers of excellence at five universities to pursue high-end computing systems and simulation software and is working with the developers of these systems.[9] Meanwhile, NASA pursues a more limited program of IT research to develop tools and integrated systems for the design and manufacture of flight vehicles, to manage complex flight and aviation operation systems, and to automatically generate and verify flight-crucial software. The DOD research labs support a range of fundamental and applied research programs to serve military needs.

A new multiagency initiative, proposed under the name Information Technology for the Twenty-First Century (IT²) by the NSF is intended to boost fundamental IT research, particularly in the areas of scalability and software. In its first year (FY00), the initiative provided an additional $366 million in federal funding for IT R&D to support (1) long-term research in software, human-computer interfaces and information management, scalable information infrastructure, and high-end computing; (2) the procurement and deployment of advanced computers that are 100 to 1,000 times more powerful than those available in 1999, simulation software and tools to make the computers useful in scientific and engineering applications, and teams of researchers to work on them to solve challenging problems, and (3) research on the social and economic impacts of IT that will enhance the usefulness of IT systems, limit potential misuses of such systems (such as potential violations of privacy), and lead to better understanding of the ways in which knowledge, values, and systems of society influence the spread of IT and the acceptability of IT systems in various applications (NSTC, 1999a). The long-term research component, in particular, is an attempt to recapture the past success of federal funding for IT research and "lead to fundamental breakthroughs in computing and communications, in the same way that government investment beginning in the 1960s led to today's Internet" (PITAC, 1999). The initiative is to be coordinated jointly with the HPCC programs and the NGI initiative. The Clinton Administration proposed an additional $605 million in IT R&D funding in its FY01 budget to support research in priority areas, such as infrastructure for advanced computational modeling and simulation; storing, managing, and preserving data; security and privacy of information; ubiquitous computing and wireless networks; intelligent machines and networks of robots; more reliable software; broadband optical networks; and future generations of computers. It will also support partnerships to pursue research breakthroughs in particular application areas, such as health care and education (White House, 2000).

Six federal agencies are participating in the IT^2 initiative: DOD, DOE, NASA, NIH, the National Oceanic and Atmospheric Administration (NOAA), and NSF. Each has developed new programs or expanded existing ones to meet the objectives of IT^2. Some of these programs will address elements of large-scale systems and social applications of IT, but not to the full extent needed (see Chapters 3 and 4). Although it is too soon to evaluate these efforts, early indicators point to some practical challenges. The largest federal supporter of computing research, DARPA, attempted to jump-start its efforts to promote path-breaking IT research by issuing a broad agency announcement (BAA) in late 1998 (immediately after PITAC released a draft version of its report) calling for "radically new visions" of the future of information technology (Box 2.1). Anecdotal reports suggest that the results were disappointing to DARPA, perhaps because the research community was uncertain about the new effort. Nevertheless, several projects were funded as a result of this announcement, including Project Oxygen at the Massachusetts Institute of Technology (MIT) Laboratory for Computer Science;[10] the Endeavor expedition at the University of California at Berkeley;[11] Portolano/Workscape at the University of Washington;[12] and another expedition at Carnegie Mellon University. Each of these is exploring different aspects of the post-PC era in which computing will be embedded into a range of information devices.[13]

In late 1999, NSF issued a solicitation for proposals under its agency-wide Information Technology Research (ITR) program, which called for research in eight areas related to IT: software, IT education and workforce, human-computer interfaces, information management, advanced computational science, scalable information infrastructure, social and economic implications of computing and communications, and revolutionary computing (NSF, 1999). Awards are anticipated in September 2000, but anecdotal reports on this effort point to the stresses on NSF program management caused by a large influx of researcher communications (e.g., letters of intent, preproposals, and proposals) that need to be evaluated

---

BOX 2.1
Expeditions into the Twenty-first Century

"The goal of Expeditions into the 21st Century, a broad agency announcement (BAA) issued by the Defense Advanced Research Projects Agency, is to encourage vigorous and revolutionary research in information technology (IT). The funded efforts will set out to invent the future of IT by exploring alternative visions and their impact on society. The ideas pursued by expedition teams are expected to lead to unexpected results, thereby nourishing the information infrastructure and industries of the future.

"The BAA solicits proposals for radically new visions that step outside of the present and anticipated models of both IT itself (i.e., hardware, software, etc.) and the domains and modes in which it is applied. There are a number of precedents for the 'expedition' approach. A famous example is the Xerox Palo Alto Research Center, where researchers created an experimental network of computers for use by individuals doing office work. This effort pioneered many of the revolutionary technologies that led to today's personal computers—graphical user interfaces, pointing devices, laser printing, distributed file systems, and 'what you see is what you get' word processing. This expedition was rooted in an alternative vision regarding how IT could be organized and used by individuals (i.e., distributed computing) as opposed to a more predictable goal of increasing the raw capability of then-dominant mainframe computers.

"An expedition may focus on either a discipline-based theme, such as bioinformatics, or an infrastructure-based theme, such as ubiquitous computing. To establish a context, each expedition must be based on assumptions not true today; for example, one could assume the worldwide availability of near-infinite bandwidth. An expedition need not be limited to a single such assumption; however, proposals are expected to outline an approach to the exploration of a vision within the context of the assumptions. The bottom line: Think big and bold."

SOURCE: Reproduced from the Defense Advanced Research Projects Agency (1999).

---

and responded to by a fixed staff already busy with ongoing responsibilities. Extraordinary efforts were made to recruit experts to participate in the necessary peer review. It will be years before the results of these recent efforts by DARPA, NSF, and other participants in the IT^2 initiative can be evaluated, but current indications underscore the importance of the human infrastructure associated with the design and implementation of federal programs.

INDUSTRY SUPPORT FOR INFORMATION
TECHNOLOGY RESEARCH

In the United States, industry is the leading supporter of IT R&D overall, according to available statistics—although these statistics raise as many questions as they appear to answer.[14] The committee chose to analyze the available, albeit flawed, information in the belief that rough dimensions could be discerned and would be relevant to thinking about how to make progress, notably because the conduct and capacity of industry research are key to policy debates about whether and why the federal government should support more IT research. In an attempt to understand the sources of variation in reported aggregate data and to devise a more consistent set of data covering the 1990s, the committee made special arrangements with the Census Bureau to secure access to the raw data it collects on corporate R&D expenditures. In addition, committee members were able to enhance the utility of the data with quantitative and qualitative insights based on their own experiences. That said, the committee underscores the inadvisability of reading too much into specific numbers and other details.

Federal statistics indicate that companies in the six industry sectors most closely related to the manufacture and supply of IT products and provision of information services—office, computing, and accounting machines, communications equipment, electronic components, computer and data processing services, professional and commercial equipment and supplies, and communications services—invested some $52 billion in R&D in 1998. Detailed data are not available for the professional and commercial equipment and supplies industry. The five remaining sectors had combined R&D expenditures of $45 billion in 1998 (Table 2.3). This figure represents 7.3 percent of the combined annual sales revenues of the companies in these industries. More than one-quarter of these R&D expenditures, or $12.7 billion, was spent on research, with roughly 20 percent of research funding, or $2.7 billion, classified as basic research— the best approximation of fundamental research that is available using federal statistics.[15]

As the data in Table 2.3 indicate, there are considerable sector-to-sector differences in the support of R&D. For example, in the office, computing, and accounting equipment industry, R&D expenditures totaled more than 9 percent of sales revenues in 1998, whereas in the communications services industry (which might include companies such as AT&T, MCI, Sprint, and the regional Bell operating companies), expenditures on R&D represented less than 1 percent of sales revenues. Equally significant differences exist in support for research. Manufacturers of office, computing, and accounting machines, communications equipment, and

TABLE 2.3 Company Investment in Research and Development in Information Technology Industries, 1998 (millions of dollars)

Industry Sector	R&D as % of Sales	Investment		
		Total R&D	Total Research	Basic Research
Office, computing, and accounting equipment	9.2	8,890	3,441	276
Communications equipment	11.2	10,173	2,296	1,148
Electronic components	8.4	9,776	4,661	635
Communications services	0.9	1,768	349	56
Computing and data processing services[a]	12.4	14,297	1,996	599
Total	7.3	44,904	12,743	2,714

NOTE: Does not include data for the professional and commercial equipment and supplies industry, which had estimated R&D investments of $7.2 billion in 1998.

[a]Computing and data processing services includes prepackaged software, programming services, systems integration, and other computer-related services.

SOURCE: National Science Foundation (2000b).

electronic devices (including semiconductors)—"component vendors" in the terminology developed in Chapter 1—funded more than 80 percent of the research reported by IT firms in 1998. Communications service providers—which can be considered "end users" in the terminology of Chapter 1—funded less than 6 percent of the total. The computer and data processing services industry, despite its significant R&D expenditures both in nominal terms and as a percentage of sales, also invests relatively little in research: its research expenditures accounted for just 14 percent of the IT industry total in 1998. The computer and data processing services industry encompasses firms engaged in a wide variety of activities, from the development of prepackaged software (another "component") to custom programming and systems integration ("systems" work in the terminology of Chapter 1) to computer support and repairs. As the analysis below demonstrates, much of the R&D in this industry is attributable to software developers, such as Microsoft, implying that systems integrators themselves fund little research.

Most industry-funded IT research targets the discovery of new technical opportunities, usually within the sponsor's line of business. The time horizon is longer and the risk is higher than would be the case for product development, but the work does not pursue fundamental knowledge and it typically is completed within 3 years. Targeted research usually is done only by larger companies with $3 billion or more in annual revenues; smaller companies do little or no explicit research. A few large companies, such as IBM Corporation, Lucent Technologies, Microsoft Corporation, and Xerox Corporation, support fundamental research conducted in their own laboratories and, to a much lesser extent, in universities. This research addresses fundamental questions not necessarily limited to the sponsor's line of business, and it has resulted in a number of major industry innovations, from the transistor to relational databases. Without exception, such work accounts for only a small fraction of the sponsor's overall research portfolio, because the emphasis is on targeted work.

The following sections examine trends in industrial research support, R&D at large companies, disincentives to corporate R&D investment, gaps in systems integration research, research by end-user organizations, and venture capital support for innovation.

Trends in Industry Support

Trends in industrial support for IT research over the past decade are difficult to discern because of limitations in data collection and inconsistencies in the available data. Over the past 20 years, the Census Bureau has expanded the three relevant Standard Industrial Classification (SIC) categories—business services, electronics, and computing equipment—on two different occasions, meaning that each one has twice been segmented into a larger number of subsectors.[16] The reclassification of IT companies cannot be tracked because the Census Bureau cannot say which companies are in which categories. (The business category declared by a company in its filings to the Securities and Exchange Commission (SEC) is not relevant because Census makes its own classification decisions based on the composition of the company's domestic payroll.) To complicate matters, a change in a firm's business focus (e.g., from telephone services to equipment manufacturing or communications business consulting) also leads to a reclassification of the firm and its research.[17] There are also data gaps because the Census Bureau did not collect R&D statistics from service-sector companies (whether in telecommunications or banking) prior to 1995, nor does it break out the IT-related component of R&D expenditures by firms in other industries (i.e., end users of IT), such as the Boeing Company, General Motors Corporation, and Merrill Lynch. Furthermore, companies have different cultures and definitions for research; even within a single company it is often impossible to get an accurate estimate of spending on research that is spread thinly among divisions and researchers. Often the most important research is conducted informally by individuals without explicit corporate approval. In the past, it was somewhat easier to estimate spending because research was concentrated in the centralized laboratories of a few large companies.

Industry support for IT research is in the midst of significant transformation, driven in large part by burgeoning demand for IT-based products and services. Large IT firms and start-ups are attempting to meet the demand by bringing new technologies to market at an increasing rate, a trend that has profound implications for research. As new competitors enter the industry, the traditional process of performing in-house research and incorporating the results into new products and services is being supplemented by some firms' attempts to, in effect, purchase research results. Some companies buy research explicitly by supporting university research, buying other companies (e.g., start-ups that have developed innovative products or technologies), or licensing technology from them, thereby obviating the need to fund their own research directed at developing similar solutions. Many companies engage in no explicit research, instead buying it indirectly through the activities of their vendors. Some assemblers of personal computers, such as Dell Computer Corporation and Gateway, Inc., for example, conduct virtually no research, choosing instead to assemble components (e.g., microprocessors, disk drives, operating systems) purchased from vendors such as Intel Corporation, Seagate Technologies, and Microsoft, which do conduct R&D. The same is true for many communications service providers, which perform limited R&D because they build networks out of communications equipment developed by vendors (although they often participate in testing equipment supplied by vendors and are actively involved in designing their own networks). Supply chains in IT industries are, therefore, important to understanding the flow of innovation, in addition to furnishing components for larger products and services. This trend has significant implications for research throughout the IT industry.

Federal statistics suggest that industry spending on IT R&D grew rapidly between 1990 and 1998 (Figure 2.4). The sheer magnitude of the swings in the reported data for individual industry sectors calls into question the reliability of the data and indicates the degree of reclassification of firms among sectors over time.[18] Nevertheless, the data suggest that firms in the office, computing, and accounting industry and in the professional equipment industry reduced their R&D expenditures in the early 1990s before boosting them later in the decade. R&D in computing and data processing services appear to have grown, while R&D in communications services declined.

These trends mirror the data on R&D reported by firms in their annual filings to the Securities and Exchange Commission, although the magnitude of the changes is considerably less dramatic (Table 2.4). Among a dozen or so top IT firms whose combined R&D investments constituted

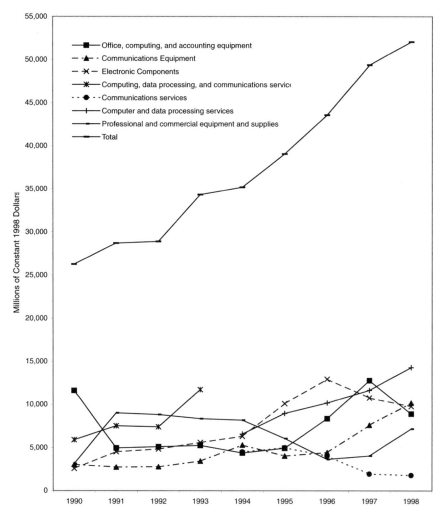

FIGURE 2.4 Reported company investments in research and development in IT industries, 1990 to 1998. Data for the professional and commercial equipment and supplies industry estimated in 1998. SOURCE: Compiled from U.S. Census Bureau statistics.

almost three-quarters of all reported IT industry R&D in 1998,[19] such spending declined moderately in real terms between 1991 and 1994 and then grew rapidly between 1995 and 1999. Only three companies reported 1999 R&D investments lower than those of 1991 (in real terms). IBM's investments in R&D declined from $7.6 billion in 1991 to $4.4 billion in 1995 before rising to $5.2 billion in 1999, Digital Equipment's investments

TABLE 2.4 Research and Development Investment by Large Information Technology Companies, 1991-1999 (millions of constant 1998 dollars)

Company	1991	1992	1993	1994	1995	1996	1997	1998	1999
IBM	7,644	7,334	6,095	4,677	4,378	4,794	4,939	5,046	5,205
AT&T	3,583	3,288	3,412	3,334	3,903	847	862	662	543
Lucent Technologies						2,628	3,226	3,903	4,452
NCR						389	388	360	336
Hewlett-Packard	1,683	1,822	1,931	2,173	2,417	2,800	3,110	3,328	3,393
Motorola	1,303	1,469	1,668	1,994	2,307	2,466	2,783	2,893	3,394
Intel	711	877	1,064	1,191	1,361	1,862	2,377	2,509	3,071
Microsoft	270	396	515	654	903	1,366	1,887	2,601	2,932
Texas Instruments	1,053	1,002	1,076	1,120	884	1,216	1,576	1,225	1,316
Sun Microsystems	410	430	488	536	591	673	837	1,014	1,246
Xerox	1,024	1,037	968	959	998	1,075	1,079	1,043	966
Digital Equipment	1,857	1,854	1,924	1,640	1,092	1,094	1,027	533	0
Compaq Computer	489	464	478	491	580	716	827	1,353	1,639
Cisco Systems	0	0	48	115	222	411	711	1,026	1,574
Total	23,608	23,259	23,080	22,219	23,537	26,199	30,104	32,421	35,397

NOTE: AT&T spun off Lucent Technologies and NCR in 1996. Digital Equipment Corporation was purchased by Compaq Computer in June 1998; the data shown for Digital's 1998 R&D expenditures are estimates for the two quarters of the year during which it operated as a separate company. Compaq's 1998 and 1999 figures reflect its acquisition of Digital's R&D operations. SOURCE: Company annual reports.

dropped from $1.9 billion in 1991 to $1 billion in 1997 before the company was purchased by Compaq Computer in 1998, and Xerox's R&D spending dropped slightly, from $1.02 billion to $966 million. Most companies posted real gains in R&D spending during the course of the decade. Microsoft's R&D spending jumped from $270 million to $2.9 billion in real terms between 1991 and 1999 and Intel's leapt from $711 million to $3.1 billion. Cisco Systems, a relative newcomer to the field, increased its R&D investment to more than $1.5 billion in 1999. People in these industries or knowledgeable about them recognize that the figures apply primarily to development or highly applied activity rather than to more fundamental research, but the figures do suggest an increase in innovative activity in the IT industry.

Despite impressive gains, company-financed R&D has not grown as quickly as have the sales of IT goods and services. Several of the companies listed in Table 2.4 saw their R&D investments decline as a percentage of net sales between 1991 and 1999 (Table 2.5), despite growing absolute R&D investments by many of them. Intel, for example, boosted its R&D spending almost fivefold between 1991 and 1999, but its R&D as a percentage of sales dropped from 13 percent to 10.5 percent. Although there were signs that many of the numbers improved in the late 1990s, the data overall indicate that R&D funding by large IT companies has declined in proportion to the IT marketplace, as noted earlier in this chapter.

Furthermore, the decline in the rate of R&D investment has been magnified by a shift toward more near-term, targeted research or development in many industry labs. Over the past decade, the share of IT R&D conducted by the 12 largest firms—those most likely to conduct long-term research—has declined by more than 10 percentage points. In addition, several large IT companies that operate central research divisions have redirected their research to track more closely areas of clear business interest. These changes have been driven by a desire to (1) better couple research activities with product development as a means of bringing new technologies to market more quickly and improving overall corporate performance,[20] (2) shift resources into computing and communications systems research, and (3) emphasize a more problem-oriented way of selecting research topics (Box 2.2). Research is coupled more closely now to the needs of the marketplace. IBM, for example, still supports the industry's largest in-house research program, but more of its work is concentrated on systems and software, the underpinnings of e-commerce, than on mathematics and physics.

Disincentives to Corporate Investment in Research and Development

Like most commercial enterprises, IT firms have strong economic reasons to refrain from investing in research, especially long-term research.

TABLE 2.5 Research and Development as a Percentage of Sales in Large Information Technology Companies, 1991 to 1999

Company	1991	1992	1993	1994	1995	1996	1997	1998	1999
IBM	10.3	10.1	8.9	6.8	5.8	6.1	6.2	6.2	6.0
AT&T	4.8	4.4	4.5	4.1	4.7	1.6	1.6	1.2	0.9
Lucent Technologies						11.0	12.1	12.3	11.8
NCR						5.4	5.8	5.5	5.5
Hewlett-Packard	10.1	9.7	8.5	8.0	7.0	7.0	7.1	7.0	6.8
Motorola	10.0	9.8	9.0	8.4	8.1	8.6	9.2	9.8	11.1
Intel	12.9	13.3	11.0	9.6	8.0	8.7	9.4	9.5	10.6
Microsoft	12.7	12.7	12.4	12.9	14.2	14.7	15.6	17.0	15.0
Texas Instruments	13.5	12.0	11.5	10.1	7.4	11.9	15.6	14.2	14.1
Sun Microsystems	11.1	10.6	10.3	10.7	9.5	9.2	9.6	10.4	10.8
Xerox	6.6	6.4	6.2	5.9	5.7	6.0	5.5	5.4	5.4
Digital Equipment	11.6	11.8	12.6	10.6	7.5	7.3	7.8	8.2	0.0
Compaq Computer	7.3	7.1	4.9	3.6	3.3	3.5	3.3	4.3	4.3
Cisco Systems			6.8	8.0	9.5	9.7	10.9	12.1	13.1

NOTE: AT&T spun off Lucent Technologies and NCR in 1996. Digital Equipment Corporation was purchased by Compaq Computer in June 1998; the data shown for Digital's 1998 R&D expenditures are estimates for the two quarters of the year during which it operated as a separate company. Compaq's 1998 and 1999 figures reflect its acquisition of Digital's R&D operations. SOURCE: Company annual reports.

BOX 2.2
Redirection of Research at Large Industrial Laboratories

IBM Corporation

When IBM Corporation experienced substantial operating losses in the early 1990s, IBM Research underwent significant restructuring. Skeptical of the Research Division's contributions to the company's bottom line, IBM executives cut the company's total research and development (R&D) expenditures from $7.7 billion in 1991 to $4.4 billion in 1995, and the division's budget dropped from $550 million to $430 million. Although most of the cuts were accommodated by trimming overhead and eliminating redundant or unpromising programs, total R&D employment declined from a peak of about 3,400 to approximately 2,800 in late 1997.

To deal with this situation, IBM managers attempted to couple research more closely to corporate objectives. IBM reoriented its research to focus less on physics and materials science and more on information systems, storage, software, applications, and solutions. Accordingly, the number of researchers working on networking, Internet technologies, solutions, and services grew, whereas the number of physicists and materials scientists declined. Electronic commerce emerged as a main focus of research. This research is clearly market-driven but still requires fundamental advances in computing and mathematics. It has produced innovations such as secure encrypted transactions.

In recent years, IBM Research has experienced a resurgence. By 1999, IBM's R&D spending had increased 19 percent (in real terms) over its 1995 level, and the Research Division's budget reached an all-time high. Between 1995 and 1999, IBM established three new research facilities across the world: a lab in Austin, Texas (1995) that works on microprocessor technology; a lab in Beijing (1995) that focuses on speech recognition and digital library applications; and a facility in India (1998) that addresses cutting-edge customer solutions. IBM Research also has produced some much-heralded successes. Work on speech recognition contributed to the successful ViaVoice product; researchers found a way to replace aluminum with copper in microprocessors, paving the way for smaller, faster chips; and work on magnetoresistive data recording technology enabled IBM to capture 40 percent of the laptop storage market and produced the Microdrive, a 1-square-inch storage device for digital cameras and handheld computers. Paul Horn, director of research, says these technologies and others derived from the company's research contribute $25 billion a year in revenues for IBM—one-third of its total.

AT&T and Lucent Technologies

Since splitting off from AT&T in 1996, Lucent Technologies (which retained Bell Laboratories) committed itself to funding research at 1 percent of total revenues, which gives researchers an incentive to contribute to the company's growth. Research expenditures have grown with the company at roughly 19 percent a year since 1996, reaching $4.5 billion in 1999. To increase the value and effectiveness of its research, Lucent established a variety of mechanisms to accelerate the commercialization of research results. It established an internal venture capital operation to fund innovative ideas that do not fit into existing business units. It has launched a dozen or so internal businesses that have their own presidents and virtual stock, as well as several independent spin-offs, such as Visual Insights, which sells software that can detect billing fraud by analyzing large amounts of

continued

BOX 2.2 Continued

data; Veridicom, Inc., which markets Bell Labs' patented fingerprint-authentication technology; Lucent Digital Radio, which is developing technology to convert analog FM radio signals to high-quality digital sound for broadcasters and greatly improve the quality of AM radio; and Persystant Technologies, which offers a software server that creates virtual environments linking networked users—whether on wired or wireless phones, laptops, or multimedia personal computers—over the public Internet or corporate intranets. Some of these ventures have moved their research results to the marketplace in just 8 months.

AT&T also remains committed to funding research, but at a level not to exceed 0.3 percent of total revenues. Actual expenditures for research at AT&T have been closer to 0.2 percent of revenues since the two companies split, because the size of the staff grew more slowly than had originally been anticipated. AT&T also has allied research programs with newly defined strategic initiatives of its business units, especially those focusing on Internet-related technologies. For example, AT&T formed a subsidiary, a2b music, in November 1997 to provide secure downloading of music over the Internet. The company uses AT&T's encryption technology to protect the digital content rights of music labels and artists.

Xerox Corporation

Most of Xerox Corporation's computing- and communications-related research is conducted at its Palo Alto Research Center (PARC), which views itself as providing the equivalent of genetic diversity for Xerox. PARC's goals are to create surprising technological opportunities and ensure resilience against dramatic changes in the information technology industry. The center maintains small research programs in several topical areas that are expanded or contracted as technology trajectories and each program's relative importance to the company become clearer. Over time, PARC's research agenda has shifted to emphasize computing over areas such as mathematics and physics, and the center's overall level of effort has increased slightly, reflecting Xerox's commitment to research.

To avoid repeating past mistakes, Xerox PARC has established mechanisms to improve its ability to capture the value of its research. Researchers are encouraged to work more closely with Xerox business units, and PARC routinely uses "spin-ins" (cases in which Xerox forms a corporation to develop a technology, takes a majority ownership position, and offers participants stock) and "spin-outs" (in which separately operating companies are formed that license the technology from Xerox) to encourage the commercialization of research results. Research problems still are chosen in a highly decentralized fashion, with researchers proposing new projects, but PARC has emphasized a problem-oriented approach to project selection. The idea is to focus on projects that are important to the company, such as how to make a totally silent copier. A challenge like this allows a range of responses, from incorporating sound-deadening devices in the copiers to facilitating the use of computer displays instead of paper copies. Such problem-oriented research often results in multidisciplinary work teams. Work on "smart matter" (the creation of materials with embedded computing capabilities), for example, involves both solid-state physicists and computer scientists.

SOURCES: Buderi (1999); Carey (1999); Neil Marx, Internet Division Finance, IBM Software Group, personal communication, November 20, 1997.

Within their relatively small research budgets, vendors are understandably reluctant to invest in projects from which they are unlikely to reap many or all of the benefits. Economists call this the "appropriability" problem: because good ideas diffuse rapidly and can be only partially protected by patents, individual firms cannot be assured of reaping (or appropriating) the benefits of their investments. Practical companies therefore tend to underinvest in the generation of new knowledge and technologies (see Box 2.3).

But IT firms face additional hurdles that make the problem of funding research especially acute. First, the IT industry is known for a rapid pace of innovation, which by all reports has accelerated in recent years. With product cycles as short as 6 to 9 months in many areas of IT, companies must pour resources into product development or risk being quickly left behind. The future is harder for research managers to predict than it was in the 1980s, a shift that increases the perceived risk for companies that invest too much in a particular vision of the future. IT companies that commit resources to projects that extend more than 3 years or so can find themselves abandoned by an unexpected direction of the industry. In such an environment, long-term research is risky unless broadly distributed across a portfolio—as prescribed by the diversity principle explained at the beginning of this chapter.

Other disincentives may be further reducing interest in IT research. One is the so-called network effect: the value of a networked application grows with the number of its users.[21] Because of this effect, the market can lock in popular applications, which quickly become difficult to displace. The value of prototype applications in such an environment is small. For example, there is little incentive to do research on technically superior alternatives to common standards such as TCP/IP, Microsoft Windows, or the Intel microprocessor architecture; the rewards are more obvious for products that leverage these de facto standards.[22] In this environment, there is less innovation in the form of fundamental improvements, which would challenge the dominant technologies; instead, innovation tends to be seen in new products and services that cleverly adapt these technologies to new market needs.[23] For example, the Internet's basic protocol, IPv4, which provides only about 4.3 billion unique addresses, may not provide a large enough address space to meet future demands as the Internet grows. A replacement, IPv6, which is generally thought to not only provide a vastly larger address space but other technically superior features, was developed in anticipation of this need, but because of the high cost of getting everyone to switch protocols it has thus far failed to catch on in the marketplace. To surmount the switching problem, a variety of coexistence strategies are being pursued in the Internet community, but none have yet caught on with a large

BOX 2.3
The Economics of Research Funding

Over the past 30 years, economists have developed a solid body of theory that demonstrates the limitations of the marketplace in supporting research, as well as the need for public support. This theory is based on the observation that knowledge—especially scientific and technical knowledge generated by research—has many of the characteristics of so-called public goods: research results are widely available to people and organizations whether or not they paid for or participated in their creation, and the discoverers of new knowledge cannot easily prevent others from making use of the knowledge without imposing additional costs on themselves and society. In economic terms, these characteristics are referred to as "nonrival use" and "costly exclusion," respectively. These characteristics are associated especially with long-term, fundamental research. Together, they make it difficult for firms that fund research to fully capture (or appropriate) the benefits of the resulting knowledge or to keep others from doing so. Competitive markets work well when the incremental costs and benefits of using a commodity can be assigned to the user; they do not work well for the creation of scientific and technical knowledge, and firms tend to underinvest in research.

Firms can try to protect new knowledge by seeking patent or copyright protection or by trying to keep it secret. Patents and copyrights provide legally enforceable means of protecting knowledge, but they require public disclosure, enabling others to learn from the work (by, for example, reverse engineering) and to find alternative means of achieving the same end. By keeping trade secrets, companies can avoid public disclosure, but this approach offers little means for legal recourse should others learn the secret (unless they use unlawful means to do so). Neither set of mechanisms, therefore, provides foolproof protection for new knowledge. Moreover, each imposes some economic inefficiencies, akin to those of a monopoly, that result from the restrictions placed on the use of the ideas. Such restrictions can result in duplicative research programs in different firms and the insufficient exploitation of new ideas.

Despite appropriability problems, firms do support some fundamental research. Their motives range from monitoring progress at the frontiers of science, to identifying ideas for potential lines of innovation that may emerge from the research of others, to better positioning themselves to penetrate the secrets of rivals' technical practices. By conducting fundamental research, firms can also hope to attract top technical and scientific talent, who can contribute to research as well as development activities. Cohen and Levinthal (1990), in their theory of absorptive capacity, argue that firm-level investment in research creates an absorptive capacity in the firm that makes it better able to realize the benefits of research conducted by others. Nevertheless, funding fundamental research is a long-term strategy that is sensitive to commercial pressures to shift the research toward developing new products and services and improving existing ones.

SOURCE: Condensed from Chapter 2 of Computer Science and Telecommunications Board (1999); additional discussion of the appropriability problem can be found in Nelson (1959) and Arrow (1962).

number of users. So Internet users have been forced to adopt various work-arounds, such as network address translation, that provide a quick fix for the address shortage but have significant side effects. The ultimate outcome is, as of this writing, unclear.

Further pressure to reduce expenditures on long-term research is being created by companies that successfully compete in certain segments of IT markets without incurring research expenses. As noted earlier, companies such as Dell Computer and Gateway have captured large shares of the market for PCs by offering products that incorporate standard components purchased from other vendors. Their products exploit technical advances made by supplier firms—many of which maintain extensive R&D programs.[24] In effect, these assemblers buy research conducted by their component vendors and benefit from the economies of scale that the vendors enjoy by selling to numerous assemblers.

Another disincentive to fundamental innovation may be the limited capacity of users to absorb new technology.[25] For example, the difficulty and risk associated with upgrading software can deter users from adopting new programs as quickly as vendors can generate them; similarly, end users may not be able to incorporate increases in processing speeds as fast as manufactures can provide them. Another limiting factor is the nature of the customer base for potential IT innovations. Because many potential users (both individuals and organizations) are less sophisticated and able than the early adopters of IT, vendors have limited incentive to invest in fundamental research unless they can hope to penetrate new markets with rapidly improving technology. Considerable energy is instead devoted to launching tactical product innovations and letting the marketplace sort out the winners from the losers. The enormous amount of activity and marketing hype should not be confused with fundamental advances in IT.

A Countertrend in Central Research Laboratories

Competitive pressures have not forced the traditional IT research labs to give up on fundamental research entirely. For example, Lucent Technologies supported a Bell Labs cosmologist who was attempting to detect hidden dark matter in the universe. Interestingly, the work contributed to a software product that detects billing fraud by analyzing patterns in large amounts of data. Other Lucent researchers are investigating neural pathways of the slug to learn how to build self-healing information networks or exploring computers based on quantum mechanics and the information processing capabilities of genetic material (Carey, 1999). Nevertheless, the breakup and divestiture of AT&T has steadily diminished the flow of fundamental IT research historically associated with the Bell Labs name (see Box 2.4).

BOX 2.4
Changes in Telecommunications Research

The telecommunications sector provides a compelling example of the transformation from a vertically structured to a horizontally stratified industry. Before 1984, AT&T maintained a regulated monopoly over the nation's telecommunications services. As both an equipment manufacturer and a service provider, the company had strong interests in end-to-end systems issues, and its research laboratories (most notably Bell Laboratories) supported those interests. With its divestiture in 1984, AT&T's research divisions were divided between AT&T and the Bell Communications Research Corporation (Bellcore), which was formed to conduct research in support of the seven newly established local exchange service providers, the regional Bell operating companies (RBOCs). Bellcore's applied research organization started out with approximately 350 professional research staff, drawn almost entirely from the original Bell Laboratories, and grew to its target staff size of 501 within 3 years. By 1990, its budget peaked at about $135 million—nearly all of which was provided by the RBOCs.[1]

Then, amid increasing competition in the telecommunications sector, the RBOCs' funding for applied research at Bellcore steadily and rapidly declined, and by 1998 Bellcore's applied research staff was back down to about 350. Approximately 20 percent of Bellcore's researchers were funded by government contracts in 1998; another 50 percent were funded by Bellcore's business units to support the company's Software System and Professional Services products (e.g., technology and architectures for Internet telephony products, new types of software-based tools for efficiently finding Y2K problems, and, more generally, for testing software). Less than 30 percent of Bellcore's research budget was directed at broader industry research issues. Furthermore, Bellcore's customer base had grown substantially beyond the RBOCs, so the share of Bellcore's research supported by the RBOCs declined. Further separating Bellcore from the service providers, the RBOCs sold Bellcore (now called Telcordia Technologies) to Science Applications International Corporation in 1998, divesting themselves of their core research capability.

Some of the RBOCs (e.g., NYNEX, U S WEST) supported large internal research organizations in 1990, with combined research expenditures of $75 million to $100 million. But these research programs were eliminated or dramatically scaled back during the 1990s. As a result, by 1999, the RBOCs no longer supported fundamental research (i.e., research that may not generate a return on investment until more than 3 years in the future), and even their support for more targeted research (i.e., attempts to discover innovative approaches for addressing clearly defined immediate problems) declined precipitously. The spin-off of Lucent Technologies from AT&T in 1996 reinforced the separation between equipment providers and service providers, as roughly two-thirds of AT&T's original research capacity (including Bell Labs) went to Lucent Technologies and only one-third remained within AT&T (in the form of AT&T Research). Research at Lucent continues to move toward systems and software, but with a less direct connection to the operational issues faced by telecommunications service companies.

continued

BOX 2.4 Continued

All of these changes occurred during a 15-year time period when the need to better understand how to design large, complex information networks, including their associated applications, greatly increased.[2]   As a result, the majority of research supporting the nation's telecommunications industry now is conducted by equipment suppliers, such as Lucent Technologies, Nortel, and Cisco Systems, with fundamental research performed by some of the largest of these firms. These organizations, in effect, conduct research for a rapidly growing sector comprising RBOCs, long-distance carriers (such as MCI and Sprint), and Internet service providers.

---

[1]A small portion came from Southern New England Telephone and Cincinnati Bell (independent entities that purchased Bellcore's products as part of a package).
[2]The history recounted here, and the estimates of R&D support by the RBOCs, were provided by Stewart Personick, former vice president of information networking at Bellcore, personal communication, April 26, 1999.

Some IT companies have created new corporate research laboratories to extend their horizons. Intel, for example, established a microcomputer lab in 1996 to conduct pioneering research on microprocessors. With an original staff of 70, the group's objective was to identify technical roadblocks to improved microprocessor performance and find ways to overcome them (Takashi, 1996). In November of 1998, Motorola created a central research lab, Motorola Labs, as a way of combining and better managing the approximately 1,000 researchers who had previously worked in separate research groups focusing on wireless communications, semiconductors, and other products. At the same time, Motorola began increasing its funding for research, especially fundamental research, to bring it up to what it describes as a standard level of research funding among larger IT companies, 1 percent of the prior year's revenues.[26] Research topics range from high-quality displays for cellular phones to work with genetic material aimed at finding ways of using the attraction between pairs of organic acids to lay down patterns of circuitry on integrated circuits (Hardy, 1999).

The most obvious newcomer to corporate research is Microsoft, which in 1991 established a research division that has attracted some of the top talent in IT. Microsoft Research grew to some 200 researchers by 1999, even expanding to include a facility in England, and further growth has been planned. Research groups are maintained in a dozen areas, including speech recognition, decision theory, and computer graphics. They pursue research with long-term implications for the company that also may also feed into ongoing development projects.[27] Systems to check spelling and grammar, assist users in real time, facilitate remote collaboration, and translate among languages are among the fruits of Microsoft's R&D that have been commercialized; more speculative work includes efforts to develop a tablet computer—a portable, wireless device without a keyboard that could serve a range of personal computing and communications purposes—and to develop large-scale-image databases with intuitive interfaces (Markoff, 1999; Barclay et al., 1999).

Gaps in the Research Base: Systems Integration

As noted in an earlier report by the Computer Science and Telecommunications Board (CSTB, 1992), systems integration first became an issue in the 1960s, when federal agencies began hiring contractors to design large-scale systems for data processing, communications, and aerospace and defense applications. Over the next 40 years, the emergence of distributed personal computing, local area networks, and, more recently, the Internet, drove a growing need for systems integration. The integration challenge goes beyond making incompatible machines communicate with each other; it is a problem-solving activity that harnesses and coordinates the power and capabilities of IT to meet customers' needs. The result is generally one-of-a-kind systems that increase productivity, flexibility, responsiveness, and competitive advantage. Considerable effort is expended on customized consulting—modification, interfacing, coding, and installing hardware and software—to integrate the individual components into a cohesive whole.

Systems integration is now a thriving U.S. industry that is finding new opportunities in the efforts across the economy to engage in e-commerce. Total revenues for custom integrated system design and custom programming services topped $76 billion in 1997, up from $34 billion in 1990.[28] Different types of firms provide such services. Companies such as Andersen Consulting, Electronic Data Services (EDS), and Computer Sciences Corporation earn the majority of their revenues from systems integration activities. Many of the large accounting/business services firms, including PricewaterhouseCoopers, KPMG, and Ernst & Young, also have established systems integration and services practices. Large diversified computer manufacturers, such as IBM and Hewlett-Packard, have moved into systems integration and related services, creating new divisions for these activities. IBM's Global Services Division is the fastest-growing part of the company; its revenues increased almost 30 percent between 1997 and 1999 and accounted for 37 percent of the company's revenues in 1999. Also participating in the industry are a number of defense contractors, such as Lockheed Martin and the Boeing Company, which developed their systems integration experience by designing complex weapons or command-and-control systems for the military and by operating their own substantial information and communications systems.

In general, systems integrators support limited R&D, and most of what is funded is development. Neither Andersen Consulting nor EDS— two of the largest systems integration firms—report R&D expenditures in their annual reports (Table 2.6). Andersen does have a small research division that employs about 200 computer scientists and business analysts to identify interesting technologies and build prototype applications for testing with potential customers; however, the division constitutes a small part of the company.[29] Its work focuses on areas such as e-commerce, intellectual asset management, and work group productivity.[30] Lockheed Martin, a diversified company with approximately $1 billion in R&D

TABLE 2.6 Research and Development Investments of Representative Systems Integrators, 1998 (millions of dollars)

Company	Systems Integration Revenues	Systems Integration R&D
Services-only firms[a]		
Andersen Consulting	8,307	0
American Management Systems	1,058	77
Computer Sciences Corporation	7,660	0
Electronic Data Services	16,891	0
Keane	1,076	3.5
Diversified firms[b]		
IBM	28,916	25% of research division budget
Hewlett-Packard	6,956	50
Lockheed Martin	5,212	36.4

[a]Data on the services-only firms was taken from annual reports to the Securities and Exchange Commission. Andersen Consulting reports no research and development expenditures in its annual filings to the Securities and Exchange Commission, but it does operate a research group with about 200 members.
[b]Data for the diversified firms shows systems integration revenues out of total corporate revenues and systems integration R&D out of total R&D. Data on IBM provided by Irving Wladawsky-Berger, vice president of technology and strategy at IBM, personal communication, October 6, 1999. Data on Hewlett-Packard provided by Curtis Hoyle, special assistant to the director, Hewlett-Packard Laboratories, personal communication, November 2, 1999. Data on Lockheed Martin provided by B. Clovis Landry, vice president of technology, Lockheed Martin Information and Services Sector, personal communication, October 11, 1999.

expenditures, spends only 0.7 percent of its IT systems integration revenues on R&D, reflecting its reliance on off-the-shelf components researched and developed by IT vendors and the academic research community.[31]

Taken together, these facts suggest that most of the research included in federal statistics for computer and data processing services is performed by firms in the prepackaged software industry (e.g., Microsoft, Oracle, and SAP) rather than firms in the custom programming and systems integration industries, and insiders discount the amount of research reflected in the figures. Indeed, the largest supporter of research on systems and services appears to be IBM. Although detailed breakouts of the company's R&D expenditures are not available, managers in the Research Division estimate that about 25 percent of the company's research budget is devoted to services and solutions. This figure is only a rough approximation, because some software research (e.g., speech recognition) could have been considered part of services and solution work but was not. But the 25 percent share is much higher than the corresponding share in the early 1990s, when services and solutions accounted for just a tiny percentage of the research budget.[32]

The apparent lack of attention to large-scale systems issues is accentuated by changes in the structure of the IT industry. Historically, large vendors of computer and communications technology such as IBM and AT&T were vertically structured. They enjoyed both significant returns on investment that could be devoted to systems research and a clear competitive advantage from doing so. Over the past decade, the IT industry structure has changed, becoming horizontal rather than vertical, with individual companies focusing on only certain portions of the IT value chain—microprocessors, software, or PCs—and addressing a full range of applications within that functional group. Examples of horizontal structure are evident in the computer industry, with Microsoft specializing in operating systems and applications software, Intel in microprocessors, Compaq in computer platforms, and SAP in systems integration and business applications. The communications industry exhibits a similar pattern, with the separation of voice and data communications service providers (such as AT&T and America Online) from manufacturers of networking equipment (such as Lucent Technologies and Cisco Systems) and underlying communications facilities (see Box 2.4). Horizontally structured companies have less incentive to invest in large-scale systems research, because each is responsible for only a piece of the overall infrastructure and none has a holistic view of the systems created from its components. Although IBM has increased its emphasis on systems, few other IT companies conduct research in these areas—and, as suggested earlier and elaborated upon in the next section, organizations that integrate systems or build custom applications do not support research.

Research by End-User Organizations

Most large companies in industries as disparate as automobiles, banking, and health care maintain a growing staff of IT professionals whose work consists primarily of deploying, operating, and supporting the company's information systems. Many of these companies develop IT applications to suit their specific needs; a handful engage in highly targeted IT-related research.[33] *Information Week* magazine recently polled 500 organizations considered to be top end users of IT regarding their IT budgets and R&D activities. The poll revealed that these organizations planned to spend an average of 3.6 percent of their expected annual revenues on IT in 1999, and that 4 percent of the IT share would support related R&D (Table 2.7). Banking and financial services firms topped the rankings by a wide margin, with IT R&D budgets equivalent to 0.45 per-

TABLE 2.7 R&D Spending on IT in 500 End-User Organizations (percentage)

Industry	IT Budget As Share of Projected Revenues	R&D Budget As Share of IT	Estimated IT R&D As Share of Projected Sales Revenues
Banking and financial services	9	5	0.45
Professional services	7	4	0.28
Telecommunications	6	4	0.24
Health care	4.5	4	0.18
Construction and engineering	3	6	0.18
Information technology	4	4	0.16
Pharmaceuticals and medical equipment	3	5	0.15
Transportation	3	4	0.12
Media and entertainment	4	3	0.12
Insurance	3.5	3	0.11
Manufacturing	2.5	4	0.10
Metals and natural resources	2	5	0.10
Retail and distribution	2.5	4	0.10
Energy	3	3	0.09
Utilities	2.5	3	0.08
Chemicals	2.5	3	0.07
Consumer goods	3.5	2	0.07
Electronics	3	2	0.06
Hospitality and travel	2	4	0.06
Food and beverage processing	1.5	3	0.05
Median/average	3.6	4	0.14

SOURCE: *Information Week* (1999).

cent of their sales revenues; professional services and telecommunications followed with IT R&D budgets of 0.28 and 0.24 percent of sales revenues, respectively (*Information Week*, 1999). Food and beverage processing firms came in at the low end, with IT R&D expenditures of 0.05 percent of their projected sales (*Information Week*, 1999). The figures show that on average, even in the 500 most IT-intensive end-user organizations, less than 0.15 percent of sales revenues are devoted to IT R&D.

In short, most large end users who invest massively in developing and deploying IT systems fund only limited research, although they often do invest in developing custom applications for their own purposes. These are the companies most likely to benefit from attention to the research challenges inherent in IT applications (discussed in Chapter 3 and Chapter 5), yet they are the least likely to support research. The companies that do support research, mostly equipment suppliers, do not benefit directly from research on large-scale systems and applications and cannot be expected to assume the entire burden of supporting such work. Clearly, the industry as a whole underinvests in this type of research.

End users of IT focus almost exclusively on applied R&D. For example, a large hospital or health care system might conduct applied research to evaluate whether expert systems reduce the inappropriate use of medications and which system features are needed. Boeing employed approximately 150 workers (out of its total workforce of 231,000) in its computer science area in 1998 to develop systems to support aircraft manufacturing operations (e.g., tools for collaborative design of aircraft, advanced computer-aided design (CAD) technologies); to implement corporate information infrastructures; and to design systems for Boeing aircraft (e.g., onboard networks, entertainment systems).[34] Online retailer Amazon.com spent $47 million to enhance the features, content, and functionality of its Web sites and transaction-processing systems and upgrade its systems and telecommunications infrastructure.[35] Merrill Lynch spent hundreds of millions of dollars to develop a new computing platform for its financial advisors and a Web-based interface that allows customers to access their accounts and company research, consult with their financial advisors, and conduct e-commerce. [36] The much smaller online investment firm, E*Trade, spent $33 million—13 percent of its total revenues—on technology development in 1998 to enhance its product offerings and maintain its Web site.

Such efforts can result in innovative technologies. Companies such as Aetna, Amazon.com, Citicorp, Merrill Lynch, and the Sabre Group (which processes airline reservations) have been awarded a handful of patents on inventions related to IT and related systems (Table 2.8).[37] E*Trade has applied for a patent on its proprietary Stateless Architecture, which enables its Web site to handle more than 1 million visitors and place up to

TABLE 2.8 Representative IT-Related Patents Assigned to End-User Organizations

Company	Patent Title
Aetna	Insurance classification plan loss control system.
	Expert system for providing interactive assistance in solving problems such as health care management.
	Three-level distributed control for networking input/output devices.
Amazon.com	System and method for providing multimedia bookmarks for hypertext markup language files.
	Secure method for communicating credit card data when placing an order on a nonsecure network.
	Secure method and system for communicating a list of credit card numbers over a nonsecure network.
Citicorp	System and method for delivering financial services.
Merrill Lynch	Distributed network agents.
	Check alteration detection system and method.
	Integrated system for controlling master account and nested subaccount(s).
	Securities trading workstation.
Sabre Group	Information aggregation and synthesization system.
	System to predict optimum computer platform.

SOURCE: Compiled from information contained in the U.S. Patent and Trademark Office's Web patent database. Available online at <http://www.uspto.gov>.

150,000 orders at the same time. Although the total number of patents held by these companies is dwarfed by the hundreds of thousands of patents held by major IT vendors such as IBM, AT&T, and Xerox, end users are clearly pursuing innovative work to address their IT needs.[38]

Innovation by end users is not a new phenomenon, nor is it limited to the IT arena. Research conducted by Eric von Hippel in the Sloan School of Management at MIT found that well over half of the innovations in scientific instruments, semiconductor and printed circuit board equipment, and pultrusion equipment (used for making fiber-reinforced plastic products) were attributable to end users as opposed to vendors of such products (von Hippel, 1988). Such end users tend to have an understanding of their particular needs, the expertise to satisfy their needs through innovation, and an expectation that they can improve their competitive positions through innovation. End users who must apply technology to a particular need often have greater insight into the issues involved than do equipment vendors, but they are limited with regard to the types of R&D they can perform. Indeed, many lack the expertise to conduct research altogether. They may have intelligent, capable staffs in their IT departments, but they typically lack computer scientists who can contribute to fundamental as opposed to applied research. Furthermore, investments in R&D are examined closely to make sure they have a good chance of improving organizational performance. Many organizations run on tight margins, and if the expected returns are too far into the future or are only weakly linked to profit margins and overall performance, then the proposed R&D generally does not survive the budget process. Also, contemporary management's focus on core competencies—the essential business of a company—encourages skepticism about R&D.

Venture Capital Support for Innovation

Venture capital (VC) plays a significant role in accelerating innovation in IT in the United States, although not necessarily through direct support of R&D. VC firms are concerned primarily with earning a return on investment. They raise funds from private investors to make equity investments in new firms. They also provide management and other nontechnical assistance to the firms in which they invest, serving on boards of directors and helping to attract top management talent to these firms. The technologies developed by VC-backed companies typically draw on research conducted in other corporate or university laboratories. Indeed, VC firms tend not to invest in companies that require technological breakthroughs; instead, recipients of VC must have viable technologies—and business plans—in hand. Much of the work conducted with VC relates to marketing and business development.

Yet VC funding does contribute to innovation and, less directly, to research. By helping to establish and expand companies, VC enables novel ideas generated by previous research to be exploited and brought to the marketplace through continued development. As the Congressional Budget Office (1999) has noted, "venture capitalists increase the number of new ideas introduced into the economy from the stock of ideas generated in the laboratory," thereby enhancing the efficiency of R&D. Start-up companies do a lot of work on systems architectures and design trade-offs, understanding of user needs and refinement of applications, and ancillary tools (e.g., CAD tools, verification methodologies). They tend not to focus on long-term research or on developing a deep understanding of the phenomena exploited in their innovations. Although this work is not intended to be research in the narrow sense of the word and is not published in academic papers, it does generate new knowledge, and that knowledge diffuses through the industry in the form of patents and, more importantly, a flow of people among companies.[39]

From another perspective, VC firms are even more fundamental to innovation in Internet and IT technologies than in other venues. Increasingly, much of the innovation in these areas is related to new business models and social innovation rather than technology. An example is the use of the Internet to bring together buyers and sellers at online auctions. The research related to these models seems to be carried out by starting new companies that succeed or fail in the real marketplace. Looked at in this way, the market itself is the laboratory and arbiter of success, and the whole system of VC firms can be thought of as a new way of conducting research.

Studies demonstrate that venture capitalists have a disproportionate impact on technological innovation relative to the size of their investments. Although they fund only a few hundred of the nearly 1 million businesses begun in the United States each year, venture capitalists backed roughly one-third of all the companies that went public in the past two decades—including several of the most successful IT firms, namely Amazon.com, Cisco Systems, Microsoft, Intel, and Yahoo (Gompers and Cohen, 1999; Lerner, 1999a,b). These companies have a significant impact on the economy. A study conducted by the venture firm Kleiner, Perkins, Caufield, and Byers found that the companies it had financed since its founding in 1971 had created 131,000 jobs, generated $44 billion in annual revenues, and had $84 billion in market capitalization (Peltz, 1996).

In the IT industry, VC firms are a growing source of funding, although insiders wonder how long the gold rush that took place during the period in which this report was written will last. Total VC investments in U.S. firms jumped from less than $4 billion in 1994 to $14.7 billion in 1998, with investments in IT-related companies rising from less than $2 billion to roughly $9 billion during that time.[40] In the 4-year period between January 1995 and December 1998, VC firms invested a total of $46.6 billion in start-up companies in all industries; of that amount, $26 billion—or 56 percent—was invested in the IT sector. Roughly half of the IT-related investments went to firms in the computer software and services sector, with investments in communications, semiconductors, and computer hardware accounting for the rest (Table 2.9).[41] Internet-related companies (e.g., Yahoo, Amazon.com, and eBay) also have garnered a growing share of VC investments. Venture capitalists reportedly invested $3.8 billion in Internet-related companies in the second quarter of 1999, up from $1.4 billion in the second quarter of 1998 and more than the $3.3 billion invested during all of 1997.[42]

In contrast to the much smaller amounts of VC in Europe and Japan, almost half of VC investments in the United States represent early-stage

TABLE 2.9 Venture Capital Investments, January 1995 Through
December 1998 (millions of dollars)

Industry	Investment
Information technology	
Computer services and software	12,722
Communications	8,054
Semiconductors and electronic components	2,659
Computer hardware	2,529
IT subtotal	25,964
Other industries	
Medical and health-related	6,624
Other products	4,786
Consumer-related	4,000
Biotechnology	3,670
Industrial and energy	1,593
Total	46,636

SOURCE: Congressional Budget Office (1999).

capital. This includes so-called seed capital that firms use to research, assess, and develop initial concepts, as well as start-up financing, which supports product development and initial marketing. Recipients of start-up funding may be in the process of setting up or may have been in business for a short time, but without selling products commercially. Early-stage financing is distinguished from expansion financing, which dominates foreign VC investments and supports the growth and expansion of firms already operating in the commercial marketplace. Expansion funds may be used to finance increased production capacity, for market or product development, or as a source of additional working capital.[43] These differences show that the VC system in the United States is more able than VC systems elsewhere to stimulate innovation.

UNIVERSITY RESEARCH

Universities play two important roles in IT research. They are major performers of research funded by both government and industry, and they are the source of the educated professionals who populate industrial and government research laboratories as well as university faculties. University research has had a significant impact on the evolution of IT and related practices. As documented in other reports (CSTB, 1995, 1999), many important information technologies were first investigated in academia or largely developed there. Significant examples include the Internet, reduced-instruction-set computing, redundant arrays of inexpensive disks for storage, object-oriented programming, CAD of integrated circuits, and computer graphics. Universities can be particularly important performers of fundamental and long-term research.

Unlike industrial research, most university research is conducted in the public domain. Results of university research are disseminated widely throughout the research community, maximizing the impact of the research, and university graduates serve as key conduits of technology transfer as they move into jobs in other universities, government, and industry. Universities are fertile sources of innovation; free from pressures to make a near-term impact on the next generation of products, they often provide new ideas for established companies and seed the establishment and growth of numerous start-up companies. Maintaining the strength of university research is therefore key to ensuring the vitality of the IT industry. The following sections discuss trends in support for university research, gaps in such research, and commercialization of the research results.

Trends in Support for University Research

The available statistics present a mixed picture of funding for university research focusing on IT. Universities report that, between 1990 and 1998, constant-dollar funding for R&D in computer science grew from $614 million to $754 million, and constant-dollar funding for R&D in electrical engineering grew from $791 million to $1.02 billion. Approximately two-thirds of those funds came from federal sources, with the balance coming from industry, state and local governments, university funds, and other sources. Statistics on federal funding for university research indicate that federal support for IT-related research in universities grew at an average annual rate of 3.3 percent between 1990 and 1998 (Figure 2.5). But these statistics indicate that the rise is attributable almost entirely to increases in federal funding for computer science research, which expanded from $336 million to $470 million during the period of interest; federal funding for university research in electrical engineering rose at a rate of only 0.9 percent between 1990 and 1998 (from $165 million to $177 million) and actually declined in real terms after 1993.[44]

Additional IT-related research is conducted in university departments other than computer science and electrical engineering, but it tends not to be captured fully in federal statistics. Historically, this work has been pursued in science and engineering departments and has been directed toward large simulations of physical phenomena and technological systems. It has been a primary driver for research into high-performance

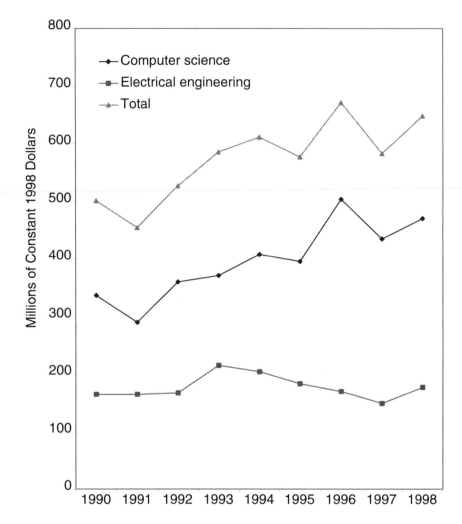

FIGURE 2.5 Federal funding for university research in IT, 1990 to 1998. SOURCE: National Science Foundation (2000a).

computing and parallel processing. More recently, the number of departments engaged in IT-related work appears to have grown as IT has become more deeply ingrained in science and engineering, as well as a host of nontechnical fields. Business schools and departments of industrial engineering, for example, are studying the ways in which IT affects business processes. Medical schools and biology departments are conducting research to enable better use of IT in providing patient care and in sequencing the human genome. The Department of Aeronautics and Astronautics at the Massachusetts Institute of Technology recently hired a computer scientist (Nancy Leveson) with expertise in software safety. As discussed in greater detail in Chapter 4, a number of universities have established new schools or departments to investigate issues at the intersection of IT and the social sciences. In all of these cases, it is difficult to determine the extent to which the work advances the state of the art in IT (i.e., should be considered IT research) versus the extent to which it is used to advance research in another discipline (i.e., supports development of IT systems to support research in another discipline). This report argues that there is great value in the former.

Industry support for university research has grown over the past decade but still represents less than 10 percent of all university research funding. Moreover, it tends to be concentrated at a select set of universities. At Carnegie Mellon University, MIT, Stanford University, and the University of California at Berkeley, funding from industry constitutes 20 to 30 percent of IT funding for research. Such support can take several forms. Companies may sponsor research of potential interest to them, providing support for a faculty member and graduate students, or they may participate in collaborative programs in which industrial and academic researchers work side by side to bring new technology to market.[45] Organizations such as the Semiconductor Research Corporation (SRC), whose members include most of the nation's largest manufacturers of integrated circuits, pool research funds and make grants to universities for nonproprietary research that will help a range of member companies. In August 1998, for example, the SRC announced that it would establish six national Focus Centers with a total of $60 million per year in new funding to pursue long-term research of interest to the semiconductor industry.[46] The trend toward IT-related start-ups originating in universities (discussed below) also fosters a type of collaboration. These varied forms of collaboration have a number of benefits: they can compensate for fluctuations in federal research budgets, increase the relevance of academic research, and, at times, generate revenues from licensing. Industry also benefits because academic research allows it to access new technologies of particular interest, keep abreast of new developments, and, perhaps most importantly, identify promising young researchers.

Gaps in Academic Research

To some extent, research conducted in academic research laboratories is aligned with the research agendas of its sponsors. Because much research funding in IT comes from government and industry, both of which appear to allocate most of their resources to component research, academic research has been slow to respond to emerging requirements for interdisciplinary research connected to the large-scale systems and IT applications that are responding to business and societal needs. This is not to say that academia has failed to develop highly innovative programs to educate students and conduct research on interdisciplinary topics but simply that there is substantial room for improvement. Just as industry research can become compartmentalized along product lines and industry sectors, academic research can track individual disciplines too closely. Faculty members tend to be rewarded on the basis of their contributions to a particular field, so setting off in new directions can have adverse consequences.

Universities face difficult problems in conducting research on networks and large-scale systems: primarily they lack access to large operational systems—most of which are owned and operated by private firms—as well as tools for simulating the performance of such systems. This problem has persisted for decades (CSTB, 1994), and its consequences have worsened as interest grows in the social applications discussed in this report. As the framers of federal networking research programs have long known, only large networks populated by real users demonstrate the behaviors that need to be studied and understood. Even if academic researchers gain access to these systems, it is extremely difficult, if not impossible, to change their operation for experimental purposes, because users and their applications demand stability and availability. This problem was first noted when the research community's use of the Internet grew rapidly in the 1980s; the commercialization of the 1990s only exacerbated the problem (CSTB, 1994).[47] The limited ability to simulate such systems is reflected in the poor understanding of their behavior.

Commercialization of University Research

University students, professors, and researchers often start new companies to commercialize the results of their research. Universities also license technology to industry, especially since the passage of the Bayh-Dole Act of 1980, which allows universities to license technologies emerging from federally funded research programs. The large number of new companies created to sell products based on university research, and the thousands of licenses that universities grant to firms, testify to the dramatic impact of university research on the private sector—and the effectiveness of the nation's innovation system in converting research results into new products and processes.

Across all industries, the number of start-up companies emerging from university research is growing rapidly. A 1998 survey by the Association of University Technology Managers (AUTM) reported that, since 1980, more than 2,200 companies had been created to commercialize the results of research conducted in U.S. and Canadian universities, research hospitals, and other research institutions (AUTM, 1998). Almost half of those companies had been created since 1993. In 1997, 258 of the 333 start-up companies in the survey came out of university research. In 1996, only 248 start-ups were reported by all the institutions combined. Although the number of start-up companies is increasing, the percentage of technologies licensed to start-up (as opposed to established) companies is decreasing. From 1977 to 1993, 50 percent of licenses were granted to start-up companies. Since 1993, only 29 percent of licenses were extended to start-up companies, and 61 percent were extended to existing companies. The implications of this trend are as yet unclear, and further study is needed; the trend could signify greater recognition within established companies of the value of university research, or it could suggest established companies' growing dependence on university research.

The IT industry is home to a large number of firms that emerged from university research. Stanford University, for example, gave rise to a number of well-known Silicon Valley companies, including Sun Microsystems and Cisco Systems. MIT also gave rise to a number of firms, ranging from Open Market, Inc., an e-commerce firm, to RSA Data Security, which specializes in public key encryption, and more recently Akamai, which streamlines the downloading of content from popular Web sites. The AUTM survey reports that MIT contributed to the creation of 17 start-up companies in 1997, second only to the University of Washington, with 25. A report by BankBoston found that MIT graduates and faculty had been involved in founding 4,000 companies that employed 1.1 million people and had annual world sales of $232 billion in 1995; 57 percent of the employment resulted from firms in electronics and instruments (BankBoston, 1997). Carnegie Mellon University has licensed technologies to many small software and robotics companies, as well as LYCOS, one of the well-known players in the Internet search engine market.

The characteristics of start-up companies that arise out of academia vary significantly among universities. For example, both Stanford and the University of California at Berkeley have provided many new technologies to Silicon Valley, but their approaches are quite different. Berkeley professors have tended to remain in academia. At Stanford, by contrast, "it's almost expected that a successful faculty member will at some point start a company" (Hamilton and Himelstein, 1997), although an individual may return to Stanford after the company is well launched. Berkeley's style is to "develop technology, convince existing companies to use the ideas, and then go back and develop more technology" (Hamilton and Himelstein, 1997). This pattern seems to be changing rapidly: in any given year about 10 percent of Berkeley's electrical engineering and computer science faculty members are on leave starting a company. Each pattern illustrates one way in which faculty and students migrate between universities and start-ups. It is too early to tell whether the late-1990s trend of faculty across the country leaving academia to establish start-ups will persist, but the prospect is debated actively among academics. All other things being equal, the trend raises questions about the long-term capabilities of universities.

CONCLUSION

This review indicates that the recent growth in spending on IT research does not alleviate all concerns about the nation's research enterprise. Several underlying trends could ultimately limit the nation's innovative capacity and hinder its ability to deploy the kinds of IT systems that could best meet personal, business, and government needs. First, expenditures on research by companies that develop IT goods and services and by the federal government have not kept pace with the expanding array of IT. The disincentives to long-term, fundamental research have become more numerous, especially in the private sector, which seems more able to lure talent from universities than the other way around. Second, and perhaps most significantly, IT research investments continue to be directed at improving the performance of IT components, with limited attention to systems issues and application-driven needs. Neither industry nor academia has kept pace with the problems posed by the large-scale IT systems used in a range of social and business contexts—problems that require fundamental research. With the exception of IBM, most companies involved in developing IT systems for end-user organizations invest little in research. Academic researchers also have tended to ignore work on large-scale systems and social applications because they require interdisciplinary teams and very large budgets and because it is hard for them to obtain access to operational systems for experimental purposes. New mechanisms may be needed to direct resources to these growing problem areas.

REFERENCES

Arrow, Kenneth. 1962. "Economic Welfare and the Allocation of Resources for Invention," in Richard Nelson, ed., *The Rate and Direction of Innovative Activity*. Princeton University Press, Princeton, N.J.

Association of University Technology Managers (AUTM). 1998. *FY 1998 AUTM Licensing Survey*. AUTM, Norwalk, Conn.

BankBoston. 1997. *MIT: The Impact of Innovation*. MIT Technology Licensing Office, Cambridge, Mass., March. Available online at <http://web.mit.edu/newsoffice/founders/>.

Barclay, Tom, Jim Gray, and Don Slutz. 1999. *Microsoft TerraServer: A Spatial Data Warehouse.* Technical Report MS-TR-99-29, Microsoft Corp., Redmond, Wash., June. Available online at <http://research.microsoft.com/~gray/Papers/MSR_TR_99_29_TerraServer.pdf>.

Buderi, Robert. 1999. "Into the Big Blue Yonder," *Technology Review*, July/August:46-53.

Carey, John. 1999. "An Ivory Tower That Spins Pure Gold," *Business Week*, April 19, pp. 167-168.

Christensen, Clayton. 1997. *The Innovator's Dilemma.* Harvard Business School Press, Boston.

Cohen, W., and D. Levinthal, 1990. "Absorptive Capacity: A New Perspective on Learning and Innovation." *Administrative Science Quarterly* 35:128-152.

Computer Science and Telecommunications Board (CSTB), National Research Council. 1992. *Keeping the U.S. Computer Industry Competitive: Systems Integration.* National Academy Press, Washington, D.C.

Computer Science and Telecommunications Board (CSTB), National Research Council. 1994. *Academic Careers for Experimental Computer Scientists and Engineers.* National Academy Press, Washington, D.C.

Computer Science and Telecommunications Board (CSTB), National Research Council. 1995. *Evolving the High Performance Computing and Communications Initiative to Support the Nation's Information Infrastructure.* National Academy Press, Washington, D.C.

Computer Science and Telecommunications Board (CSTB), National Research Council. 1999. *Funding a Revolution: Government Support for Computing Research.* National Academy Press, Washington, D.C.

Computer Science and Telecommunications Board (CSTB), National Research Council. 2000. *The Digital Dilemma: Intellectual Property in the Information Age.* National Academy Press, Washington, D.C.

Congressional Budget Office (CBO). 1999. "Current Investments in Innovation in the Information Technology Sector: Statistical Background," April. Available online at <http://www.cbo.gov>.

Defense Advanced Research Projects Agency (DARPA). 1999. "Information Technology Expeditions," BAA 99-07. Available online at <http://www.darpa.mil/ito/Solicitations/CBD_9907.html>.

Dertouzos, Michael L. 1999. "The Future of Computing," *Scientific American* 281(2):52-55.

Gompers, Paul A., and Josh Cohen. 1999. *The Venture Capital Cycle.* MIT Press, Cambridge, Mass.

Hamilton, Joan, and Linda Himelstein. 1997. "A Wellspring Called Stanford," *Business Week, Silicon Valley Special Report* (August 26). Available online at <http://www.businessweek.com/1997/34/b354112.htm>.

Hardy, Quentin. 1999. "Motorola's New Research Efforts Look Far Afield," *Wall Street Journal* (June 17):B6.

Information Week. 1999. "Information Week 500: Industries At a Glance," September 27. Available online at <http://www.informationweek.com/754/99iw500.htm.

Lerner, Josh. 1999a. "Small Business Innovation and Public Policy," in *Are Small Firms Important?* Zoltan Acs, ed. Kluwer Academic Publishing, New York.

Lerner, Josh. 1999b. "Small Business, Innovation, and Public Policy in the Information Technology Industry," paper prepared for the conference Understanding the Digital Economy: Data, Tools, and Research, Washington, D.C., May 25-26.

Markoff, John. 1999. "Microsoft Brings in Top Talent to Pursue Old Goal: The Tablet," *New York Times* (August 30):C1,C10.

National Science and Technology Council (NSTC), IT2 Working Group. 1999a. *Information Technology Research for the Twenty-First Century: A Bold Investment in America's Future. Implementation Plan.* National Coordination Office for Computing, Information, and Communications, Arlington, Va., June.

National Science and Technology Council (NSTC), Committee on Technology, Subcommittee on Computing, Information, and Communications R&D. 1999b. *Information Technology Frontiers for a New Millennium: Supplement to the President's FY 2000 Budget,* National Coordination Office for Computing, Information, and Communications, Arlington, Va., April.

National Science Foundation (NSF). 1999. "Information Technology Research: Program Solicitation, NSF 99-167," September 28, available online at <http://www.nsf.gov/pubs/1999/nsf99167/nsf99167.htm>.

National Science Foundation (NSF), Division of Science Resources Studies. 2000a. *Federal Funds for Research and Development: Fiscal Years 1998, 1999, and 2000.* Arlington, Va., forthcoming.

National Science Foundation (NSF), Division of Science Resources Studies. 2000b. *Research and Development in Industry: 1998.* Arlington, Va., forthcoming.

Nelson, Richard. 1959. "The Simple Economics of Basic Research," *Journal of Political Economy* 67(2):297-306.

Organization for Economic Cooperation and Development (OECD). 1999. *STI Scoreboard of Indicators.* OECD, Paris, France.

Peltz, Michael. 1996. "High Tech's Premier Venture Capitalist," *Institutional Investor* 30 (June):89-98.

President's Information Technology Advisory Committee (PITAC). 1999. *Information Technology Research: Investing in Our Future.* National Coordination office for Computing, Information, and Communications, Arlingon, Va., February.

Semiconductor Industry Association (SIA). 2000. *The Silicon Century.* Semiconductor Industry Association, San Jose, Calif.

Smith, Douglas K., and Robert C. Alexander. 1988. *Fumbling the Future: How Xerox Invented, Then Ignored the Personal Computer.* William Morrow and Company, New York.

Streitfeld, David. 1999. "Capital and Ideas: Financiers of the Information Age Serve Up Cachet, Cash," *Washington Post* (August 15):H1.

Takashi, Dean. 1996. "Intel Shifts Its Focus to Original Research," *WSJ Interactive Edition* (August 26):1. Available online at <http://interactive3.wsj.com/edition/articles/SB841015179745727000.htm>.

von Hippel, Eric. 1988. *The Sources of Innovation.* Oxford University Press, New York.

White House. 2000. "Information Technology Research and Development: Information Technology for the 21st Century." Press release dated January 21, Office of the Press Secretary, Washington, D.C.

NOTES

1. Diversity is not, of course, the only factor in research success. The quality of the research is also of paramount importance. Quality can be assured through mechanisms such as peer review.

2. The Internet, for example, traces its roots to the DOD's ARPANET, built in the late 1960s and 1970s. Early work in virtual reality was supported by the government, and continued government investments in the technology sustained the field even when early commercial interest waned. Many of the most important advances in artificial intelligence came from government-funded research.

3. All data on federal funding for IT research in this paragraph were derived from the National Science Foundation (2000a).

4. The growth rate cited includes sales in five industry sectors defined in the standard industrial classification (SIC) codes: office, computing, and accounting machines (SIC 357),

communications equipment (SIC 366), electronic components (SIC 367), communications services (SIC 48), and computer and data processing services (SIC 737).

5. According to preliminary estimates from the National Science Foundation, defense R&D spending will decrease even further in FY00.

6. Many important, lasting IT developments sprang from DARPA's experimental projects, such as the ARPANET (which laid the groundwork for the Internet) and the Very Large Scale Integrated Circuit program, which helped advanced reduced-instruction-set computing.

7. Research supported by the NSF has contributed significantly to the evolution of IT. An important capability, scientific visualization, grew out of NSF sponsorship of computing in the service of science. Visualization, which uses carefully designed images to allow scientists and engineers to glean insight from computer simulations of natural phenomena, is now widely used in scientific computing and advanced engineering applications such as jet engine design.

8. For more information on the NGI, see <www.ngi.gov>.

9. The university centers established as part of ASCI are the Center for Integrated Turbulence Simulation at Stanford University, the Computational Facility for Simulating the Dynamic Response of Materials at the California Institute of Technology, the Center for Astrophysical Thermonuclear Flashes at the University of Chicago, the Center for Simulation of Accidental Fires and Explosions at the University of Utah, and the Center for Simulation of Advanced Rockets at the University of Illinois at Urbana-Champaign.

10. For more information on Project Oxygen, see Dertouzos (1999).

11. Additional information on the University of California at Berkeley's Endeavor project is available online at <http://endeavor.cs.berkeley.edu>.

12. Additional information on the University of Washington's Portolano/Workscape project is available online at <http://portolano.cs.washington.edu/>.

13. As of April 2000, DARPA planned to transform its expeditions program into a program that would explore "ubiquitous computing," a term used to describe the incorporation of computing and communications capabilities into a range of everyday devices.

14. It should also be cautioned that it is notoriously difficult to separate research from development, especially given that fundamental research advances sometimes emanate from focusing on development projects. Most often research and development are lumped together in the statistics, and attempts to separate out the research should be viewed with some skepticism.

15. The 20 percent figure reported in the 1998 data is unusually high, suggesting some inconsistencies in the collection or reporting of the data. IT firms reported that 10 percent of their research dollars were allocated to basic research in 1997, which is more consistent with earlier reports and anecdotal reports from research managers.

16. The Census Bureau is in the process of shifting from the SIC to a new system, the North American Industry Classification System, which features significant changes such as the introduction of an Information Sector and is undergoing additional modification and revision. Additional information on the transition to the new industry classification system is available online at <http://www.census.gov/epcd/www/naics.html>.

17. Despite the difficulties in tracing the movements of firms among industry sectors, federal statistics are still the best source of data for tracking research in the IT industry. Corporate annual reports and other public documents cannot be used because individual companies do not report research investments in these documents, although most list combined research and development investments.

18. Indeed, there is reason to believe that much of the decline in reported research and development investments in the office and computing equipment industry between 1990 and 1991 resulted from the reclassification of large firms to other industries.

19. Combined R&D investments for these firms totaled $32 billion in 1998. R&D investments for all firms contained in the NSF survey of industrial R&D in the office and computing equipment, communications equipment, electronic components, communications services, and computing/data processing services industries in 1998 totaled $45 billion.

20. Many large IT firms were criticized in the 1980s and early 1990s for failing to take advantage of technologies developed in their own labs. Xerox, for example, developed one of the earliest personal computers (the Alto) but never successfully marketed it. See Smith and Alexander (1988).

21. Robert Metcalfe, a founder of 3Com Inc., has said that the value of the network scales as the square of the number of users. This is now called Metcalfe's law.

22. This is not to say that there will be no effort to displace the prevailing technology, as the open-source software movement and the Linux-based initial public offerings demonstrate.

23. Of course, there can be benefits to the rapid adoption of new technologies, and lock-in as well, in that they allow other innovators to build on top of a commonly accepted platform. It is only when limitations in the platform itself become evident and impede further innovation that lock-in becomes problematic.

24. Such companies have forced many of the traditional computer manufacturers, such as IBM, to streamline their PC operations, sometimes establishing them as separate business lines with their own cost structures.

25. A notable proponent of this theory is Christensen (1997).

26. For Motorola, which has roughly $30 billion in sales, this ratio would imply about $300 million in research funding.

27. For example, work in natural language processing has long-term goals, but it already has contributed to the grammar checker in Microsoft Office.

28. These activities correspond to SIC codes 7371 and 7373.

29. Andersen Consulting employs about 50,000 workers, so the research group represents just 0.4 percent of its workforce.

30. The information on Andersen Consulting's research activities was obtained from Joseph Carter, Andersen Consulting, in a presentation to the study committee in Palo Alto, California, on February 10, 1998.

31. The data on Lockheed Martin's R&D expenditures were obtained from B. Clovis Landry, vice president of technology, Lockheed Martin Information & Services Sector, October 11, 1999.

32. Personal communication from Irving Wladawsky-Berger, vice president of technology and strategy for IBM, October 6, 1999.

33. Amazon.com reported $47 million in product development expenses in 1998, most of which were related to continual enhancement of the features, content, and functionality of the company's Web sites and transaction processing systems, as well as investments in systems and telecommunications infrastructure. Merrill Lynch reported in 1997 that it would spend $200 million to complete the development of a technology platform for its financial consultants by the third quarter of 1998.

34. Needless to say, most of Boeing's $1.9 billion R&D budget is allocated to non-IT activities.

35. These data are from Amazon.com's annual 10-K report to the SEC.

36. Merrill Lynch reported in 1997 that it was investing some $200 million in the development of a new platform for its financial consultants called the Trusted Global Advisor system. In keeping with new accounting standards, Merrill Lynch amortized $72 million in development costs for internal-use software in 1998. These amounts are amortized over the useful life of the developed software (generally 3 years).

37. Most of these patents have been awarded since 1998, although the patent applications were submitted several years before the awards.

38. In the late 1990s, end-user organizations also began applying for—and receiving—patents covering methods of doing business. Considerable controversy has arisen around this subject. The Computer Science and Telecommunications Board is developing a prospectus for a study of this issue. For additional background on the patenting of business practices, see CSTB (2000), especially pp. 192-198.

39. Anoop Gupta, a Stanford University professor on leave at Microsoft at the time, characterized this distinction to the committee on February 10, 1998, as follows: "The difference between black and white magic is really in its symbolism and intent." Symbolism and intent seem to determine the perceptions of whether something is research or not. Whether knowledge is created is often overlooked. From this "intent-based" perspective, the work of start-ups is not research, whereas from the perspective of producing knowledge, it certainly is.

40. These data are from a PricewaterhouseCoopers MoneyTree survey.

41. Preliminary statistics from PricewaterhouseCoopers indicated that for the second quarter of 1999, 63 percent of VC investments went to firms in the communications, software and information, and computers and peripherals industries.

42. Data from VentureOne Corporation, as reported in Streitfeld (1999).

43. The definitions of seed, start-up, and expansion financing used here are derived from OECD (1999).

44. The apparent disparities between the research funding numbers reported by universities and by federal agencies are due largely to differences in the ways the surveys are administered to collect these data.

45. The federal government has attempted to stimulate collaboration between industry and academia as a means of improving the competitiveness of U.S. companies and of better exploiting the results of federally sponsored research. For example, NSF established the ongoing Engineering Research Centers program in the 1980s to foster partnerships among government, industry, and universities in research and engineering. This program is more fully described in Chapter 4 of this report.

46. Two Focus Centers had been established as of May 2000. The first is led by researchers at the University of California at Berkeley; the second, by researchers at the Georgia Institute of Technology. Each involves researchers from a number of other universities. Additional information on the program is available in SIA (2000).

47. Congressional hearings that predated the 1995 commercialization of the NSFnet featured debates over "experimental" versus "production" networks.

3

Research on Large-Scale Systems

S ystems research has long been a part of the information technology (IT) landscape. Computer scientists and engineers have examined ways of combining components—whether individual transistors, integrated circuits, or devices—into larger IT systems to provide improved performance and capability. The incredible improvements in the performance of computer systems seen through the past five decades attest to advances in areas such as computer architectures, compilers, and memory management. But today's large-scale IT systems, which contain thousands or even millions of interacting components of hardware and software, raise a host of technical and nontechnical issues, some of which existed in the early days of computing and have now become critical and others of which arose recently as a result of the increases in scale and the degree of interconnection of IT systems. As computing and communications systems become more distributed and more integrated into the fabric of daily life, the scope of systems research needs to be broadened to address these issues more directly and enable the development of more reliable, predictable, and adaptable large-scale IT systems. Some have argued that the notion of computer systems research needs to be reinvented (Adams, 1999).

Today's large-scale IT systems crest on a shaky foundation of ad hoc, opportunistic techniques and technologies, many of which lack an adequate intellectual basis of understanding and rigorous design. There are at least three concrete manifestations of these deficiencies. First, there has been an unacceptably high rate of failure in the development of large-scale IT systems: many systems are not deployed and used because of an outright inability to make them work, because the initial set of requirements cannot be met, or because time or budget constraints could not be met. Well-publicized failures include those of the government's tax processing and air traffic control systems (described later in this chapter), but these represent merely the tip of the iceberg. The second manifestation of these deficiencies is the prevalence of operational failures experienced by large-scale systems as a result of security vulnerabilities or, more often, programming or operational errors or simply mysterious breakdowns. The third sign of these deficiencies is the systems' lack of scalability; that is, their performance parameters cannot be expanded to maintain adequate responsiveness as the number of users increases. This problem is becoming particularly evident in consumer-oriented electronic commerce (e-commerce); many popular sites are uncomfortably close to falling behind demand. Without adequate attention from the research community, these problems will only get worse as large-scale IT systems become more widely deployed.

This chapter reviews the research needs in large-scale IT systems. It begins by describing some of the more obvious failures of such systems and then describes the primary technical challenges that large-scale IT systems present. Finally, it sketches out the kind of research program that is needed to make progress on these issues. The analysis considers the generic issues endemic to all large IT systems, whether they are systems that combine hardware, software, and large databases to perform a particular set of functions (such as e-commerce or knowledge management); large-scale infrastructures (such as the Internet) that underlie a range of functions and support a growing number of users; or large-scale software systems that run on individual or multiple devices. A defining characteristic of all these systems is that they combine large numbers of components in complicated ways to produce complex behaviors. The chapter considers a range of issues, such as scale and complexity, interoperability among heterogeneous components, flexibility, trustworthiness, and emergent behavior in systems. It argues that many of these issues are receiving far too little attention from the research community.

WHAT IS THE PROBLEM WITH LARGE-SCALE SYSTEMS?

Since its early use to automate the switching of telephone calls—thereby enabling networks to operate more efficiently and support a growing number of callers—IT has come to perform more and more critical roles in many of society's most important infrastructures, including those used to support banking, health care, air traffic control, telephony, government payments to individuals (e.g., Social Security), and individuals' payments to the government (e.g., taxes). Typical uses of IT within companies are being complemented, or transformed, by the use of more IT to support supply-chain management systems connecting multiple enterprises, enabling closer collaboration among suppliers and purchasers.

Many of the systems in these contexts are very large in scale: they consist of hundreds or thousands of computers and millions of lines of code and they conduct transactions almost continuously. They increasingly span multiple departments within organizations (enterprisewide) or multiple organizations (interenterprise) or they connect enterprises to the general population.[1] Many of these systems and applications have come to be known as "critical infrastructure," meaning that they are integral to the very functioning of society and its organizations and that their failure would have widespread and immediate consequences. The critical nature of these applications raises concerns about the risks and consequences of system failures and makes it imperative to better understand the nature of the systems and their interdependencies.[2]

The IT systems used in critical intra- and interorganizational applications have several characteristics in common. First, they are all large, distributed, complex, and subject to high and variable levels of use.[3] Second, they perform critical functions that have extraordinary requirements for trustworthiness and reliability, such as a need to operate with minimal outages or corruption of information and/or a need to continue to function even while being serviced. Third, the systems depend on IT-based automation for expansion, monitoring, operations, maintenance, and other supporting activities.

All three of these characteristics give rise to problems in building and operating large-scale IT systems. For example, applications that run on distributed systems are much more complicated to design than corresponding applications that run on more centralized systems, such as a mainframe computer. Distributed systems must tolerate the failure of one or more component computers without compromising any critical application data or consistency, and preferably without crashing the system. The designs, algorithms, and programming techniques required to build high-quality distributed systems are much more complex than those for older, more conventional applications.

Large-scale IT systems are notoriously difficult to design, develop, and operate reliably. The list of problematic system development efforts is long and growing (Table 3.1 provides an illustrative set of failures). In some cases, difficulties in design and development have resulted in significant cost overruns and/or a lack of desired functionality in fielded systems. In others, major IT systems were cancelled before they were ever fielded because of problems in development. To be sure, the reasons

TABLE 3.1 Examples of Troubled Large-Scale Information Technology Systems

Project	Problem
Federal Aviation Administration air traffic control modernization	Project begun in 1981 is still ongoing; major pieces of project were canceled, others are over budget and/or delayed. The total cost estimate now stands at $42 billion through the year 2004.
Internal Revenue Service tax systems modernization	In early 1997, the modernization project was cancelled, after expenditures of $4 billion and 8 years of work.
National Weather Service technology modernization	Project begun in 1982 to modernize systems for observing and forecasting weather was over budget and behind schedule as of January 2000. The cost of the system is estimated to be $4.5 billion.
Bureau of Land Management automated land and mineral records system	After spending more than 15 years and approximately $411 million, the program was canceled in 1999.
California vehicle registration, driver's license database	Vehicle registration and driver's license database was never deployed after $44 million in development costs—three times the original cost estimate.
California deadbeat dads/ moms database	Even at a total cost of $300 million (three times the original budget estimate), the system was still flawed, and the project was canceled.
Florida fingerprint system	Incompatible upgrades resulted in inability of the Palm Beach County police to connect to the main state fingerprint database (a failure that prevents the catching of criminals).
Hershey Foods, Inc., order and distribution system	A $112 million system for placing and filling store orders has problems getting orders into the system and transmitting order information to warehouses for fulfillment. As of October 1999, the source of the problem had not been identified.
Bell Atlantic 411 system	On November 25, 1996, Bell Atlantic experienced a directory service outage for several hours after the database server operating system was upgraded and the backup system failed.
New York Stock Exchange upgrade	The stock exchange opened late on December 18, 1995 (the first such delay in 5 years) because of problems with communications software.
Denver International Airport baggage system	In 1994, problems with routing baggage delayed the airport opening by 11 months at a cost of $1 million per day.
CONFIRM reservations system (Hilton, Marriott, and Budget Rent-a-Car, with American Airlines Information Services)	The project was canceled in 1992 after 32 years of work in which $125 million was spent on a failed development effort.

for failures in the development of large-scale systems are not purely technological. Many are plagued by management problems as well (see Box 3.1). But management problems and technical problems are often interrelated. If system design techniques were simpler and could accommodate changing sets of requirements, then management challenges would be greatly eased. Conversely, if management could find ways of better defining and controlling system requirements—and could create a process for doing so—then the technical problems could be reduced. This dilemma has existed from the earliest development of computer systems.

The direct economic costs of failed developments and systems failures is great. U.S. companies spend more than $275 billion a year on approximately 200,000 system development projects (Johnson, 1999). By some estimates, 70 to 80 percent of major system development projects either are never finished or seriously overrun cost and development time objectives (Gibbs, 1994; Jones, 1996; Barr and Tessler, 1998).[4] The reported data may well underestimate the problem, given that many entities would (understandably) prefer to avoid adverse publicity. However, the accountability required of government programs ensures that system problems in government at all levels do get publicized, and a steady stream of reports attest to the ongoing challenges.[5] Individual failures can be expensive. For example, the state of California abandoned systems development projects in recent years worth over $200 million (*Sunday Examiner and Chronicle*, 1999). The Federal Aviation Administration (FAA) will have spent some $42 billion over 20 years in a much-maligned attempt to modernize the nation's air traffic control system (see Box 3.2), and the Internal Revenue Service (IRS) has spent more than $3 billion to date on tax systems modernization.[6] The potential cost of economic damage from a single widespread failure of critical infrastructure (such as the telephone system, the Internet, or an electric power system) could be much greater than this.[7]

The potential consequences of problems with large-scale systems will only become worse. The ability to develop large-scale systems has improved over the past decade thanks to techniques such as reusability and object-oriented programming (described below), but even if the rate of problem generation has declined, the number of systems susceptible to problems continues to grow. A large number of system failures and cost overruns in system development continue to plague the developers and users of critical IT systems (Gibbs, 1994; Jones, 1996). As recently as October 1999, Hershey Foods, Inc., was attempting to understand why its new, $112-million, computer-based order and distribution system was unable to properly accept orders and transmit the details to warehouses for fulfillment (Nelson and Ramstad, 1999). Several universities also reported difficulties with a new software package designed to allow stu-

BOX 3.1
The CONFIRM Hotel Reservation System

The CONFIRM hotel reservation system is one of the best-documented cases of system development failure in industry. The CONFIRM system was intended to be a state-of-the-art travel reservation system for Marriott Hotels, Hilton Hotels, and Budget Rent-A-Car. The three companies contracted with AMRIS, a subsidiary of American Airlines, to build the system. The four companies formed the Intrico consortium in 1988 to manage the development of the system. AMRIS originally estimated the cost of the project to be $55.7 million. By the time the project was canceled 4 years later, the Intrico consortium had already paid AMRIS $125 million, more than twice the original cost estimate.

AMRIS was unable to overcome the technical complexities involved in creating CONFIRM. One problem arose from the computer-aided software engineering (CASE) tool used to develop the database and the interface. The tool's purpose was to automatically create the database structure for the application, but the task ended up being too complex for the tool. As a result, the AMRIS development team was unable to integrate the two main components of CONFIRM—the interactive database component and the pricing and yield-management component. An AMRIS vice president involved in the development eventually conceded that integration was simply not possible. Another problem was that the developers could not make the system's database fault-tolerant, a necessity for the system. The database structure chosen was such that, if the database crashed, the data would be unrecoverable. In addition, the development team was unable to make booking reservations cost-effective for the participating firms. Originally, AMRIS estimated that booking a reservation would cost approximately $1.05, but the cost estimates rapidly grew to $2.00 per reservation.

The difficulties plaguing CONFIRM were exacerbated by problems with the project's management, both on AMRIS's side and on the side of the end users. Even though the Marriott, Hilton, and Budget executives considered CONFIRM to be a high priority, they spent little time involved directly with the project, meeting with the project team only once a month. An executive at AMRIS said, "CONFIRM's fatal flaw was a management structure. . . . You cannot manage a development effort of this magnitude by getting together once a month. . . . A system of this magnitude requires quintessential teamwork. We essentially had four different groups. . . . It was a formula for failure."

The actions of AMRIS middle managers also contributed to the delays and eventual complete failure of CONFIRM. Some AMRIS managers communicated only good news to upper management. They refrained from passing on news of problems, delays, and cost overruns. There were allegations that "AMRIS forced employees to artificially change their timetable to reflect the new schedule, and those that refused either were reassigned to other projects, resigned, or were fired." The project employees were so displeased with management actions that, by the middle of 1991 (1 year before the project was canceled), half of the AMRIS employees working on CONFIRM were seeking new jobs. Had developers at AMRIS informed upper AMRIS management or the other members of Intrico about the problems they faced with CONFIRM, it might have been possible to correct the problems. If not, then at least the end users would have had the opportunity to cancel the project before its budget exploded.

SOURCES: Ewusi-Mensah (1997), Oz (1997), and Davies (1998).

BOX 3.2
Modernization of the Air Traffic Control System

The Federal Aviation Administration (FAA) began modernizing its air traffic control (ATC) system in 1981 to handle expected substantial growth in air traffic, replace old equipment, and add functionality. The plan included replacing or upgrading ATC facilities, radar arrays, data processing systems, and communications equipment. Since that time, the system has been plagued by significant cost overruns, delays, and performance shortfalls, with the General Accounting Office (GAO) having designated it as a high-risk information technology initiative in 1995. As of early 1999, the FAA had spent $25 billion on the project. It estimated that another $17 billion would be spent before the project is completed in 2004—$8 billion more and 1 year later than the agency estimated in 1997.

The GAO has blamed the problems largely on the FAA's failure to develop or design an overall system architecture that had the flexibility to accommodate changing requirements and technologies. When the ATC program began, it was composed of 80 separate projects, but at one point it grew to include more than 200 projects. By 1999, only 89 projects had been completed, and 129 were still in progress[1]—not including several projects that had been canceled or restructured at a cost of $2.8 billion. The largest of these canceled projects was the Advanced Automation System (AAS), which began as the centerpiece of the modernization effort and was supposed to replace and update the ATC computer hardware and software, adding new automation functions to help handle the expected increase in air traffic and allow pilots to use more fuel-efficient flight paths. Between 1981 and 1994, the estimated cost of the AAS more than doubled, from $2.5 billion to $5.9 billion, and the completion date was expected to be delayed by more than 4 years. Much of the delay was due to the need to rework portions of code to handle changing system requirements. As a result of the continuing difficulties, the AAS was replaced in 1994 by a scaled-back plan, known as the Display System Replacement program, scheduled for completion in May 2000. A related piece of the modernization program, the $1 billion Standard Terminal Automation Replacement System, which was to be installed at its first airport in June 1998 has also been delayed until at least early 2000.

The FAA is beginning to change its practices in the hope of reducing the cost escalation and time delays that have plagued the modernization effort. In particular, it has begun to develop an overall architecture for the project and announced plans to hire a new chief information officer who will report directly to the FAA administrator. In addition, instead of pursuing its prior "all at once" development and deployment strategy, the FAA plans on using a phased approach as a means of better monitoring project progress and incorporating technological advances.

---

[1]Some of the high-priority projects that remain to be completed include the Integrated Terminal Weather System, intended to automatically compile real-time weather data from several sources and provide short-term weather forecasting; the Global Positioning System Augmentation Program, transferring ground-based navigation and landing systems to a system based on DOD satellites; and the Airport Surface Detection Equipment, which encompasses three projects to replace the airport radar equipment that monitors traffic on runways and taxiways. See U.S. GAO (1998), p. 9.

SOURCES: U.S. General Accounting Office (1994, 1997, 1998, 1999a,b,c), Li (1994), and O'Hara (1999).

dents to register online for classes.[8] As networking and computing become more pervasive in business and government organizations and in society at large, IT systems will become larger in all dimensions—in numbers of users, subsystems, and interconnections.

Future IT applications will further challenge the state of the art in system development and technical infrastructure:

• Information management will continue to transition from isolated databases supporting online transaction processing to federations of multiple databases across one or more enterprises supporting business process automation or supply-chain management. "Supply-chain management" is not possible on a large scale with existing database technology and can require technical approaches other than data warehouses.[9]

• Knowledge discovery—which incorporates the acquisition of data from multiple databases across an enterprise, together with complex data mining and online analytical processing applications—will become more automated as, for example, networked distributed sensors are used to collect more information and user and transaction information is captured on the World Wide Web. These applications severely strain the state of the art in both infrastructure and database technology. Data will be stored in massive data warehouses in forms ranging from structured databases to unstructured text documents. Search and retrieval techniques need to be able to access all of these different repositories and merge the results for the user. This is not feasible today on any large scale.

• Large financial services Web sites will support large and rapidly expanding customer bases using transactions that involve processing-intensive security protocols such as encryption. Today's mainframe and server technology is strained severely by these requirements.

• Collaboration applications are moving from centralized deferred applications such as e-mail to complicated, multipoint interconnection topologies for distributed collaboration, with complex coordination protocols connecting tens or hundreds of millions of people. The deployment of technology to support distance education is a good example. Today's Internet is able to support these requirements only on a relatively modest scale.

• Advances in microelectromechanical systems (MEMS) and nanoscale devices presage an era in which large numbers of very small sensors, actuators, and processors are networked together to perform a range of tasks, whether deployed over large or small geographic areas.[10] The sheer number of such devices and the large number of interconnections among them could far exceed the number of more conventional computing and communications devices, exacerbating the problems of large-scale systems.

   • Information appliances allow computing capabilities to be embedded in small devices, often portable, that realize single functions or small numbers of dedicated applications.[11] Information appliances will greatly increase the number of devices connected to the network, increasing the scalability problem. They will also magnify problems of mobility. As users roam, all the while accessing their standard suite of applications, their connectivity (in both the topological and performance dimensions) shifts with them. From an application perspective, the infrastructure becomes much more dynamic, creating a need to adapt in various ways.

   These applications exemplify a technology infrastructure strained by current and evolving requirements. Obviously, many systems are fielded and used to good effect. But as the requirements and level of sophistication grow, old approaches for coping and compensating when problems arise become less effective if they remain feasible at all.[12] This situation—a proliferation of systems and of interconnections among them—calls for better understanding and greater rigor in the design of large-scale systems to better anticipate and address potential problems and to maximize the net potential for benefit to society. Achieving that understanding and rigor will require research—research that will develop a better scientific basis for understanding large-scale IT systems and new engineering methodologies for constructing them. The high cost of failures suggests that even modest improvements in system design and reliability could justify substantial investments in research (the federal government's budget for IT research totaled $1.7 billion in fiscal year 2000). Of course, the goal of further systems research should be more than just modest improvements—it should be no less than a revolution in the way such large-scale systems are designed.

TECHNICAL CHALLENGES ASSOCIATED WITH LARGE-SCALE SYSTEMS

   Why are large-scale systems so difficult to design, build, and operate? As evidenced by their many failures, delays, and cost overruns, large-scale systems present a number of technical challenges that IT research has not yet resolved. These challenges are related to the characteristics of the systems themselves—largeness of scale, complexity, and heterogeneity—and those of the context in which they operate, which demands extreme flexibility, trustworthiness, and distributed operation and administration. Although the characteristics may be identified with specific application requirements, they are common across a growing number of systems used in a diversity of applications. As explored in greater detail below, fundamental research will be required to meet these challenges.

Large Scale

By definition, scale is a distinguishing feature of large-scale systems. Scale is gauged by several metrics, including the number of components contained within a system and the number of users supported by the system. As systems incorporate more components and serve increasingly large numbers of users (either individuals or organizations), the challenges of achieving scalability become more severe. Both metrics are on the rise, which raises the question, How can systems be developed that are relatively easily scaled by one or more orders of magnitude?[13]

The Internet provides an example of the need to scale the hardware and software infrastructure by several orders of magnitude as the user base grows and new services require more network capacity per user. The Internet contains millions of interconnected computers, and it experiences scaling problems in its algorithms for routing traffic, naming entities connected to the network, and congestion control. The computers attached to the network are increasing in capability at a pace tied to Moore's law, which promises significant improvements in a matter of months. Because so much of the activity surrounding the Internet in the late 1990s was based in industry, the academic research community has been challenged to define and execute effective contributions. The nature of the research that would arise from the research community is not obvious, and the activities in current networking research programs—as clustered under the Next Generation Internet (NGI) program or other programs aimed at networking research—seem not to satisfy either the research community or industry.

Complexity

Large systems are not complex by definition; they can be simple if, for example, the components are linked in a linear fashion and information flows in a single direction. But almost all large-scale IT systems are complex, because the system components interact with each other in complicated, tightly coupled ways—often with unanticipated results.[14] By contrast, consider the U.S. highway system: it contains millions of automobiles (i.e., the system is large in scale), but at any given time most of them do not interact (i.e., the system is low in complexity).[15] Much more complex are IT systems, which contain thousands of hardware components linked by millions of lines of code and elements that interact and share information in a multitude of ways, with numerous feedback loops. Indeed, it is often impossible for a single individual, or even a small group of individuals, to understand the overall functioning of the system. As a result, predicting performance is incredibly difficult, and failures in one part of the system can propagate throughout the system in unexpected ways (Box 3.3). Although nature has succeeded in composing systems far more complex than any information system, large-scale information systems are among the most complex products designed by humans.

Scale and complexity interact strongly. As IT systems become larger, they also tend to become more complex. The as-yet-unattained goal is to build systems that do not get more complex as they are scaled up. If

---

BOX 3.3
Performance Prediction in Large-Scale Systems

The performance of large-scale systems is difficult to predict, because of both the large numbers of interacting components and the uncertain patterns of usage presented to the system. Performance can seldom be predicted by modeling, simulation, or experimentation before the final deployment. As a result, complex systems of dynamically interacting components often behave in ways that their designers did not intend. At times, they display emergent behavior—behaviors not intentionally designed into the system but that emerge from unanticipated interactions among components. Such behaviors can sometimes benefit a system, but they are usually undesirable.

An example of an emergent behavior is the convoying of packets that was observed in the packet-switched communications networks in the late 1980s. Although the routing software was not programmed to do so, the system sent packets through the network in bursts. Subsequent analysis (using fluid flow models) discovered that certain network configurations could cause oscillations in the routing of packets, not unlike the vibration of a water pipe with air in it. This type of behavior had not been intended and was corrected by upgrading routing protocols.

Unexpected performance issues (including emergent behaviors) are among the most common causes of failure in software projects. Improved methodologies for characterizing and predicting the performance of large, complex, distributed systems could help enhance performance and avoid dysfunction before systems are deployed. More powerful mechanisms are needed to deal effectively with emergent behavior in complex hardware and software systems. Design methodologies are needed that incorporate into a system some type of structure that limits system behavior and can reason about subsystem interaction. Also needed are more effective ways of modeling and simulating or otherwise testing large-system behavior.

scaling can be achieved merely by replicating existing components, and if the management and operation of components do not change as their numbers grow, then the system has been scaled up successfully. On the other hand, if software must be rewritten or reconfigured, or if new hardware structures must be introduced to achieve larger scale, then complexity increases as well. For example, the demand for database storage and query speed is growing at a rate of 100 percent per year, a rate faster than the improvement in processor performance predicted by Moore's law. As a result, demand must be satisfied not by scaling up the system directly, but by parallel and distributed processing, which introduces additional complexity associated with the replication and reconciliation of data.

Heterogeneity

Large-scale IT systems are increasingly heterogeneous. In the past, computing capabilities generally were provided by stand-alone systems supplied by a single vendor who designed the system from the top down. Today, large-scale systems are stitched together from components and subsystems drawn from many vendors; they are increasingly constructed from commercial off-the-shelf (COTS) technology, and the products of any one vendor (equipment or software) must fit into a larger system containing components from many other vendors. This process results in a high level of heterogeneity within systems and heightens the need for interoperability among components. It requires sound techniques for designing large systems from components "out of the box," especially when they are mixed and matched in ways unanticipated by their makers—a process that makes systems difficult to design and maintain. A related problem of growing importance is how to design trustworthy systems from untrustworthy components, as articulated by another CSTB committee.[16]

Heterogeneity means much more than accommodating different processor architectures or different operating systems, which are daunting problems in their own right. Systems increasingly are composed of software objects and components that are written by different entities, perhaps using different object architectures. These parts may be built on top of different operating systems or middleware architectures.[17] It is often not feasible to determine ahead of time which sets of objects will interact when any given user (with a particular machine, operating system, browser, etc.) connects to the system and requests a service. Nomadicity— the mobility of individuals and their use of different hardware and software under different circumstances—adds to the uncertainty. Techniques are needed to help design robust, reliable, and secure software in this new and highly challenging environment.[18]

Further complicating matters is the reality that large-scale IT systems do not generally come out of a centralized, top-down design process. Rather, they often result from the bottom-up integration of many individual components and subsystems. Systems are not designed as a whole; instead, each added component must incorporate, elaborate on, and interoperate with the preexisting parts. Large-scale IT systems (and personal systems) tend to be custom-configured for particular users and applications, compounding the difficulties associated with testing (Box 3.4). [19] Furthermore, interoperability is needed over the lifetime of a system (which can be years, if not decades) because the ensemble must continue to evolve as new hardware replaces old or as software is repaired or enhanced. These requirements are difficult to accommodate using traditional reductionist engineering approaches, and methodologies to successfully engineer such systems are poorly understood. The publicized system failures presented in Table 3.1 and Boxes 3.1 and 3.2 reflect the situation: the design of large-scale IT systems is characterized not by consistent, well-understood engineering methodology but rather by considerable trial and error.

Flexibility

The ad hoc nature of design as a consequence of the heterogeneity described above suggests another challenging characteristic of large-scale IT systems: the need for flexibility. Flexibility is important both during the design process and after deployment. The development of large-scale IT systems can take so long that mission requirements and component technologies change before the system is fielded.[20] An inability to accommodate these changes and to integrate subsystems that were designed and implemented separately is a main reason that many major IT systems are never deployed.[21] Once deployed, large IT systems tend to have long lifetimes, during which additional functionality is often desired, old components must be replaced—often with more modern technology—or the scale of the system must be expanded. The need for system upgrades and expansions can be particularly pressing for businesses, whose requirements evolve more rapidly than those of government. Companies want to establish new products and services quickly, either to beat competitors to market or to match their innovations. Doing so almost always requires reconfigured information systems; the challenge is to "change the software as fast as the business."

A complementary trend driving the need for flexibility is a shift away from the standardization of products and toward rapid innovation, short product cycles, and "mass customization." This trend has been forecast by business analysts since at least the 1980s, but it is becoming a reality

BOX 3.4
The Challenges of Testing Large-Scale Systems

Tiny programs (systems) can be tested exhaustively by enumerating every state the system can enter and checking to be sure that, when started in that state, the system conforms to its specification. But the combinatorial explosion of possible states in a large-scale system defeats this technique very quickly. Testing a hardware design for a 32-bit adder or multiplier (as in the case of the famous Intel failure) is not practical. There are techniques, including theorem proving and model checking, for verifying the correctness of somewhat larger designs. These techniques have been used recently to find errors in network protocol designs, (hardware) bus designs, and the like. These are subsystems of interesting size but still far smaller than any product component as the term is used in this report (see Chapter 1).

At the level of a modest-sized computer program, such as a word processor or a World Wide Web browser, proof techniques cannot be applied. Instead, testing is used in various forms. Two forms of testing are common. In unit testing, the main modules of a system are tested separately, each against test cases derived from its specification. This technique takes advantage of hierarchical decomposition used in the design of the system. It helps reduce testing time by not testing modules that have not changed. Often modules have simple, easy-to-understand interfaces, which lead to good, thorough test suites, thereby also improving testing. When code does not have simple specifications, a form of testing called path coverage is used, in which every possible path through the system is executed at least once as part of a test program. To do so may require writing a huge quantity of test cases. These techniques are used in both hardware and software designs (in hardware, it is often called simulation, whereby a chip design is simulated against a large number of test cases before it is fabricated).

Testing can demonstrate the presence of bugs but never their absence. It does not enumerate all the possible states into which a system can enter or all combinations of paths through the system, so it is not definitive. Furthermore, testing becomes costly as systems become large. Today, a serious limitation on the ability to design microprocessors (and in their time-to-market) is the amount of simulation that must be done.

The forms of testing described apply to a single system of modest size. When the system is a large, distributed system-of-systems, the cost of testing becomes so high that only a tiny fraction of possible system behaviors is tested. The scale problem means that either (1) testers cannot afford to assemble a large enough system to test all interesting cases (e.g., for routers, lines, clients) or (2) they cannot explore a significant fraction of the system states or configurations (e.g., loads on the network, routing table entries, link congestion, routing policies). Thus, testing can quickly get out of hand.

Another complicating aspect of large-scale systems is that they have very complex failure modes. When a single personal computer running a single system stops, it is obvious that it is broken, and users no longer expect the system to meet its specification until the problem is fixed. However, when a single element of a large system (such as the Internet) fails, the rest of the system is often required to continue functioning properly. System designs are often intended to remain robust despite this type of failure, but testing in the presence of all these failure modes is more difficult still. In addition, testing is of little use in identifying security vulnerabilities in an IT system, because it is hard to determine what to test for.

now because of the cumulative advances in IT. As a result, flexibility—specifically, the ability to meet changing needs rapidly—has become one of the most fundamental and important requirements of many applications. The pursuit of flexibility is complicated by the context in pre-existing organizations, where new enterprise applications usually need to incorporate legacy departmental applications and thus cannot be developed from scratch. In the case of a merger or divestiture, information systems may need to be integrated or dismantled. Another source of complication that is growing along with economic globalization is the internationalization of functions within businesses. Such internationalization demands multifaceted support, not only for multiple languages but also for business processes that differ from one geographic area to another. The Internet is a global phenomenon, and research needs to be sensitive to international differences, including differences in technology and in issues of privacy, taxation, content regulation, and so on. Technologies such as automated language translation, which could be easily customized for different countries, would facilitate the internationalization of IT. Research is needed to understand the other differences mentioned above, perhaps through international or comparative research projects.[22]

System upgrades and expansions have proven particularly difficult in practice. One reason is that the original system may not be fully understood, and the developers attempting to augment it may have played no role in its design. Changes or additions to the system can therefore produce unexpected and unanticipated results.[23] Another source of difficulty is that many systems are designed without the modularity and encapsulation of functionality needed to facilitate future upgrades. In many hardware and software projects, the emphasis is on getting a system up and running. Less attention is paid to designing large-scale applications that will be easy to modify and maintain over a long lifetime. As a result, many systems—sometimes poorly designed in the first place—are modified repeatedly with great effort, to the point where their complexity virtually precludes further modification. Such systems may have to be scrapped long before they ordinarily would have been, at a high cost to the organizations that created them. An additional complication is a dearth of expertise in systems architecture. Some large government IT systems that have experienced problems, for example, have been faulted for the lack of architecture planning and perspective.[24]

Large-scale systems require architectures that are flexible enough that necessary modifications can be made easily, at low cost, and with little impact on system availability. Beyond paying more attention to IT designs that support flexibility, it will be important to gain an understanding of which forms of flexibility are desirable and which are unnecessary.

Unfettered flexibility can lead to too many options for end users to consider, making interactions cumbersome. When a system is customized for a particular application, interactions tend to become relatively short and efficient, but the system itself is less capable of accommodating changing specifications. A balance needs to be struck between unfettered flexibility (which doubtless would be too expensive and also degrade performance) and the present state of inflexibility, which increasingly cannot meet the needs of real-world systems. This is a variation on a traditional engineering theme: the trade-off between specialized and flexible technology.

Trustworthiness

Because they increasingly support mission-critical functions in industry, government, and other societal organizations, large-scale IT systems must also be extremely trustworthy. That is, they must do what they are required to do—and nothing else—despite environmental disruption, human user and operator error, and attacks by hostile parties (CSTB, 1999a). They must be available for service when needed (perhaps continuously) and perform their tasks reliably, with adequate security and without error. Failure to meet these standards can disrupt the service the IT systems provide, causing loss of business revenues or even human life. Trustworthiness increasingly is recognized as one of the most important challenges in IT, because systems are increasingly used to support critical functions and are increasingly networked, which can introduce new vulnerabilities. Ensuring trustworthiness is particularly difficult in large-scale IT systems because of their size and complexity.

The challenges are much broader and deeper than security alone. The trustworthiness of systems and applications encompasses a number of issues, including correctness, reliability, availability, robustness, and security; some analysts would also include privacy and other issues that add more subjective coloring to the trade-offs by clearly blending technical and social elements. For example, how one approaches the need for accountability and the value of anonymous speech will affect approaches to system design. These issues are central to ongoing discussions and developments relating to electronic identity. Gaining a deeper understanding of trustworthiness, and measures to ensure it, is in large part an operational and managerial challenge as well as a technical problem. Even the most secure installations or reliable systems are subject to human error, inattention, or dishonesty.[25]

Security

Large-scale information systems are vulnerable to malicious attacks that can render them unable to perform their intended tasks; result in the loss of confidential information; or cause information to be lost, modified, or destroyed. The security issue is obvious in areas such as e-commerce, where the potential for financial loss is huge, and in health care, where divulging a patient's medical record could result in an irreparable loss of privacy. But security gaps in any sort of IT system can lead to widespread system failure and disruption, financial loss, or theft of private or proprietary information in a very short time. The Defense Information Systems Agency (DISA) estimates that the Department of Defense (DOD) may have experienced as many as 250,000 attacks on its computer systems in a recent year, and that the number of such attacks may be doubling annually. Most of these attacks have been unsuccessful, but in some cases intruders have been able to take control of systems, steal passwords, and retrieve classified information (e.g., about troop movements in the Gulf War). A Swedish hacker shut down a 911 emergency call system in Florida for an hour, according to the FBI, and in March 1997 a series of commands sent from a hacker's personal computer disabled vital services to the FAA's control tower in Worcester, Massachusetts.[26] Such vulnerabilities are not limited to government computer systems, whose problems are more likely to be publicized; they apply as well to a growing number of private-sector systems, which become attractive targets of corporate espionage as attackers come to recognize that proprietary information is stored on networked systems. The wave of denial-of-service attacks launched against high-profile commercial Web sites in February 2000 underscores the vulnerability of such systems.

Large-scale systems are especially vulnerable to security flaws. The large number of client computers attached to them means an even larger number of portals at which a lapse in security (e.g., a weak or divulged password) can allow entry into a system. Furthermore, many such systems are distributed among several administrative domains, making security more difficult to manage and assure. Additional vulnerabilities are introduced by the connection of large-scale IT systems to the Internet. Although the attraction of many of today's large-scale systems stems from their attachment to the global network, this network connection also makes the systems vulnerable to misuse or attack.

How can systems be designed to retain information securely and operate correctly while under attack from intruders? How can intruders be deterred, while accommodating more open or less predictable interactions over computer networks? Existing technologies such as encryption, authentication, signatures, and firewalls can provide some degree of protection. But flaws in these systems and in operating systems are found and exploited regularly, leading to incremental improvements while also raising fundamental questions about the state of the art. More research on new methodologies for creating secure and trusted software systems would be of great benefit to the nation.

Availability and Reliability

As IT applications increasingly address critical needs such as disaster recovery, e-commerce, and health care, the requirements for availability (i.e., assurance that a system is available for use when and as needed) and fault tolerance (i.e., assurance that a system can function even when problems arise) have increased dramatically. Large-scale system designs clearly differ from, say, desktop office suites in that they must operate in unknown, changing environments. Unfortunately, most algorithms and design techniques for computer hardware and software assume a benign environment and the correct operation of every component. There is an urgent need for new algorithms based on different assumptions that will lead to algorithms that work correctly in spite of failures. The study of distributed computing (i.e., computer systems interconnected by networks) has begun to address the problem. Algorithms have been developed that work correctly even when a data packet sent into the network from a computer fails to arrive at its intended destination. The algorithms used to route packets through the Internet are not only robust in the presence of dropped packets but also adapt to changing network performance (e.g., when a communication link fails or resumes operation after failure). Although considerable progress has been made in critical algorithms, they are far from perfect (e.g., routing algorithms cannot always prevent network congestion), and they fulfill only a small fraction of the requirements of today's large-scale systems.

Ensuring the availability and reliability of large-scale IT systems is especially challenging (Box 3.5). As noted earlier, the number of components in these systems and the deep-seated interactions among them make attempts to predict performance especially difficult. The fact that they are usually custom-built for a particular application makes testing them extremely difficult—especially when they may be operated by a large number of users under a wide variety of operating conditions and when companies are under intense competitive pressure to field new systems quickly. In this environment, how can a large-scale system be designed to be so robust that it is guaranteed to be available all but, say, 30 seconds per year no matter what, even in cases of hardware failure, software bugs, or human error? Individual components of IT systems (such as routers and computing platforms) can be made reliable,[27] but making the large-

---

BOX 3.5
Availability Problems Experienced in
Information Technology Systems

Numerous well-publicized failures of major systems show that current technology and operating practices are not meeting expectations. For example, the 3-year-old central computer system that monitors the position of trains in the Washington, D.C., Metrorail system reportedly crashed 50 times in the first 15 months after its deployment. In September 1999, it failed for unknown reasons, delaying morning startup by 45 minutes and causing significant delays in the rush hour. A number of high-profile Internet companies have also experienced problems with World Wide Web sites for electronic commerce, many stemming from problems in upgrading systems and growing traffic volume. Charles Schwab's online brokerage service, for example, experienced more than a dozen outages in 1999, during which users could not access real-time quotes, check account information and margin balances, or execute trades. Online retailer Beyond.com experienced an extended outage in October 1999 as a result of complications stemming from a scheduled upgrade. In 1998, problems with unscheduled maintenance caused Amazon.com to take its site offline for several hours; eBay and E*Trade Securities are experiencing intermittent outages as the volume of visitors to their Web sites increases. Indeed, a survey conducted in late 1999 by the consulting company Deloitte & Touche found that the primary business concerns of online brokerage firms were system outages and an inability to accommodate growing numbers of online investors. Performance and reliability were also cited as significant concerns.

SOURCES: Junnarkar (1999), Layton (1999), Luenig (1999), and Meehan (2000).

---

scale systems themselves reliable is more difficult. The telephone system, which is based heavily on software, may be the closest to reaching this goal, but its robustness has been achieved only at considerable cost and with delays in development.[28] The race to develop new critical applications, driven by the rapid pace of innovation in Internet applications and services, has resulted in inadequate, even dangerously poor, robustness. Often prototypes or simplistic implementations become so popular so quickly that expectations far exceed the reliability achievable with the initial design. Moreover, even when systems are designed carefully to address reliability concerns, their complexity makes it doubly difficult to achieve reliability and robustness goals.

The spread of IT bears witness to the fact that, overall, hardware reliability has advanced significantly but software reliability has lagged (think of the frequency with which standard desktop computers crash). Techniques for assuring robustness in hardware have been of critical importance in, for example, space flight; by performing each computation using three independent hardware systems and attaching a "voting" circuit to the outcome to determine the majority answer, one can catch and overcome many hardware failure modes. However, this approach would not catch so many software bugs.[29]   The implementation of software modules in three different ways probably would catch some bugs, but at a high cost.   In a complex situation, how could one determine which version was behaving correctly?   Clearly, new ideas are needed on how to assure the robustness of complex hardware and software systems.   Experimenting with and qualifying these ideas will be a daunting challenge, given the nature of these large-scale systems and their myriad and infrequently observed failure mechanisms.

Distributed Operation and Administration

The challenges inherent in large-scale IT systems are further complicated by the frequent distribution of their operation and administration across different organizational units.   In the past, most IT applications were compartmentalized into individual organizations and independently administered.   Now, applications—whether designed for social, information access, or business purposes—are executed across a networked computing infrastructure spanning whole organizations and enterprises, and indeed multiple enterprises and consumers (see Box 3.6 for a discussion of e-commerce as a distributed system).   Such an infrastructure cannot be administered effectively in a centralized fashion—there is no central administrative authority.   New tools and automated operational support methodologies could improve the operation and administration of such distributed systems.   These potential solutions have yet to be considered seriously by the research community; network management is an area that has long needed more research (CSTB, 1994).

IMPROVING THE DESIGN AND IMPLEMENTATION OF LARGE-SCALE SYSTEMS

To date, IT research has failed to produce the techniques needed to address the challenges posed by large-scale systems.   Standard computer science approaches, such as abstraction, modularity, and layering (Box 3.7), are helpful at separating functionality and establishing clear interfaces between components, but even with these techniques engineers have great difficulty designing and refining large, complex systems.   These tools are apparently insufficient for dealing with the enormous complex-

---

BOX 3.6
Electronic Commerce Applications As Distributed Systems

Electronic commerce (e-commerce) demonstrates the issues of heterogeneity and multiple administrative domains cropping up in large-scale systems. In business-to-business e-commerce applications, the system cannot be integrated, nor is it deployed, by a single organization or professional service firm—even when parties nominally use the same product (e.g., popular enterprise resource planning systems). A vendor offering to sell its product over the Internet controls only its own servers and databases. The customer's client software is likely to be a generic World Wide Web browser; the Web, of course, is implemented by numerous Internet service providers running routers and other systems and software that has to work right to support the communications aspects of e-commerce. The vendor's software is likely to be part of a complex information technology system that must be integrated with a payment mechanism (e.g., credit card verification or maybe an electronic cash service) as well as the software of a shipping firm to track the status of orders. It also interacts with suppliers to manage and pay for the flow of materials and component parts. Such an e-commerce application spans multiple administrative domains, including firms and individual consumers. No single entity has access to, or control over, the complete system for systematic testing; nor does anyone have access to all the source code that defines the system. It is not surprising, for example, that even with the best intentions, privacy or security glitches arise because of the difficulty of assuring the appropriate design and performance of so many systems and system levels.

---

ity and cross-module, cross-layer interactions that arise in large IT systems. The IT community needs to understand better the root causes of the problems exhibited in large-scale systems and to articulate that understanding in ways that will bring more good minds and ideas to bear on the problems. Better software-based tools are needed for managing complexity, and best practices need to be codified and propagated so that, collectively, designers and engineers repeat methods and approaches that appear to work and avoid those whose failure has been demonstrated.

Limitations of Past Research

Part of the reason that better approaches to designing scalable, reliable, flexible large-scale IT systems do not yet exist is a lack of attention from the research community. Traditionally, IT systems research has emphasized advances in performance, functionality, and cost, primarily to improve device (or component) characteristics (Hennessy, 1999). The

BOX 3.7
Abstraction, Modularity, and Layering

Computer scientists have long used a set of tools known as abstraction, modularity, and layering to help them deal with the complexity of designing information technology (IT) systems. The limits of these approaches are tested by large-scale systems in a variety of ways:

• *Abstraction* is the process of simplifying the description of an element of a system to hide unnecessary details and allow greater focus on attributes that are important to system analysis or design. The trick is to select an appropriate abstraction that preserves the necessary attributes of the element without becoming unrealistic. Using abstraction, for example, one can form a simplified abstract model of a packet router and actually prove things about the interconnections of such routers. To some extent, however, performance is the enemy of abstraction. When an algorithm or system is tuned to improve performance, it usually departs from its simple, abstract form, giving up many of the benefits of reasoning about the abstraction.

• *Modularity* refers to the decomposition of a system into smaller subsystems that can be developed separately (and in parallel). Modules encapsulate the internal details of a system component and specify a set of interfaces for allowing interaction among components. As such, changes in the internal configuration of one module do not necessarily require changes to other modules. By reducing the complexity of intersystem dependencies, modularity facilitates more rapid reconfiguration of systems to meet operational requirements. As the scale and complexity of IT systems grow, however, it becomes more difficult to separate functionality cleanly, and the set of interfaces can become more complicated, increasing the possibility of errors in implementation or the possibility that particular circumstances will not be sufficiently addressed.

• *Layering* is a form of modularity that decomposes systems into horizontal strata (layers), each of which depends on the layer below and provides services to the layer above (by adding its own capabilities to those of the lower layers). Layering allows capability to be added to a system by building on what already exists in lower layers. It also allows the implementation of one layer to be changed without necessarily affecting the layers above. Layering is helpful in large-scale systems, but only to a point. It can lead to reduced performance because of the additional overhead associated with moving between layers. Furthermore, when the lower layers fail to do their jobs, the upper-level abstractions fail, and in ways that may not be easily recognizable. A common layer in networks is the transport layer, which allows users to assume that each node in a distributed computation has some number of reliable transport paths to other nodes. If one or more of these fail, then users can quickly find it hard to reason about the system as a whole, unless care has been taken when implementing the lower layers to reduce the difficulties involved in analyzing failures.

SOURCES: The definitions of abstraction, modularity, and layering derive from those in CSTB (1999b) and Messerschmitt (2000).

problems in large-scale systems stem not so much from the components but rather from the way they are customized, assembled, tested, deployed, operated, and modified to serve a particular purpose, especially when they are combined with other components into larger systems and when such systems span organizational boundaries or connect even larger numbers of embedded devices working in concert.[30] The organizations that might be best positioned to understand these issues, namely, systems integrators and end users, tend not to conduct the types of research that might yield greater insight.

This is not to say that problems of scalability, complexity, heterogeneity, flexibility, trustworthiness, and distributed management have been absent from the IT systems research agenda. Several programs over the past decade have made forays into this arena, but with shifting priorities and emphases. The High Performance Computing and Communications Initiative (HPCCI) began with a priority familiar to researchers from earlier decades—a push for higher-performance IT systems (e.g., increased processing and communications speed). By the mid-1990s, attention to issues such as scale and heterogeneity was growing; these issues were emphasized in the recommendations in CSTB's Brooks-Sutherland report, *Evolving the High Performance Computing and Communications Initiative to Support the Nation's Information Infrastructure* (CSTB, 1995b). The mid-1990s also saw concerns about information systems trustworthiness begin to coalesce, as evidenced by the 1995 workshop on high-confidence systems sponsored by the Committee on Information and Communications (CIC, 1995) and a 1997 workshop on the same topic by the committee's successor, the Committee on Computing, Information, and Communications of the National Science and Technology Council (CCIC, 1997). The High Confidence Systems research program was added under the HPCCI umbrella, but concerns about the limitations of existing research efforts were expressed in a variety of reports on critical infrastructure and in the associated calls for research.[31]

The Information Technology for the Twenty-First Century (IT²) initiative, begun in 1999, carries these themes forward. This new initiative, led by the National Science Foundation (NSF) but joined by several other federal agencies, is pursuing breakthrough research and research to apply IT successfully in applications that benefit society. To a lesser extent, it may support research directed at the challenges of building large, complex information systems. In particular, NSF's Information Technology Research (ITR) initiative will fund large research projects that bring together interdisciplinary teams for several years. Issues such as scalability and software are clearly on the agenda. Work in these areas may build on a workshop NSF convened in the summer of 1997 to identify significant new approaches to systems research. Some of the themes that emerged from that workshop included developing high-confidence systems with predictable properties at predictable cost, developing global-scale systems, and making architectures dynamic and adaptive (Kavi et al., 1999). These three themes are congruent with the research needs identified in this chapter.

A number of other programs sponsored by the NSF and the Defense Advanced Research Projects Agency (DARPA) in late 1999 and early 2000 promise continued exploration of systems issues:

• *Information Assurance and Survivability (DARPA)*—This large, multidimensional program is focused on research that will enable the DOD and the nation to build IT systems that are trustworthy, meaning that they will be able to quickly detect intrusions and attacks, be reasonably secure against them, and recover quickly from them. The program is clearly focused on systems issues, such as the joint design of new protocols, distributed intrusion-detection mechanisms, and information integration methods that can collectively be used to design, build, and operate networks that are trustworthy and secure. Program managers are making a conscious effort to bring new people with new ideas and new approaches into the program, and they are encouraging interdisciplinary approaches, with an emphasis on testbeds. Researchers are encouraged to combine their respective competencies to pursue breakthrough system approaches rather than continue work in more established directions. The projects are proposed by industry, universities, and government agencies, bringing together a wide range of perspectives.

• *Scalable Enterprise Systems (NSF)*—This is a new research program sponsored by the Engineering Directorate of NSF. A solicitation for proposals was issued in 1999, and the funding decision process is in progress for proposals submitted in late 1999. In principle, this program could be a first step toward addressing challenges related to the design, deployment, and operation of large enterprise systems that are reliable. It aims for systems that are predictable in their behavior and meet the performance requirements of their users. The NSF has asked for phase 1 proposals for small, exploratory projects, a good approach for soliciting and funding a reasonably large number of innovative approaches. It is too soon to tell whether this program will address systems needs of the sort outlined in the chapter. One issue is whether the program will attempt to develop practical engineering approaches to the full range of problems associated with scalable systems. Another concern is the traditional NSF peer review process. If the peer review process emphasizes past publications and other evidence of past results at the expense of novelty and the potential relevance of the approaches proposed, and if the peer reviewers fail to adequately appreciate proposals that bring together interdisciplinary teams with competencies that allow them to address the challenges from new perspectives (even if the teams have not addressed these particular problems in the past), then the program will discourage researchers from extending their competencies into new areas in which they can collectively have an impact. This concern is not limited to this one program—it extends to a range of initiatives NSF is entering into that attempt to push research in new directions or bring together researchers from multiple disciplines.

• *Next Generation Internet (NGI) (DARPA and NSF along with the Departments of Energy, Commerce, and Health and Human Services, and the National Aeronautics and Space Administration)*—This program is supporting a substantial number of multidisciplinary research initiatives, both large and small, aimed at understanding and addressing the challenges associated with high-speed networks capable of transmitting data at speeds 100 to 1,000 times those possible on the Internet. It has three components: (1) research on high-speed networking, (2) development of revolutionary applications that take advantage of improved networking capability, and (3) deployment of high-speed testbed networks for experimentation. Although some of the NGI research is properly directed at traditional technology problems, such as creating higher-speed devices and subsystems, a substantial portion of the projects is directed at problems associated with large, complex, distributed systems, addressing questions such as how to provide quality of service in a network constructed of distributed and autonomous subnetworks and network management.

What is missing from existing federal research programs is a coherent approach to attacking the gamut of systems problems—a thrust that specifically targets large-scale systems and their associated problems and pursues fundamental research to address them. Such an effort would need to support research along many different dimensions—theory, architecture, design methodologies, and the like—because no single approach to system design will be able to address the full scope of challenges presented by large-scale systems.[32] It is possible (although, in the committee's judgment, unlikely) that dramatically improved methodologies for the design of large-scale systems are beyond human capability—certainly, it is difficult to get one's arms around the challenge (especially for researchers who have little hands-on experience with large-scale systems) and validate the outcomes. But the problems in large systems are too pervasive, expensive, and fundamental to be largely ignored any longer.

Toward an Expanded Systems Research Agenda

Two distinct but complementary styles of research can provide insight into large-scale systems:

- *Case research*—research that attacks a specific large-scale system application (whether a distributed database or the Internet) and attempts to improve it to make it more functional, scalable, robust, and so on; and
- *Methodology research*—research that addresses the issues involved in designing large-scale systems generally, looking for architectures, techniques, and tools that can make significant advances in the ways that large-scale systems are designed.

Methodology research is distinguished from case research in that it addresses generic issues that plague most or all large-scale systems and looks for dramatic improvements in the methodologies for the design of all large-scale systems. The goal of such work is not to make incremental advances in existing systems (which is frequently the agenda of case research), but rather to create new design methodologies that result in large-scale systems that are intrinsically superior to existing systems in the dimensions of concern (such as vulnerability or flexibility or scalability). This objective makes methodology research potentially much more beneficial to the nation (financially and otherwise).

Case research and methodology research are complementary: case research identifies specific shortcomings and problems in large-scale system design methodologies that can be more fully explored through methodology research, and improved methodologies arising from methodology research can be validated by trying them out on one or more specific cases using case research. Case research is by far more common today than methodology research, in part because the latter is riskier and less likely to have near-term payoff. This is not to say that methodology research is nonexistent. There have been a few notable successes in (1) architectural techniques, including abstraction and encapsulation, that were conceptualized in the 1970s and used in the design of many IT systems, (2) transaction processing, which encompasses a collection of techniques that make large distributed systems much easier to develop—some would say even feasible (Gray and Reuter, 1993),[33] (3) application components, generic and reusable collections of functionality that contribute to system correctness and stability because elements that are widely reused are inherently more extensively tested, and (4) security, which is receiving increasing attention because of the current attention to e-commerce. Individually and collectively, these examples fall far short of resolving the serious challenges that lie ahead in the design and operation of large-scale IT systems, but they provide some indication of the advances that could come out of additional methodological research. There is a need for dramatically new ideas about how to approach the design of large-scale systems, with the goal of dramatically improving outcomes in terms of successful deployment and the desirable qualities mentioned earlier. The investment in methodology research needs to be greatly expanded to stimulate more research that pursues high-risk approaches to system design and to foster greater collaboration among IT researchers in universities and industry and end users with operational knowledge of large-scale system problems.

An expanded research agenda would need to address systems that are (1) large in *scale*, meaning there are massive numbers of elements interacting within the system, and (2) highly *complex*, meaning that the interactions among those elements are both highly heterogeneous and complicated in nature. The low rate of success in designing large-scale systems today does not mean that research should focus solely on known failures, although they would offer useful insight. Rather, much of the research should target systems that are much larger in scale and complexity than the systems that have been attempted to date. The goal of the research should be to explore methodologies for structuring and architecture that will enable practical, large-scale systems to be successfully constructed and deployed. Measures of success in this program would include the following:

- A dramatic, or at least substantial, improvement in practitioners' success in constructing and deploying large-scale systems and
- A dramatic, or at least substantial, increase in the scale and complexity of systems that practitioners will reasonably attempt to develop.

Because of the tremendous resources being wasted in large-scale IT system failures today, success in the first of these two measures alone could justify considerable investment in research. Of course, favorable outcomes will become evident only with time, as larger-scale systems are attempted. Thus, the research programs will have to rely on qualitative measures in the short term, such as a better understanding of large-scale systems, clearer reasoning about the correct behavior of such systems, and even optimism about improved prospects for large-scale systems on the part of practitioners. In the longer term, metrics and benchmarks could be developed for assessing improvements in system design and comparing the merits of competing approaches.[34]

Designing a Research Program

A range of approaches needs to be pursued if progress is to be made on large-scale IT systems. These approaches include theoretical computer science, computer systems architecture, analogies to large systems in the natural and social sciences, programming methodologies, and continued extensions of ongoing work in areas such as software components and mobile code. Experimental work will be extremely important and, in this context, inherently problematic, because the systems of interest are beyond the current capability of engineers to implement and because the construction of large-scale IT systems is especially difficult in a research environment. Nevertheless, experiments can be done in the context of existing large-scale systems, attempting incremental improvements. Furthermore, useful insights into the behavior of large-scale extensions can be inferred from small-scale prototypes. Of course, the best ideas for pursuing research in large-scale systems will come from the research community itself, but the following examples show the range of approaches needed in a comprehensive attempt to develop a stronger scientific and engineering basis for large-scale IT systems.

Theoretical Approaches

One element of any approach to studying the properties of systems of a scale and complexity exceeding current capabilities is to develop theoretical constructs of behaviors. Theoretical computer science has been quite successful in applying such methodologies to, for example, the computing requirements for algorithms of arbitrary complexity, quantifying which algorithms have desirable properties and which algorithms do not. There have also been some efforts and successes in reasoning about protocols (algorithms executed among autonomous actors), which gets closer to the heart of large-scale systems.[35] Similar methodologies could be applied to large-scale systems. One direction for research would be to construct certain constraints on the behaviors of elements of the system and then to reason deductively about desirable properties of the system as a whole. Another approach would be to define helpful properties of large-scale systems and draw inferences about the characteristics of constituent actors that ensure these properties.

Architectural Approaches

Efforts are also needed to develop further the nascent fields of system or software architecture (Shaw and Garlan, 1996; Rechtine and Maier, 1997). System architects—software architects, in particular—are similar to building architects in that they need to understand the needs and interests of their users and be aware of the characteristics of the components that the users had developed previously. The architect's job is then to marry user needs to the available resources in such a way that the resulting system will be useful for many years, even if it undergoes significant change during its lifetime.

Work on architectural approaches could help extend existing principles of abstraction, modularity, and layering to large-scale systems—or to augment them with additional architectural tools. Recent work sponsored by DARPA, for example, recognized the difficulties introduced into the modeling of complex systems by insufficient understanding, information, and computer processing power, and evaluated a number of different frameworks of abstraction for modeling such systems.[36] This work combined an architectural approach to large-scale system problems with the theoretical basis advocated above, and it illustrates the promise of architectural methodologies for large-scale system design. Another approach may be to investigate alternatives to the top-down approach to decomposing systems advocated by structured programming (which tends to work on a small scale only) and to the bottom-up approach to system design embodied in notions of component software (described below). For example, a middle-out approach that breaks systems into horizontal layers or platforms that are standardized across systems and can be tuned to particular applications might be worth further evaluation.

Inspiration from Natural and Social Systems

Work on large-scale IT systems could also draw on analogies in natural and social systems. Some natural and social systems display a scale and complexity far beyond what has been achieved in technological systems. Research may determine how such characteristics are achieved in natural and social systems, and whether those lessons can be applied to IT systems. Two such systems that are systematic and purposeful—achieving useful higher goals through the composition of many elements—are ecological systems and the economy, both of which might usefully serve as models (Box 3.8). DARPA has already supported research on information systems trustworthiness that draws on biological models, and its exploration of other intersections between computing and biology suggest the potential for more cross-fertilization between these two disciplines.[37]

Software Development Processes

The ability of programmers to design and develop large-scale software systems could, in principle, benefit from better methodologies, pro-

BOX 3.8
Ecological and Economic Systems as Models for Large-Scale
Information Technology Systems

Biological and economic systems could serve as models of complex systems. As such, they could inform the development of large-scale information technology systems. An ecological system achieves a remarkable level of diversity and heterogeneity with mutual dependence, through a process of natural selection. Researchers could examine processes like natural selection for possible applicability to technological systems and study the specific mechanisms of interaction and coordination that have evolved in such systems. Of course, analogies have been shown between technological and biological systems for many years, and the concept has been pursued concretely in, for example, genetic algorithms and neural networks.

The economy also achieves a scale of purposeful heterogeneity with mutual dependence far beyond that in any technological system. Experience suggests strongly that central planning—the systematic design of an economy top-down, much as technological systems are designed today—is not a viable methodology. The most successful economic systems are composed of semiautonomous actors who act in accordance with self-interest within the imposed constraints of an incentive system. This approach differs from technological systems in that it uses incentives rather than dogmatic behavioral expectations and in terms of the degree of autonomy delegated to its agents and the degree of intelligence (human and organizational) with which those agents are endowed. This latter feature is likely to distinguish economic systems from technological ones for some time to come, although of course there has been considerable effort to emulate human intelligence in limited ways in the context of artificial intelligence research.[1]

Arguably the greatest opportunity lies in the application of economic theory to the methodology of large-scale system design. Microeconomic and macroeconomic theories are limited by the approximations that need to be made in certain modeling assumptions about the behavior of economic actors and organizations. This same limitation need not apply to technological systems constructed in accordance with economic principles, because these systems can follow prescribed principles by construction. Theoretical economics is replete with tools, such as game theory, that are interesting to consider in this context. A handful of organizations, including the Santa Fe Institute, are pursuing interdisciplinary research along these lines, examining the way aggregate behaviors can arise from the actions of independent agents.

---

[1] This work provides an interesting link to the biological analogies mentioned above, given that human intelligence itself arose through an evolutionary process.

gramming environments, and tools for software development. The field of software engineering was created 30 years ago to deal with the predictability, time, and cost issues related to software development, and many problems identified in the 1960s persist today (as CSTB committees report regularly). Good engineering practice has contributed to improvements in the development of small and even medium-sized modules, yielding modest improvements in the productivity of programmers (Boehm, 1993).[38] Further improvements are needed in large-scale systems and in methods for addressing their inherent problems. In particular, software engineering techniques must scale to very large and complex systems. Software development is itself an intense collaborative task, which could make better use of tools that can greatly facilitate collaborative development. There is also room for improvement in software testing, a time-consuming and expensive aspect of the development process. Challenging issues include the testing of large, concurrent software systems as well as multimedia systems. Other issues include the development of processes that work well even when people have less-than-optimal skills.[39]

Extensions of Existing Approaches

Existing approaches to large-scale system design, including some that are in commercial practice, show promise for facilitating the development of large-scale systems and could benefit from greater attention from the research community. Two approaches worth mentioning are methodologies based on component software and mobile code.

The ideal of component software is to construct systems by assembling and integrating preexisting modules of code with known functionality. The elements are purchased as is, rather than constructed specifically for system needs, and combined in new ways, possibly with other newly developed elements, to create a system. Two existing approaches are the reuse of components (reusable modules) and the reuse of frameworks (reusable architectures for specific application domains). Component reuse is common in the manufacture of physical goods and was one of the major innovations of the industrial revolution.[40] Among the practical advantages of this approach are the time and cost efficiencies gained from avoiding a new development effort and the improved quality of components that are tested by reuse in many systems. The most promising approach is the containment of complexity by the substitution of assembly for traditional programming, with the possibility of this assembly being performed by end users.[41] Reuse is common in computing and networking infrastructure. Increasingly, existing software design patterns are adapted and applied as an alternative to custom-crafting major software structures. For example, many client-server applications use similar designs and code. Emerging component software frameworks, such as JavaBeans, exploit libraries of predefined elements that fit within a common design framework. Applications are built by assembling existing components as well as by creating new, unique components that fit within the framework.

Several factors, some technological and some economic, have limited the utility of component software to date (Szyperski, 1998). The biggest obstacle to software reuse is the complexity of software structure and interaction, which is much greater than that found in the physical parts and assemblies of industrial production. Reuse via very high level languages has proven effective for small systems but does not scale well (Boehm, 1999). Furthermore, the fragmentation of the software industry—resulting in part from the lower transaction and coordination costs made possible by networked computing—has made it difficult to implement reuse on a large scale, and modest improvements in programming productivity are being swamped by expanding needs. Improvements in techniques for finding and validating chunks of reusable code may improve the prospects for this technique. More research is required to determine how well this approach applies to large-scale systems.

Another approach receiving commercial attention is mobile code, which abandons the architectural principle that the elements of a system are static in their behaviors and interaction with other elements and instead allows elements to influence the behavior of other elements in richer ways beyond simple interaction. More generally, the capabilities of components can be dynamically extended and modified by providing them with programming code. Of course, simply moving the execution of code around a system provides no fundamental change in the expressiveness of such code, but it does fundamentally alter architectural assumptions about the type and flexibility of functionality encapsulated in system elements. It therefore illustrates the possibilities for substantially new architectural approaches to system design that could improve the ability to make systems more reliable or easier to build (although such potential still needs to be demonstrated). Examples of interesting research (of the case variety rather than the methodology variety) include Jini (i.e., opportunistic cooperation of Internet appliances) and active networks (i.e., using mobile code to add new flexibility and capability to networks). At the same time, mobile code can introduce new concerns regarding system trustworthiness. Addressing those concerns may add to the perceived complexity of a system.

Support for Research Infrastructure

Research on large-scale systems will have a significant experimental component and, as such, will necessitate support for research infrastructure—artifacts that researchers can use to try out new approaches and can examine closely to understand existing modes of failure.[42] Researchers need access to large, distributed systems if they are to study large systems, because the phenomena of interest are those explicitly associated with scale, and the types of problems experienced to date tend to be exhibited only on such systems. Furthermore, researchers must be able to demonstrate convincingly the capabilities of the advanced approaches that they develop. They will not be able to convince industry to adopt new practices unless they can show how well these practices have worked in an actual large-scale system. Through such demonstrations, research that leverages infrastructure can improve the performance, cost, or other properties of IT systems.[43]

Access to research infrastructure is especially problematic when working with large-scale systems because systems of such large size and scale typically cannot be constructed in a lab, and because researchers cannot generally gain access to operational systems used in industry or government. Such systems often need to operate continuously, and operators are understandably unwilling to allow experimentation with mission-critical systems. In some contexts, additional concerns may arise relating to the protection of proprietary information.[44] Such concerns have long roots. In the late 1970s, the late Jonathan Postel complained that the success of the ARPANET (a predecessor of the Internet) and its use as a production system (that is, for everyday, routine communications) was interfering with his ability to try new networking protocols that might "break" the network. In the early 1990s, with the commercialization of the Internet looming, Congress held hearings to address the question of what it means for a network to be experimental or production, and the prospects for experimental use of the Internet dimmed—even though its users at the time were limited to the research and education community. That today's Internet is much larger than the Internet of a decade ago and continuing to grow quickly makes even more remote the prospect of research access to comparably large-scale network systems. At the same time, it increases the value of researcher access to "large-enough"-scale network systems to do the research that can help to justify the dependence on the Internet that so many want to see.

Several large-scale infrastructures have been put in place by government and private-sector organizations largely for purposes of experimentation. The NGI program mentioned above, for example, is deploying testbed networks across which technologists can demonstrate and evaluate new approaches for improving security, quality of service, and network management. But even then, only "stable" technologies are to be deployed so that the network can also be used to demonstrate new, high-end applications (LSN Next Generation Implementation Team, 1998).

The Internet 2 and Abilene networks being deployed by the private sector have similar intentions. In the early and mid-1990s, the Corporation for National Research Initiatives organized the creation of a set of five testbeds to demonstrate high-speed networking technologies, systems, and applications. Participants came from industry, government, and academia, and each testbed was a relatively large research project. Many lessons were learned about the difficulties involved in implementing very high speed (1 Gbps) networks and very high speed networking applications on an end-to-end basis. Lessons learned from these testbeds have been, and continue to be, incorporated into current and emerging computers and networks. Because these testbeds brought together interdisciplinary teams and addressed complex end-to-end system issues, they were representative of the research in large-scale systems that this chapter describes; however, because the testbeds were operational over large geographical areas (spanning hundreds of miles), a large share of the effort and cost was associated with the construction and operation of the physical infrastructure rather than the research itself. With the benefit of hindsight, it might have been possible to achieve a better balance to ensure that building, maintaining, and operating a research testbed did not inadvertently become the principal objective, as opposed to gaining research insights. Yet this tension between funding for infrastructure, per se, and funding for the research that uses it continues to haunt federally funded networking research.

Existing infrastructure programs have a critical limitation with respect to the kind of research envisioned in this report: they help investigators in universities and government laboratories routinely access dedicated computers and networks used for scientific research or related technical work, but they do not provide researchers with access to experimental or operational large-scale systems used for purposes other than science—computers and networks used for everything from government functions (tax processing, benefits processing) through critical infrastructure management (air traffic control, power system management) to a wide range of business and e-commerce application systems. Given the problems experienced with large-scale IT systems, gaining some kind of access is important. Even indirect access in the form of data about system performance and other attributes could be valuable.[45] Instrumenting operational systems to collect needed data on their operations and allowing researchers to observe their operation in an active environment would greatly benefit research. Figuring out what is possible, with what kinds of precautions, compensation, and incentives, will require focused discussions and negotiation among key decision makers in the research community and among candidate system managers. The federal government can facilitate and encourage such discussions by linking the IT research community to system managers within federal agencies or by brokering access to elements of the commercial infrastructure.[46]

Experimental academic networks could, with some additional effort, be made more useful to IT researchers. Most such networks, such as the Internet 2, are limited by Acceptable Use Policies (AUPs) to carrying academic traffic and may therefore not be used to study business applications. One option would be to modify AUPs to allow some forms of business traffic to use the research Internet, so as to create a laboratory for studying the issues. Firms might be willing to bear the cost of maintaining backups for their commercial traffic on the commercial Internet if they could use the research network at below market prices.[47] Government could also fund some data collection activities by Internet service providers (ISPs) that would be helpful to researchers trying to understand the evolution of networking. The commercialization of the Internet also put an end to systematic public data collection on network traffic. Unlike the regulated common carriers, who must report minutes of telephone calling statistics to the FCC, unregulated ISPs do not regularly disclose information on aggregate traffic or traffic by type. Thus, for example, published estimates of the portion of Internet traffic that is related to the Web vary widely.

MOVING FORWARD

Despite the myriad problems associated with large-scale IT systems, a coherent, multifaceted research program combining the elements described above could improve the ability to engineer such systems. Such work would help avert continuing problems in designing, developing, and operating large-scale systems and could open the doors to many more innovative uses of IT systems. It could also lead to expanded educational programs for students in computer science and engineering that would help them better appreciate systems problems in their future work, whether as researchers or users of IT. Because IT is less limited by physical constraints than are other technologies, much of what can be imagined for IT can, with better science and engineering, be achieved. It is not clear which techniques for improving the design, development, deployment, and operation of large-scale systems will prove the most effective. Each has its strengths and weaknesses. Only with research aimed at improving both the science and the engineering of large-scale systems will this potential be unlocked. This is a challenge that has long eluded the IT research community, but given the role that large-scale IT systems play in society—and are likely to play in the future—the time has come to address it head on.

REFERENCES

Adams, Duane. 1999. "Is It Time to Reinvent Computer Science?" Working paper. Carnegie Mellon University, Pittsburgh, Pa. May 4.

Barr, Avron, and Shirley Tessler. 1998. "How Will the Software Talent Shortage End?" *American Programmer* 11(1). Available online at <http://www.cutter.com/itjournal/itjtoc.htm#jan98>.

Bernstein, Lawrence. 1997. "Software Investment Strategy," *Bell Labs Technical Journal* 2(3):233-242.

Boehm, Barry W. 1993. "Economic Analysis of Software Technology Investments," in *Analytical Methods in Software Engineering Economics*, Thomas Gulledge and William Hutzler, eds. Springer-Verlag, New York.

Boehm, Barry W. 1999. "Managing Software Productivity and Reuse," *IEEE Computer* 32(9):111-113.

Brooks, Frederick P. 1987. "No Silver Bullet: Essence and Accidents of Software Engineering," *IEEE Computer* 20(4):10-19.

Committee on Information and Communications (CIC). 1995. *America in the Age of Information*. National Science and Technology Council, Washington, D.C. Available online at <http://www.ccic.gov/ccic/cic_forum_v224/cover.html>.

Committee on Computing, Information, and Communications (CCIC). 1997. *Research Challenges in High Confidence Systems*. Proceedings of the Committee on Computing, Information, and Communications Workshop, August 6-7, National Coordination Office for Computing, Information, and Communications, Arlington, Va. Available online at <http://www.ccic.gov/pubs/hcs-Aug97/>.

Computer Science and Telecommunications Board (CSTB), National Research Council. 1994. *Academic Careers for Experimental Computer Scientists and Engineers*. National Academy Press, Washington, D.C.

Computer Science and Telecommunications Board (CSTB), National Research Council. 1995a. *Continued Review of Tax Systems Modernization for the Internal Revenue Service*. National Academy Press, Washington, D.C.

Computer Science and Telecommunications Board (CSTB), National Research Council. 1995b. *Evolving the High Performance Computing and Communications Initiative to Support the Nation's Information Infrastructure*. National Academy Press, Washington, D.C.

Computer Science and Telecommunications Board (CSTB), National Research Council. 1997. *The Evolution of Untethered Communications*. National Academy Press, Washington, D.C.

Computer Science and Telecommunications Board (CSTB), National Research Council. 1999a. *Trust in Cyberspace*, Fred B. Schneider, ed. National Academy Press, Washington, D.C.

Computer Science and Telecommunications Board (CSTB), National Research Council. 1999b. *Realizing the Potential of C4I: Fundamental Challenges*. National Academy Press, Washington, D.C.

Davies, Jennifer. 1998. *CONFIRM: Computerized Reservation System—Case Facts*. Case study material for course on ethical issues of information technology, University of Wolverhampton (U.K.), School of Computing and Information Technology, March 20. Available online at <http://www.scit.wlv.ac.uk/~cm1995/cbr/cases/case06/four.htm>.

Ewusi-Mensah, Kweku. 1997. "Critical Issues in Abandoned Information Systems Development Projects," *Communications of the ACM* 40(9):74-80.

Fishman, Charles. 1996. "They Write the Right Stuff," *Fast Company*, December. Available online at <www.fastcompany.com/online/06/writestuff.html>.

Gibbs, W.W. 1994. "Software's Chronic Crisis," *Scientific American* 264(9):86-95.

Gray, Jim, and Andreas Reuter. 1993. *Transaction Processing Concepts and Techniques*. Morgan Kaufman, San Francisco.

Hennessy, John. 1999. "The Future of Systems Research," *IEEE Computer* 32(8):27-33.

Johnson, Jim. 1999. "Turning Chaos into Success," *Software Magazine*, December. Available online at <http://www.softwaremag.com/archives/1999dec/Success.html>.

Jones, C. 1996. *Applied Software Measurement*. McGraw-Hill, New York.

Junnarkar, Sandeep. 1999. "Beyond.com Revived After Extended Outage," *CNET News.com*, October 22. Available online at <http://news.cnet.com/news/0-1007-200-922552.html>.

Kavi, Krishna, James C. Browne, and Anand Tripathi. 1999. "Computer Systems Research: The Pressure Is On," *IEEE Computer* 32(1):30-39.

Large Scale Networking (LSN) Next Generation Implementation Team. 1998. *Next Generation Internet Implementation Plan*. National Coordination Office for Computing, Information, and Communications, Arlington, Va., February.

Layton, Lyndsey. 1999. "Computer Failure Puzzles Metro: Opening Delayed, Rush Hour Slowed," *Washington Post*, September 25, p. B1.

Li, Allen. 1994. "Advance Automation System: Implications of Problems and Recent Changes." GAO/T-RCED-94-188. Statement of Allen Li, Associate Director, Transportation Issues, Resources, Community, and Economic Development Division, U.S. General Accounting Office, before the Subcommittee on Aviation, Committee on Public Works and Transportation, U.S. House of Representatives, April 13.

Luenig, Erich. 1999. "Schwab Suffers Repeated Online Outages," *CNET News.com*, October 22. Available online at <http://news.cnet.com/news/0-1007-200-922368.html>.

Lyytinen, Kalle. 1987. "Different Perspectives on Information Systems: Problems and Solutions," *ACM Computing Surveys* 19(1):5-46.

Meehan, Michael. 2000. "Update: System Outages Top Online Brokerage Execs' Concerns," *Computerworld*, April 4. Available online at <http://www.computerworld.com/home/print.nsf/all/000404D212>.

Messerschmitt, David G. 2000. *Understanding Networked Applications: A First Course*. Morgan Kaufman, San Francisco.

National Security Telecommunications Advisory Committee (NSTAC). 1997. Reports submitted for NSTAC XX (Volume I: Information Infrastructure Group Report, Network Group Intrusion Detection Subgroup Report, Network Group Widespread Outage Subgroup Report; Volume II: Legislative and Regulatory Group Report, Operations Support Group Report; Volume III: National Coordinating Center for Telecommunications Vision Subgroup Report, Information Assurance, Financial Services Risk Assessment Report, Interim Transportation Information Risk Assessment Report), Washington, D.C., December 11.

Nelson, Emily, and Evan Ramstad. 1999. "Trick or Treat: Hershey's Biggest Dud Has Turned Out to Be Its New Technology," *Wall Street Journal*, October 29, pp. A1, A6.

Network Reliability and Interoperability Council (NRIC). 1997. *Report of the Network Reliability and Interoperability Council*. NRIC, Washington, D.C.

Norman, Donald A.. 1998. *The Invisible Computer: Why Good Products Can Fail, the Personal Computer Is So Complex, and Information Appliances Are the Solution.* MIT Press, Cambridge, Mass.

O'Hara, Colleen. 1999. "STARS Delayed Again; FAA Seeks Tech Patch," *Federal Computer Week*, April 12, p. 1.

Oz, Effy. 1997. "When Professional Standards Are Lax: The CONFIRM Failure and Its Lessons," *Communications of the ACM* 37(10):29-36.

Perrow, Charles. 1984. *Normal Accidents: Living With High-Risk Technologies.* Basic Books, New York.

President's Commission on Critical Infrastructure Protection (PCCIP). 1997. *Critical Foundations.* Washington, D.C.

Ralston, Anthony, ed. 1993. *Encyclopedia of Computer Science,* 3rd ed., International Thomson Publishers.

Reason, James. 1990. *Human Error.* Cambridge University Press, Cambridge, U.K.

Rechtine, E., and M.W. Maier. 1997. *The Art of Systems Architecting.* CRC Press, New York.

Shaw, M., and D. Garlan. 1996. *Software Architecture.* Prentice-Hall, New York.

Standish Group International, Inc. 1995. *The Chaos.* Standish Group International, West Yarmouth, Mass. Available online at <http://www.standishgroup.com/chaos.html>.

Sunday Examiner and Chronicle. 1999. "Silicon Valley Expertise Stops at Capitol Steps," August 8, editorial, Sunday section, p. 6.

Szyperski, C. 1998. *Component Software: Beyond Object-Oriented Programming.* Addison-Wesley, Reading, Mass.

Transition Office of the President's Commission on Critical Infrastructure Protection (TOPCCIP). 1998. "Preliminary Research and Development Roadmap for Protecting and Assuring Critical National Infrastructures."

U.S. General Accounting Office (GAO). 1994. *Air Traffic Control: Status of FAA's Modernization Program.* GAO/RCED-94-167FS. U.S. Government Printing Office, Washington, D.C., April.

U.S. General Accounting Office (GAO). 1997. *Air Traffic Control: Immature Software Acquisition Processes Increase FAA System Acquisition Risks.* GAO/AIMD-97-47. U.S. Government Printing Office, Washington, D.C., March.

U.S. General Accounting Office (GAO). 1998. *Air Traffic Control: Status of FAA's Modernization Program.* GAO/RCED-99-25. U.S. Government Printing Office, Washington, D.C., December.

U.S. General Accounting Office (GAO). 1999a. *Major Performance and Management Issues: DOT Challenges.* GAO/OCG-99-13. U.S. Government Printing Office, Washington, D.C.

U.S. General Accounting Office (GAO). 1999b. *High Risk Update.* GAO/HR-99-1. U.S. Government Printing Office, Washington, D.C., January.

U.S. General Accounting Office (GAO). 1999c. *Air Traffic Control: Observations on FAA's Air Traffic Control Modernization Program.* GAO/T-RCED/AIMD-99-137. U.S. Government Printing Office, Washington, D.C., March.

NOTES

1. The term "enterprise" is used here in its general sense to encompass corporations, governments, and universities; typical applications include e-commerce, tax collection, air traffic control, and remote learning. A previous CSTB report used the term "networked information system" to cover the range of such systems. See CSTB (1999a).

2. See, for example PCCIP (1997), TOPCCIP (1998), NSTAC (1997), and NRIC (1997).

3. The complexity of some components is so great that they easily meet the definition

of system. For example, no single individual can understand all aspects of the design of a modern microprocessor, but compared to numbers of large-scale IT infrastructures, few such designs are created. Because microprocessors tend to be manufactured in great quantity, huge efforts are mounted to test designs. In fact, more effort is spent in verifying the performance of microprocessors than in designing them. In the original Pentium Pro, which had about 5.5 million transistors in the central processing unit, Intel found and corrected 1,200 design errors prior to production; in its forthcoming Willamette processor, which has 30 million transistors in the central processing unit, engineers have found and corrected 8,500 design flaws (data from Robert Colwell, Intel, personal communication, March 14, 2000). Despite these efforts, bugs in microprocessors occasionally slip through. For example, Intel shipped many thousands of microprocessors that computed the wrong answer for certain arithmetic division problems.

4. A 1995 study of system development efforts by the Standish Group found that only 16 percent of projects were completed on time and within the predicted budget. Approximately one-third were never completed, and more than half were completed later than expected, exceeded the budget, or lacked the planned functionality. Projects that either exceeded budget or were canceled cost, on average, 89 percent more than originally estimated, with more than 10 percent of projects costing more than twice the original estimate. Approximately 32 percent of the completed projects had less than half the functionality originally envisioned, and fewer than 8 percent were fully functional. See Standish Group International, Inc. (1995). A subsequent study (Johnson, 1999) showed some improvement in large-scale system development, but continuing failures. The study reports that 28 percent of projects were canceled before completion and 46 percent were completed over budget. The remaining 26 percent were completed on time and within the predicted budget.

5. The General Accounting Office is a regular source of reports on federal system problems, for example.

6. Data on IRS expenditures come from the GAO (1999b). For a discussion of the problems facing the IRS tax systems modernization project, see CSTB (1995a).

7. In the late 1990s, concern about the Y2K computer problem led to both overhauls of existing systems and projects to develop new systems to replace older ones. These activities put a spotlight on systems issues, but it is important to understand that they involved the application of existing knowledge and technology rather than fundamental advances. They are believed to have reduced the number of relatively old systems still in use, but they may have introduced new problems because of the haste with which much of the work was undertaken. It will be a while before the effects of Y2K fixes can be assessed.

8. These problems have been reported in several articles in the *Chronicle of Higher Education*'s online edition.

9. There are many examples that demonstrate why it is a good idea to have separate knowledge management systems and data warehouses, not the least of which is a social one. An information system that people will use to make informed decisions relies on a very different database design than a system for managing the integrity of transactions.

10. MEMS technology is exploding in terms of its applicability. In a few years, MEMS wallpaper will be able to sense and condition an environment. It could be used to create active wing surfaces on aircraft that can respond to changes in wind speed and desired flight characteristics to minimize drag. On a larger scale, a square mile of MEMS wallpaper may have more nodes than the entire Internet will have at that time. Clearly, scalability will be a key factor.

11. For a discussion of information appliances, see Norman (1998).

12. For example, in some instances, a manual fallback option may no longer exist or be practical.

13. As an example of the increasing scale of usage consider the following statistic:

between January 1997 and January 2000, the percentage of commission-based trades being conducted online by Boston-based Fidelity Investments Institutional Services Company, Inc., jumped from 7 percent to 85 percent. Many online brokerages have discussed the possibility of turning down potential online accounts as a means of addressing such growth. See Meehan (2000).

14. This discussion of complexity borrows from the work of Perrow (1984) and Reason (1990).

15. However, as any commuter knows, just one small accident or other disturbance in normal traffic patterns can create significant delays on busy roadways.

16. See CSTB (1999a), especially Chapter 5, "Trustworthy Systems from Untrustworthy Components."

17. Middleware is a layer of software that lies between the operating system and the application software. Different middleware solutions support different classes of applications; two distinct types support storage and communications. See Messerschmitt (2000).

18. A discussion of the fundamental problems in mobile and wireless communications can be found in CSTB (1997).

19. For example, a typical desktop computer contains an operating system and application software developed by many different companies. Although an automobile may also be composed of components from a number of suppliers, they tend to be fitted together into a test car before manufacture, and final assembly of each car takes place in a limited number of locations. A desktop computer is essentially assembled in each home or office—an assembly line of one.

20. This phenomenon is seen in the FAA and IRS systems modernization efforts.

21. In the Standish Group's survey cited earlier in this chapter, respondents blamed incomplete or changing requirements for many of the problems they faced in system development efforts. The more a project's requirements and specifications changed, the more likely it was that the project would take longer than originally planned. And the longer a project took to complete, the more likely it was that the aims of the organization requesting the system would change. In some cases, a project was delayed so long that the larger initiative it was designed to support was discontinued.

22. Indeed, the very notion of sociotechnical systems that is discussed in this report has been more thoroughly investigated outside the United States. U.S. researchers could benefit from more international cooperation. See, for example, Lyytinen (1987).

23. For example, simply upgrading the memory in a personal computer can lead to timing mismatches that cause memory failures that, in turn, lead to the loss of application data—even if the memory chips themselves are functioning perfectly. In other words, the system fails to work even if all of its components work. Similar problems can occur when a server is upgraded in a large network.

24. Architecture relates to interoperability and to ease of upgrading IT systems. A useful definition of the term "architecture" is the development and specification of the overall structure, logical components, and logical interrelationships of a computer, its operating system, a network, or other conception. An architecture can be a reference model for use with specific product architectures or it can be a specific product architecture, such as that for an Intel Pentium microprocessor or for IBM's OS/390 operating system. An architecture differs from a design in that it is broader in scope. An architecture is a design, but most designs are not architectures. A single component or a new function has a design that has to fit within the overall architecture. This definition is derived from the online resource whatis.com (<www.whatis.com>) and is based on Ralston (1976).

25. For decades, financial services have been delivered by organizations composed of elements that themselves are not perfectly trustworthy. Few, if any, of the techniques

developed by this industry have been adapted for use in software systems outside the financial services industry itself.

26. The examples of attacks on critical infrastructures and IT systems cited in this paragraph are derived from CSTB (1999a).

27. Hewlett-Packard, for example, claims that it can achieve 99.999 percent reliability in some of its hardware systems.

28. As the telephone industry has become more competitive, with more providers of telecommunications services and more suppliers of telecommunications equipment, the potential for compatibility and reliability problems has grown.

29. Other techniques have been used to create highly reliable software, suggesting hope for improvement in general practice. The software for the space shuttle system, for example, has performed with a high level of reliability because it is well maintained and the programmers are intimately familiar with it. They also use a number of the tools discussed in this chapter. See Fishman (1996).

30. As an example, customization usually is accomplished through the programming of general-purpose computers; huge computer programs often are built to form the core functionality of the system. How to design and construct such large computer programs is the focus of research in software engineering. Current research efforts, however, do not go far enough, as discussed later in this chapter. For a lengthier discussion of the challenges of developing better "glue" to hold together compound systems, see CSTB (1999a).

31. See TOPCCIP (1998) and CSTB (1999a).

32. In fact, a famous paper by Fred Brooks argues that there will be no single major improvement in the ability to develop large-scale software. See Brooks (1987).

33. Transaction processing does this by capturing some inherent challenges (such as an explosion of failure modes and resource conflicts due to concurrency) that plague all distributed systems and by providing countermeasures within an infrastructure supporting the application development.

34. Benchmarks play an important role in driving innovation by focusing system designers on improving particular attributes of a system. If the benchmark does not truly reflect the capabilities of the system, then engineering effort—and consumers—can be misdirected. An example might be the focus on microprocessor clock speeds as an indicator of performance. Consumers tend to look at such statistics when they purchase computers even though the architecture of a microprocessor can significantly influence the performance actually delivered.

35. As a simple example, automata theory can reason about the properties (such as decidability) of finite automata of arbitrary complexity. Here, the term "complexity" is interpreted differently than in the systems sense, in terms of the number of elements or operations but not necessarily their heterogeneity or the intricacy of their interaction.

36. To quote from the abstract of this study, titled *Representation and Analysis for Modeling, Specification, Design, Prediction, Control and Assurance of Large Scale, Complex Systems:* "Complete modeling of complex systems is not possible because of insufficient understanding, insufficient information, or insufficient computer cycles. This study focuses on the use of abstraction in modeling such systems. Abstraction of such systems is based on a semantic framework, and the choice of semantic framework affects the ability to model particular features of the system such as concurrency, adaptability, security, robustness in the presence of faults, and real-time performance. A rich variety of semantic frameworks have been developed over time. This study will examine their usefulness for modeling complex systems. In particular, questions to be addressed include the scalability (Do the semantics support hierarchy? Is it practical to have a very large number of components?), heterogeneity (Can it be combined with other semantic frameworks at multiple levels of abstraction?), and formalism (Are the formal properties of the semantics useful?). The study will also

address how to choose semantic frameworks, how to ensure model fidelity (Does the model behavior match the system being modeled?), how to recognize and manage emergent behavior, and how to specify and guarantee behavior constraints." Additional information about this project is available online at <http://ptolemy.eecs.berkeley.edu/~eal/towers/index.html>.

37. The Computer Science and Telecommunications Board initiated a study in early 2000 that will examine a range of possible interactions between computer science and the biological sciences, such as the use of biologically inspired models in the design of IT systems. Additional information is available on the CSTB home page, <www.cstb.org>.

38. By one estimate, based on the ratio of machine lines of code to source lines of code, the productivity of programmers has increased by a factor of ten every 20 years (or 12 percent a year) since the mid-1960s (see Bernstein, 1997).

39. Problem-ridden federal systems have been associated with personnel who may have less, or less current, training than their counterparts in leading private-sector environments. The association lends credence to the notion that the effectiveness of a process can vary with the people using it. See CSTB (1995a).

40. Reuse was one of the foundations of the industrial revolution. Standard, interchangeable parts used in industrial production can be equated to IT components. The analogy to IT frameworks came later in the industrial world but recently has become common. For example, today's automobiles usually are designed around common platforms that permit the design of different car models without major new investments in the underbody and drive train.

41. The ability to define, manipulate, and test software interfaces is valuable to any software project. If interfaces could be designed in such a way that software modules could first be tested separately and then assembled with the assurance of correct operation, then large-scale system engineering would become simpler. Much of the theory and engineering practice and many of the tools developed as part of IT research can be applied to these big systems.

42. An "artifact" in the terminology of experimental computer science and engineering refers to an instance or implementation of one or more computational phenomena, such as hardware, software, or a combination of the two. Artifacts provide researchers with testbeds for direct measurement and experimentation; proving new concepts (i.e., that a particular assembly of components can perform a particular set of functions or meet a particular set of requirements); and demonstrating the existence and feasibility of certain phenomena. See CSTB (1994).

43. For example, when the Defense Department's ARPANET was first built in the 1970s, it used the Network Control Protocol, which was designed in parallel with the network. Over time, it became apparent that networks built with quite different technologies would need to be connected, and users gained experience with the network and NCP. These two problems provoked research that eventually led to the development of the TCP/IP protocol, which became the standard way that computers could communicate over any network. As the network grew into a large Internet and applications emerged that require large bandwidth, congestion became a problem in the network. This, too, has led to research into adaptive control algorithms that the computers attached to the network must use to detect and mitigate congestion. Even so, the Internet is far from perfect. Research is under way into methods to guarantee quality of service for data transmission that could support, for example, robust transmission of digitized voice and video. Extending the Internet to connect mobile computers using radio communications is also an area of active research.

44. Generally speaking, industry-university IT research collaboration has been constrained by intellectual property protection arrangements, generating enough expressions of concern that CSTB is exploring how to organize a project on that topic.

45. Networking researchers, for example, have been clamoring for better data about Internet traffic and performance. They have been attempting to develop broader and more accurate Internet traffic and performance data for some time. Federal support associated with networking research might provide vehicles for better Internet Service Provider data collection.

46. The new Digital Government program being coordinated by the National Science Foundation may yield valuable experience in the practical aspects of engaging organizations with production systems problems for the purpose of collaborating with IT researchers. More information on this program is contained in Chapter 4.

47. On the one hand, business users should not benefit from subsidies intended for researchers (if they did, there would be a risk of overloading the academic-research networks). On the other hand, given the expectation that a research network is less stable than a production one, business users would be expected to pay for backup commercial networking and would be motivated to use a research network only at a discount. Systematic examination of actual users and applications would be necessary for concrete assessment of the traffic trade-offs.

4

Research Motivated by Social Applications of Information Technology

The diffusion of the Internet, combined with advances in basic computing and communications technologies, is poised to fundamentally alter the nature of information technology (IT) research. As IT continues to move from the relatively simple realm of back-office transactions processing and personal productivity-enhancement tools into less specialized, mass-market contexts that support electronic commerce (e-commerce), delivery of government services, and personal interactions, the set of problems that motivates IT research is continuing to change. Many of the new applications are *social applications* that serve groups of people in shared activities. Simple social applications support the collaboration of geographically dispersed groups of people engaged in a shared task, such as designing a new product or writing a report. More sophisticated social applications support a range of business, economic, and societal functions, such as manufacturing processes or distance education. Social applications tend to integrate IT into larger *sociotechnical* systems that involve people, organizations, and other technologies and that derive their functionality from the complex interactions of IT with nontechnical system elements. Many of the social applications comprise large-scale systems of the kind described in Chapter 3, but social applications of IT pose a number of additional interesting research problems, the solutions to which will require more explicit collaboration among IT researchers, end users, and researchers in other disciplines. Progress along purely technical dimensions, such as processing power, communications speed, and data storage densities, will no longer suffice; a more holistic view is needed (Brown and Duguid, 2000).

This chapter examines the increasing integration of IT into larger, social applications and the shortcomings of today's technology relative to a complex set of expectations. The first two sections lay the groundwork for the analysis by identifying the characteristics of social applications and the many challenges they present. Underlying this discussion is the idea that, because IT is proliferating in social applications, research on social applications should be expanded in amount, scope, and depth and, furthermore, that this new research will require approaches that are somewhat different from those taken in much of the more narrowly technology-oriented research that is common today.

The third section discusses ways in which interdisciplinary research can play an important role in this arena and identifies some initial steps in this direction. Just as scientific computing has benefited from closer interaction between technologists and natural scientists, so can the more-social applications of IT deployed today benefit from collaboration between technologists and social scientists (including experts in law and business as well as psychology, sociology, anthropology, and economics). The fourth section examines mechanisms for pursuing technical and nontechnical research that could increase understanding of social applications of IT and thereby enhance capabilities to design, develop, deploy, and operate them. Building on the groundwork laid in the present chapter, Chapter 5 identifies specific steps that could be taken to stimulate more of this type of research.

The development of appropriate mechanisms for funding and conducting research on the sociotechnical dimensions of IT systems will be a significant challenge. This work can build on some important foundations, notably research on human-computer interactions and computer-supported cooperative work. These existing research efforts are inherently multidisciplinary in outlook because they are concerned with the ways in which people relate to systems. Experience to date in these areas illustrates both the promise of social applications and the practical problems involved. Multidisciplinary research is always problematic because of the difficulties inherent in bridging the gaps separating different communities of researchers. Compounding these problems is the need implied by the concept of social applications to engage not only established researchers in other disciplines but also end users of IT systems who understand the context in which IT systems operate and directly confront problems of implementation, ease of use, performance, and operation. Many end-user organizations have little or no history of conducting research, especially IT-related research. New mechanisms may therefore be needed, and some ongoing activities are suggestive of the types of structures that may be effective.

The discussion proceeds at a high level because it is intended to bridge research themes each of which could justify detailed examination. Such examinations have been provided already by the Computer Science and Telecommunications Board (CSTB) in more focused assessments. This chapter points to that other work, which established an intellectual history developed through separate engagements with segments of the research community. That this chapter echoes and amplifies ideas raised previously is important enough to be acknowledged explicitly: research ideas and suggestions for how to make progress in the field either recur or linger largely unaddressed because the problems are difficult, because the recommendations are aimed at subsets of the research community despite broader relevance, and/or because there is a lack of readiness, whether due to insufficient insight and understanding of the needs or inadequate capabilities. The committee recognizes that it has focused on difficult problems but believes that the time is right to address them; its recommendations are aimed at promoting both understanding and capability.

SOCIAL APPLICATIONS OF INFORMATION TECHNOLOGY

Thanks in large part to networking, IT has become a factor in large organizational constructs, whether whole enterprises, groups of enterprises that interact in commerce, or the overarching mix of enterprises and activities (economic and other) that constitute the nation's economy of social structure. It also supports interactions among smaller groups of uses (e.g., in chat rooms and discussion groups). Information technology stands poised to dramatically transform the way people live, work, and play and the way organizations large and small conduct business. With continued research, development, and deployment, IT systems could enable users to routinely access information of many types (text, images, video, etc.) from any location, participate in continuing education programs from the home or office, shop at their convenience, work from home rather than commute to a central office, consult with medical practitioners remotely, or access government services and receive government benefits electronically.[1]

As such, IT joins mass transportation and more traditional telecommunications (i.e., telephony, broadcast media) as a foundation for the social interactions that form one basis of society, industry, and commerce (Mitchell, 1996). Those long-standing societal infrastructures—transportation and telecommunications—profoundly affected aspects of society, contributing to the rise of suburbs, the globalization of industry, and the decreasing isolation of political economies. Similarly, networked IT is increasingly affecting society, as today's debates about topics such as technological literacy and the digital divide attest (Cairncross, 1997). These issues are not necessarily unanticipated—one of the pioneers of the Internet, Leonard Kleinrock, recognized and wrote about some of these challenges in 1974 (Kleinrock, 1974), but they have not been adequately addressed by researchers in technology areas or other fields, and they are growing in importance as IT becomes more pervasive in society.

Today's IT systems put a premium on the explicit consideration of the context (e.g., organizational, societal, or business) in which IT systems are deployed and the organizational structures, human factors, and other types of technology (e.g., transportation and materials transformation) that are involved in completing a certain task. In these social applications of IT, computing, storage, and communications technologies are profoundly influenced by the people involved, the choices they make, and various aspects of human behavior in the design and implementation of the system. Such systems often display a host of other features that make them especially challenging topics for research:

- They are often large in scale and high in complexity (see Chapter 3).
- They can be geographically distributed and vulnerable to malicious attacks or unintentional errors.
- They are often deployed and operated in an environment that is largely uncoordinated.
- They have critical requirements for availability and security, with the potential for significant losses (financial, human, or otherwise) if they fail.
- They include people and organizations, along with technology, as essential elements.
- They are deeply affected by social, economic, and political considerations, such as privacy, productivity, strategic business advantage, national security, poverty, equitable access, and so on.
- Their design must take into consideration the human and organizational context in which the systems are deployed and the interactions among people, organizations, and technology.

Although the first four of these characteristics are common to many large-scale IT systems discussed in Chapter 3, the last three characteristics are especially true of social applications and demand special attention. Consider, for example, the systems used in e-commerce or air traffic control. In both of these cases, the interactions among IT, people, and organizational structures are fundamental to system performance. The IT is placed in an existing social and organizational environment in an attempt to improve quality, productivity, speed, and other performance attributes.[2]

Overwhelmingly, the most important opportunities lie not in simply automating existing applications, but rather in rethinking and remolding the structure and organization of the business process to reflect the best uses of IT and in redesigning and remolding the technology to make it most valuable in its (rethought) application context. The challenge is to *reinvent* both the application and the supporting technology to make the combination of technology and applications effective. In business, this is often called *reengineering* or *transforming* a business process, but the concept applies to the full range of social applications of IT.

Transformation requires a rethinking of the entire sociotechnical system, not just the IT portion. Because most social applications involve individuals, brought together in organizations, and technologies that relate to the movement or alteration of materials or other physical items, a critical part of such a transformation is the identification of the capabilities that each element—people, IT, and other technologies—most beneficially contribute to the process, and the determination of how these elements can best work together. These processes are often constrained by complex social and regulatory issues and must take into account a number of nontechnical factors, such as capital budgets, work rules, skill sets, and administrative organizations. Nevertheless, the creative use of new IT capabilities can result in new, transforming applications. E-commerce, for example, has given rise to electronic auctions. The auction concept is not new, of course; what is new is its application to the selling of common goods and services, both new and used, and the participation of large numbers of buyers and sellers in an electronic marketplace, with new ways for individuals to research price and value and new ways to negotiate. Another example is air traffic control. Advances in technology have produced a fundamental change in the way these systems are conceptualized and designed, moving away from a centralized command-and-control model that controls all aspects of an aircraft's flight plan to a system known as free flight, which will give individual pilots greater autonomy—and more information on which to base judgments (Wald, 2000).

The changing nature of work is broadening the contexts in which IT must operate. Employees are no longer expected to sit at a single computer in an assigned office to complete their work. Even a simple application to enter employee expense reports must be accessible via many different devices in different locations: a desktop computer at work, a desktop computer at home, a laptop computer or handheld devices when traveling, and perhaps even a wireless phone. If an organization cannot offer remote access to IT services, it may limit the effectiveness of its staff. As IT systems are used to manage more aspects of a business, the properties of the IT system and the behavior of employees become more tightly interlinked.

IT-inspired transformations occur at all levels within organizations, as is evidenced in, for example, the flattening of traditional hierarchies, globalization of many business organizations and activities, and emergence of new classes of nomadic workers who are not even assigned permanent offices. As these trends demonstrate, the design of organizations is a matter of both people and IT, leveraging the strongest capabilities of each (Walton, 1989). New methodologies are needed for the design of enterprise applications that more deeply integrate the organizational design and the IT system design. Such methodologies can be developed only through collaborative research in the disciplines concerned, including technology, industrial engineering, business, psychology, and others. The challenges are compounded by the reality that all the information systems that must work together in support of an organization or society cannot be developed at once; rather, new elements are continually added to an existing mix of legacy technologies and applications. Capricious organizational requirements, particularly in a competitive business context, add another dimension to the challenge that has proven difficult to overcome.

Of course, IT has always been designed and used in one context or another. Even traditional applications (e.g., word processing) that could be used on individual computers without networking or pursued independently of other applications have had important interactions with job definitions and human relationships within organizations.[3] Social scientists studying such applications have reported on changes in status, hierarchy, work flow, job design, job satisfaction, productivity, and so on, all of which have contributed to ideas for enhancing early applications and evolving new ones.[4] Some of these ideas have contributed to computer science in arenas such as human-computer interaction (HCI, which includes the design of interfaces between people and systems and the design of systems for computer-supported cooperative work), but compared to the opportunities emerging now, those instances of interdisciplinary research are too few and too isolated.[5] The evolution of HCI is a promising indicator that progress is possible if social applications are addressed through IT research that draws on multiple disciplines: the subdisciplines "form intertwined roots in computer graphics, operating systems, human factors, ergonomics, industrial engineering, cognitive psychology, and the systems part of computer science" and draw from "supporting knowledge on both the machine and the human side" (ACM, 1992).

A much greater degree of interaction between IT applications and context is now possible.[6] Interest in optimizing that interaction—while addressing issues of complexity and scale—creates an imperative for explicit and substantial attention to context in application design and implementation, which, in turn, implies explicit and substantial attention to the behavior of people as individuals and as members of groups.

Great opportunities await progress in the sociotechnical systems that underlie IT, because such progress would enable far greater capabilities than have yet been implemented in all existing feature sets and their combinations. The IT itself can be used more effectively—and it can be combined better with people and their activities as they work, live, and play. The challenge is twofold: (1) to reinvent social applications to improve the combinations of behavior and IT with the aim of producing better economic and social outcomes and (2) to invent new social applications that enhance the economy, culture, or quality of life.[7] Both processes build on past experience with IT, which has demonstrated that tasks are typically automated directly at first and subsequently reconceptualized or reinvented to take better advantage of new technology. Both processes focus on the role of individual users and organizations as major players in social applications.

RESEARCH CHALLENGES IN SOCIAL APPLICATIONS OF INFORMATION TECHNOLOGY

Social applications of IT can motivate research on a range of questions as broad as the applications themselves, with the questions reflecting the particular circumstances in which specific applications are deployed. Some social applications are associated with a given industry or industry sector (e.g., online stock trading systems or flight reservations systems), some cut across the economy (e.g., business-to-business e-commerce systems), and others are specific to a particular organization or function. Despite the fact that it is motivated by applications, the research that results from an examination of social applications can be highly fundamental, in that it requires investigations into, and the development of, basic IT capabilities that are widely applicable to a wide range of systems. The research also tends to be highly interdisciplinary, drawing on the expertise of people in the IT and social science communities, as well as end users who understand the way systems are used in different industries and functions.

Despite their diversity, the social applications of IT tend to have in common a set of elements that support (1) group interaction, (2) knowledge management, (3) commerce, and (4) control and coordination. Although some social applications of IT emphasize one or another of these elements, they usually emphasize at least two (Box 4.1). Each of these types of functionality presents a set of interesting research challenges. An examination of each one will provide a sampling of the types of problems

---

BOX 4.1
Social Applications of Information Technology:
Examples and Features

• *Electronic commerce*—Business-to-business procurement of goods and services involves the capture and presentation of large amounts of information on available goods and services (knowledge-based features); negotiation of terms and conditions for sale and fulfillment between purchasing agents in one organization and sales agents in another organization (group-based features); periodic ordering and shipment of, and payment for, goods and services in accordance with those terms and conditions (commerce-based features); infrastructure supporting payments by credit card or bank transfer (control-based features), and post-sale support (group-based features).

• *Delivery of government services*—Government tax-collection applications involve the gathering and assimilation of data from throughout the economy (knowledge-based features); conveying of tax returns with tax payments (commerce-based features); infrastructure supporting payments and refunds (control-based features); and interactions among tax agents, citizens, and accountants in dealing with exceptional cases (group-based features).

• *Manufacturing design*—Computer-aided automotive design involves large repositories of design information (knowledge-based features), coordination of concurrent design activities distributed over global design centers (control-based features), and collaboration of the designers (group-based features).

• *Air traffic control*—Air traffic control systems are critical infrastructures that combine the coordination of planes and airport facilities (control-based features) with the collaboration of pilots and air controllers (group-based features) and information on aircraft type, flight plans and carriers, weather, and so on (knowledge-based features). Air traffic control uses information technology of increasing sophistication to reduce the incidence of human error and extend human controller capabilities to manage a volume of air traffic.

---

that could be addressed if social applications were to play a more significant role in motivating IT research.

Group Applications

An important feature of social applications and their context is that they involve people as members of groups. With networking, computing moves from enhancing the productivity of individuals in tasks they perform alone to supporting the needs and enhancing the productivity or social interactions of groups of people, or helping people find other, like-minded people—a class of applications called *group applications* in this report. Group-based elements support activities, including interaction or collaboration, among groups of individual users. Individuals and groups can now publish and manage information, literally on a global scale, as illustrated by many of the well-known Internet applications, such as electronic mail (e-mail), discussion forums, and the World Wide Web. But the Web affords comparatively static, passive information sharing with relatively little accommodation for variation in individual capabilities or preferences. To improve on this technology—and support a wider range of interactions—researchers must delve into group dynamics and interaction, human learning and cognition, human impairments, and other variations on these themes and how they might be supported by IT. Such research depends on insight from psychology and sociology as well as computer science and electrical engineering. It also depends on insight from specific domains that may shape real-world contexts: for example, different requirements will be associated with groups engaged in routine teaching and learning as opposed to groups collaborating on responses to natural disasters, when one can expect extreme variations in available technology, skill sets, responsibilities, and work environments and where crisis conditions affect needs for the type, delivery rate, and comprehensibility of information gathered, analyzed, and shared (CSTB, 1996, 1999).

Knowledge Management

Knowledge-based elements support the capture, retrieval, and manipulation of knowledge, typically drawing on massive collections of information. Although more and more data are being generated or recorded in networked computers, finding essential information is increasingly difficult. As the nation shifts from an industrial to an information economy (Shapiro and Varian, 1998), the role of physical assets as a source of competitive advantage is diminishing. To see the role that knowledge is playing in the economy, one need look no further than stock market valuations of Internet start-ups that have negligible physical assets but considerable intellectual property. The acquisition or discovery of knowledge (which is derived from information), plus the strategic management and exploitation of that knowledge—a process called knowledge management—are therefore an increasing focus of many companies, both new and established (O'Leary, 1998).[8] The goal is to be able to find, understand, and use the massive amounts of information and knowledge that reside within an enterprise.

Tools for searching for information remain frustratingly poor. While it may seem easy enough for people to express their information needs to one another, computer retrieval techniques are unable to filter out a large number of useless search results. To counter the technology shortcomings, organizations today manage knowledge using a combination of people and computers. Much as a library contains books that record information, as well as librarians to organize and index it, computers are used to store and transmit information but are able to organize and index only data that have a precise, logical structure. Managing knowledge that is encoded as expository text is largely beyond today's IT capabilities.

Historically, IT contributed to information management through systems for collecting and storing information (i.e., databases), finding and retrieving it (i.e., information retrieval), and processing online transactions. These systems provided experience with the types of functions that people now want to extend, combine, and enhance in new and more powerful ways. Data warehousing, which captures a historical record of an entire enterprise's transactions, and data mining, which attempts to analyze data to identify hidden trends and correlations, represent the current state of the art in knowledge discovery and management. For the most part, knowledge discovery and management strain current IT.

Distributed transaction databases with properties such as automatic load balancing and historical archiving have been suggested, but they are beyond the current state of the art.[9] In addition, end users are beginning to recognize that knowledge management projects require as much social science as computer science because the systems must serve the evolving mission needs of their users. According to some industry analysts, data warehousing projects fail more often for organizational reasons than for technical ones (Deck, 1999).

Commerce

Commerce-based elements support the interaction of organizations (including businesses, government entities, and universities) with other organizations and with individuals, whether consumers, citizens and tax-payers, or students. Today's most obvious example is e-commerce, the buying and selling of goods and services, especially among organizations. Business-to-business applications of IT have expanded dramatically from straightforward replacement of paper documentation (such as purchase orders and invoices) in electronic data interchange and electronic bank-to-bank wiring of funds, both of which have been in use for some time. In the emerging model, IT is integrated into all business-to-business operational activities except for the flow of material goods. This new e-commerce (Keen and Balance, 1997) includes activities such as electronic money management (direct transfers of money in electronic forms between businesses), electronic business logistics (coordination of suppliers and customers) and supply chain management (integration of business processes across businesses with supplier/customer relationships).

Most of these activities also apply to nonbusiness organizations, such as government entities involved in procurement, tax collection, licensing fees, and so on.

The development of Internet-based e-commerce has important implications for IT and related research. First, it has amplified the role of information about individuals as an element of business strategy and therefore of knowledge management. Now IT is being used to collect and analyze information about individuals as actual or potential customers—information that can be used for product design, marketing, and customer service. The result is a predictable tension between those interested in the commercial exploitation of information about individuals and those concerned about protecting privacy (Diffie and Landau, 1997). New questions are being asked: Who knows what about whom? Who owns information about individuals? Who is authorized to use that information and for what purposes? These concerns are related to those surrounding the protection of intellectual property in a digital environment.[10] Second, as illustrated by the growing attention to privacy as well as the concerns about reliability, dependability, and trustworthiness discussed in Chapter 3, government entities are scrutinizing the nature and use of IT in e-commerce. The result may well involve a combination of voluntary industry actions and government-mandated actions to promote or avoid certain uses of IT, which would have implications for system design and implementation constraints. One certain result would be a further change in the nature and impact of government, which—like businesses and other organizations—is itself affected by the use of IT.[11]

Finally, e-commerce is redefining the business processes that span traditional administrative and organizational boundaries (Davenport, 1993) and altering the relationships among organizations.[12] Even before the commercialization of the Internet, industry witnessed a strong trend away from vertical integration and toward more specialized or horizontally diversified firms, driven in part by lower coordination and transaction costs enabled by IT. There is speculation about the prospects for consolidation and concentration. The equilibrium boundary of a firm is largely set by the relationship between internal and external transaction and coordination costs, and those costs are being profoundly influenced by IT (Grenier and Metes, 1996). Furthermore, the judicious application of new IT can greatly influence these boundaries and the efficiency of the economy as a whole—another area deserving of research.

Coordination and Control

Control- or coordination-based features support the coordination of large numbers of distributed elements—often a combination of technological, informational, and human—in achieving the reliable operation of a large-scale system. They are especially prevalent in infrastructure systems that perform critical support functions for society as a whole, such as the systems used in utilities (electric, gas, telephone, and networking), finance (electronic funds transfer and auction markets), and transportation (air and rail networks). These systems place extreme requirements on features such as reliability and trustworthiness (see Chapter 3). Many require real-time operation and decision making, some of which will be done in consultation with users and some of which must occur automatically. The specific needs, and the ways in which these needs are met, are closely tied to the nature of the application. For example, security practices limiting access to a system may need to incorporate different override features depending, for example, on whether the system is being used to transfer funds between banks or to allow a doctor emergency access to a patient's medical record.

Common Challenges

Despite the diversity in social applications and the IT systems that support them, there are common elements, and they can motivate research that could inform the development of all such systems. Obviously, the broader the range of applications that benefit from particular technological and methodological innovations, the greater the overall value of the research. This is an argument for focusing a large portion of IT research on highly generic problems, such as the following:

• *Social trust*—How can people communicating with strangers in electronic communities know who is trustworthy and who is not?
• *Coordinating expertise*—How can systems and procedures make it easier to elicit and coordinate the expertise of individuals, whether they are doing system development or participating in discussion groups?
• *Personal privacy and identity*—How can systems and procedures make it easier for people to disclose as much as, but no more than, they wish about their identity and personal information in online contexts?
• *Agency*—How can people better instruct IT systems to make decisions on their behalf, e.g., to coordinate calendars and to process and route messages (such as e-mail, faxes, and voice messages)?
• *Community and collaboration*—How can IT better support the activities of groups of individuals seeking to communicate and collaborate more effectively?
• *Knowledge content*—How can the collection of, access to, and extraction of value from vast amounts of information be made more effective?

How can these tasks be better distributed among people and systems of different types?

- *Business processes*—How are repetitive, ongoing activities that meet a business goal best organized around technology, and how is technology best organized around such processes? Can common elements or strategies be used?
- *Security*—How can researchers rethink IT to reduce the vulnerability of the infrastructure, applications, and people to various risks and system failures?
- *Operations and administration*—How can IT be designed for enhanced operation and administration, particularly in a world in which many applications need to interoperate with other applications and across organizational and political boundaries?
- *Development methodologies*—How can software applications be developed more effectively, with the goal of improving outcomes in terms of meeting application needs for functionality, interoperability with other applications, and the flexibility to change in the future?

All of these issues are common to a number of different applications, and all are receiving attention today by researchers in disciplines such as computer science and engineering, information management and science, the social sciences (particularly economics, psychology, and sociology), and business. However, this attention often has too narrow a disciplinary focus. Research in these areas would benefit from a multidisciplinary approach because it pays more attention to application contexts and could define new issues and requirements to inform the research.

System-Specific Research

In addition to research in generic areas of concern such as those listed above, IT research can address more specific application contexts as well. The purpose, again, is to inform the research on IT by considering realistic needs and contexts, with the goal of molding the technology to be more powerful, effective, and secure.[13] There are important reasons for doing this. First, any particular area of technological research is more critical to some applications than to others. Some applications stress a particular facet of technology. By identifying and studying the applications that are most challenging, the IT research outcomes can have a broader and greater impact. Second, researchers pursuing generic technological concerns tend to ignore interactions with other concerns or miss opportunities to address different areas of concern with more holistic solutions. The only practical way to appreciate a full range of issues and how they interact with and buttress one another is to look at the whole problem in specific application contexts. Finally, as the application domain of research narrows, the impact of technology improvements to that application domain are likely to be greater.

As an example, consider the IT research objective "greater flexibility to meet changing needs." Can flexibility be addressed generically? Certainly, as outlined in Chapter 3, and indeed it is worthwhile to search for general approaches and principles. But it is also worthwhile to first identify more specifically what sort of flexibility is needed, as informed by particular applications domains. Does flexibility imply the merging of information systems when firms merge? Does it mean adding new applications to a mix and ensuring that those new applications are interoperable with the old? Does it mean adding features or modifying the features of existing applications? Does it mean layering new applications on top of old ones? Are there other options to explore? To what extent is the definition of flexibility itself flexible? By examining particular application domains, researchers can answer such questions with greater specificity, and the results may be more immediately useful. At the same time, of course, the results become less generally applicable; yet it is often possible to generalize from the specific case studied to a broader range of similar cases.

An essential part of research on the social applications of IT is building and deploying experimental systems. Often the utility of an application cannot be predicted by its designers or by past experience. For many IT applications, the task is more like one of industrial product design than business process reengineering. Standards for IT research need to acknowledge emerging social effects, not focus exclusively on the technology. The World Wide Web, for example, is based on extant technologies for document management and hypertext, but the unique combination of these technologies addressed a social need (to publish and communicate) with a power that could not have been predicted from previous experience with the technologies.

CONDUCTING RESEARCH ON SOCIAL APPLICATIONS

A Plausible Approach

Research that addresses the social applications of IT would need to target applications that serve groups of users, organizations (including government, businesses, and others), the citizenry at large, and critical infrastructure systems. Examples include the following:

- *Groups*—Collaboration, political activism, battlefield management, community development;

- *Organizations*—Tax collection, census collection, military logistics, e-commerce;
- *Citizens*—The political process (polling and voting, citizen involvement in decision making), continuing education, entertainment, cultural opportunities; and
- *Critical infrastructure*—Transportation and communication networks, intelligence gathering, nuclear power, and financial markets.

The research would not only address today's nascent social applications (such as e-commerce) but also explore visionary new possibilities that are unimagined today or even unimaginable owing to their scale and complexity. Much of this research would aim for visionary and revolutionary advances through the creative application of technology. Some research would work from the bottom up, envisioning the potential capabilities of technologies and identifying new opportunities that exploit those capabilities. Other research would work from the top down, categorizing the major challenges experienced in the world today or tomorrow that might be overcome by the creative application of existing and new technology. The research would aim to enhance the positive effects of IT while identifying and minimizing its negative effects.[14]

Similar to systems research, which needs to pursue both case research and methodology research (as discussed in Chapter 3), research on social applications would need to pursue both case research and generic research. Case research would identify target application areas such as "digital democracy" (i.e., public participation in collective decision making) and address the role IT could play in them. Such research would also seek new mechanisms for the political process and supporting technologies. Generic research addresses issues such as group dynamics, decision making, collaboration, enjoyment and satisfaction, and competition and looks at how they apply to and can be mediated in social applications. Generic research could also address how technology can be molded to help in balancing economic benefits to organizations against the rights or quality of life of individuals. An important example of a generic research topic is privacy; research would attempt to define what privacy entails in different contexts and identify technological means to control the degree of privacy as a function of circumstance and objectives.

Outcomes of the research into the social applications of IT could be evaluated in terms of criteria such as (1) the extent to which society and organizations benefit more from technological progress than they would otherwise, with respect to whatever dimensions make sense in context (e.g., productivity, quality, or effectiveness), (2) the extent to which the negative consequences of technological progress are avoided or mitigated, and (3) the extent to which technology is influenced by beneficial long-term, visionary ideas rather than being simply the result of incremental improvements and near-term commercial exploitation.

Research of the sort suggested in this chapter would help society reap the rewards of "learning by doing" and would accelerate that process. It would help researchers recognize patterns in their results and develop new theories and would enable them to select better research targets and exploit their work more effectively. The new approach to research would take nothing away from the tried-and-true work that continues to offer many benefits; it would be an additional, complementary asset in the overall production system.

New Research Teams

The tight linkages between the technical and nontechnical components of sociotechnical systems mean that effective research will have to draw on a broad range of constituencies, much as work in civil engineering is influenced by architects, urban planners, and transportation engineers (Box 4.2). Technology researchers, social scientists, and domain experts will have to work together to identify and solve problems related to the social applications of IT.

To date, research on the social applications of IT has tended to fall into one of four categories:

• Research on IT systems addressing generic issues of technology, informed (it is hoped) by a knowledge of application needs and addressing a broad swath of application contexts rather than focusing on a single context (examples include many of the issues mentioned in Chapter 3, such as security, administration, and flexibility);
• Applications research that addresses a specific context, trying to see how existing technologies can provide value to that application and how that application context (such as an organization) can be reorganized around IT technologies;
• Software engineering research that explores generic techniques for developing and deploying new IT-based applications; examples include the processes involved in understanding the application context, translating this understanding into requirements and specifications, implementing the applications, measuring and refining their behavior, deploying the application, training users, and supporting the deployed application and its users; and
• Social science research that explores how people undertake different activities and exercise their different physical and mental abilities to engage IT and other resources and research that explores how people adapt the structure of organizations and activities in response to the intro-

---

BOX 4.2
Social Applications of Technology in the Construction Industry

The interplay among civil engineering, architecture, transportation engineering, and urban planning demonstrates the multiple influences that impinge on social applications of technology, in a setting that many people find somewhat more familiar than the information technology (IT) industry. As such, the construction industry provides a useful illustration of the direction in which IT is heading.

Civil engineers are adept at achieving cost-effective structures based on well-specified plans provided by an architect. The architect is adept at generating those plans by understanding the local conditions and environment and interviewing future occupants of the building about their needs and wishes. But neither of these professionals can work in isolation. Their work relates to both transportation engineering and to land-use planning, and it is not difficult to see that isolated decisions by architects and civil engineers can have unintended consequences in one of those domains, perhaps interrupting traffic patterns or altering the character of a neighborhood. Local interests, which may be expressed in plans for a given structure, can be varied, but they must be aggregated for purposes of transportation and land-use planning decisions.

The construction process is clearly complicated by the involvement of three or four professions with distinct cultures and perspectives. However, this is one arena in which there is a history of interaction and a comparatively mature legal and political environment that impinges on the engineering activity, which—until the recent advent of intelligent transportation systems and the prospect of smart homes, thanks to progress in IT—has itself been comparatively mature and stable for a long time.

---

duction of IT. This category includes the classical social science disciplines themselves—e.g., psychology, social psychology, sociology, and anthropology.

Clearly, a great deal of valuable research can be performed in these four categories. Much of the research agenda discussed in Chapter 3 can be cast into the first category, as can the research into component technologies that can and should be pursued (discussed in Chapter 1). Much of the research carried out in social-science-based disciplines, such as information and library sciences and business, can be cast into the second and fourth categories. A modest amount of research (in comparison to the size of the challenges) has been conducted in the third category. It has been pursued most notably by organizations such as the Software Engineering Institute at Carnegie Mellon University and some academic computer science departments.

Each of the four kinds of research has limitations if it becomes the sole lens through which to examine the social applications of IT. Because social applications of IT link technology so tightly to people and organizations, a more integrative approach is needed. In the technology arena, IT is subject to few physical limits, so it can be molded in many different ways. To consider the technology in isolation is to miss opportunities to mold it in directions that make it more useful. Similarly, because a great deal of research in application areas takes the current observed state of technology as a given, it misses opportunities to think about ways in which the technology could be different that would make it much more useful. One of the great unsolved problems is how, as a part of software application conceptualization and development, to take into account the rich interaction between the application context and the architectural assumptions in the software application, as well as the issues of legacy technology and applications and changing requirements. This last challenge clearly embodies the consideration of technology (as it is and as it could be) in conjunction with a deep understanding of the context.

There is tremendous potential for expanded research agendas that fall between these categories and combine multiple perspectives into a more cohesive, holistic view. Research that examines the impact of IT on society and the economy is certainly needed, but equally important is research on the impact that application contexts have on IT development and software development methodologies as a part of the larger process of application conceptualization and refinement. New science and engineering may arise from such research. The discussion in this report emphasizes research in which the goal is to refine the IT itself, often in conjunction with meeting application needs more effectively. Impact remains an important issue, but there is an explicit goal of modifying the technology to maximize the beneficial impacts and mitigate the adverse ones.

Who is in the best position to make contributions to IT as informed by applications—especially the social applications of IT—and how can research on this topic best be organized? The most effective researchers will have an understanding of the potential of IT, both what might be possible technically as well as what has already been achieved, as well as an understanding of the application context. In general, opportunities for advancing application areas using existing technologies are best addressed by application domain experts who have acquired a fairly substantial understanding of the technology. (There are certainly opportunities for technology experts to participate in this research in consulting roles, but such participation is generally not greeted with enthusiasm.) The use of application domains to inspire technology is a role predominantly for technology researchers who inform themselves about the characteristics and challenges inherent in particular problem domains. Such knowledge can be gained in at least two ways: (1) by working directly with the end users (individuals and organizations) in that application domain or (2) by collaborating with researchers who have the appropriate domain expertise or expertise in disciplines directly relevant to the domain.

Where the goal is to advance both the technologies and the ways of addressing application domain challenges, interdisciplinary research collaboration is generally needed. Although some degree of collaboration has always been necessary, the need for it is growing quickly, driven by the availability of the Internet, the proliferation of IT applications in consumer and other layperson contexts, and the rapid expansion of social applications of IT generally. These trends also argue for substantially expanding the involvement of end users in setting the research agendas and articulating the goals and constraints of the research, for it is the end users who experience the opportunities and challenges in an immediate and detailed fashion. Although several programs have been established to bring together the diverse set of stakeholders needed to make progress on social applications of IT, it is increasingly apparent that a broader and more substantial effort is needed that uses multiple mechanisms to stimulate the type of research that will make significant progress. There are many practical barriers to the desired intellectual cross-fertilization, but mechanisms exist for overcoming them, as outlined in the next section.

MECHANISMS FOR SOCIAL APPLICATIONS RESEARCH

Participation of End-User Organizations

To date, end-user organizations have relied largely on their vendors to perform long-term research in IT. Vendor research, which emphasizes components, needs to continue unabated if rapid advances in the speed and capacity of IT are to be maintained. However, when it comes to research that affects the uses of IT, the constituencies who understand and benefit from those uses—that is, end-user organizations—must participate. These organizations include (1) companies that are strongly dependent on IT, including firms in almost all industries but especially those in business and financial services and online commerce; (2) suppliers of enterprise software used to automate major processes for corporations, universities, and government agencies; (3) application developers that develop customized software for large companies and government agencies; and (4) systems integrators that integrate major infrastructure components (hardware and software) to meet the needs of large-scale applications.

End users also include government agencies that depend heavily on IT systems—especially those that have considerable difficulty deploying such systems effectively. This group includes both traditional federal supporters of IT research—the Department of Defense, the National Science Foundation, the Department of Energy, and the National Aeronautics and Space Administration—as well as agencies that have a more limited history of supporting research on IT, such as the Internal Revenue Service, the Social Security Administration , and the Federal Aviation Administration. All parts of the government are increasingly dependent on IT. In FY00, federal agencies were budgeted to spend more than $34 billion on IT systems, up more than $1 billion over FY99.[15] Information technology is used both to run the back offices that store data and record transactions and to interact with citizens doing business with the government. Arguably, the funding of basic IT research directly supports the missions of these agencies (Wulf, 1999). If new IT developments can increase the effectiveness of these functions or reduce their cost, then the nation as a whole will benefit.

The greater participation of end-user organizations in IT research could have numerous benefits. First, these organizations can bring substantive intellectual insight to the research process. Research on social applications of IT demands an understanding of the ways in which IT is deployed in different organizations, the missions it supports, the requirements it must meet, and the problems that are experienced. Such insight can come only from end-user organizations that work with such systems routinely and can foresee the ways in which such systems might be used in the future. Recognition of the benefits of researcher access to real systems in situ is not new. The CSTB, for example, first recommended such access in 1989 in a report that provided recommendations for research on complex software systems. The participants at the time noted that the problems identified dated back to the 1960s, and a reading today suggests that many of the same problems persist now in software engineering and related research (see Box 4.3).

Second, end-user organizations could contribute funding, thereby expanding the financial base for research related to IT. Such an expansion is necessary if research motivated by social applications is to grow without crowding out existing research on components. The well-publicized and expensive failures of IT in end-user organizations also make a compelling case for the expansion of research funding from all sources, including the government. Finally, end-user organizations will insist (appropriately) that the research have an identifiable impact on the problems they experience. Thus, their involvement will focus the research community's

BOX 4.3
Excerpts from
Scaling Up: A Research Agenda for Software Engineering

Short-Term Actions: Foster Practitioner and Researcher Interactions

• "There is little academic investigation of the practices, techniques, or problems out in the field today. To rectify this situation, greater interaction among researchers and practitioners is needed. . . ."
• "That academic computer scientists do not often study large software systems and the process of developing them is one reason that practitioners often feel that the issues studied by academia do not adequately address the problems and challenges. . . ."
• "Academics do not study large systems because they do not have them or have access to them. . . ."
• "The disparity in perspective and exposure. . . hinders U.S. progress in developing complex software systems."

Long-Term Actions: Legitimize Academic Exploration of Large Software Systems

• "Academic investigation of research topics based on problems encountered in the 'real world' by software developers could help. . . ."
• "Funding is a major consideration. . . . [It] is difficult to study large systems cost-effectively."
• "One way to get around some of the difficulties of studying large systems in corporate settings would be to facilitate the study of large systems in government settings. . . ."

Glean Insights from Behavioral and Managerial Sciences

• "There is a need to better understand how groups of people collaborate in large projects. . . ."

SOURCE: Computer Science and Technology Board (1989), pp. 19-21.

attention on social applications of IT to a much greater extent than would otherwise be expected.

Engaging end users more directly in IT research will not be easy. Many cultural differences must be bridged, and practical issues in the management of research must be resolved. A sociotechnical systems perspective on any large-scale IT in context requires the identification and analysis of human and organizational shortcomings as well as technical ones. It is difficult to gain access to organizations, let alone financial support, for projects that are likely to identify human shortcomings (as well as technical ones) and publish them in the open literature. Organizations may pay consultants for such work already, but contractual terms of nondisclosure guarantee that the findings will not be subject to the scrutiny of peer review and will not become general knowledge. Furthermore, because end users and systems integrators have not been actively engaged in IT research, few have any internal research capacity or ability to manage outside research and ensure its quality and relevance. Consequently, they may be unable (at least at first) to participate effectively in the conduct of research. If research is conducted by parties outside the organizations, mechanisms will be needed to ensure that the research will benefit the end-user community and influence actual practices. Researchers themselves will need active and ongoing contacts with end-user organizations to gain hands-on experience with real issues and problems and the ability to validate their ideas empirically in realistic environments.

One approach would be for end-user organizations to pool their resources and fund external research related to their interests, whether at universities or industrial research labs, or in consortia established expressly for this purpose. This approach has been used by IT firms to support research of mutual interest through organizations such as SEMATECH, the Microelectronics and Computer Technology Corporation, the Semiconductor Research Corporation, and others (see Box 4.4). Such arrangements have produced mixed results to date; their success depends on many factors, including the ability of the member organizations to agree on a set of issues to address, the leadership of the consortia, and the quality of the researchers (many are drawn from member companies). When this model is used for research on the social applications of IT, the mechanisms for transferring technology back to the end users could be a problem. There is ample evidence that before they can benefit from research consortia, firms must have their own research and development (R&D) operations in place. Professor Wes Cohen of Carnegie Mellon University has referred to this characteristic as "absorptive capacity." Consortia in e-commerce or medical informatics, for example, would not succeed if banks or health maintenance organizations did not have their own internal research operations under way.

Accordingly, one element of a larger strategy would be to try to increase the amount of direct R&D conducted by firms that use IT systems. Many an applied research organization leverages external research outcomes—whether funded by that organization or not—for internal benefit. These organizations could be involved in choosing the recipients of research funding. Importantly, they have experience in identifying inter-

---

BOX 4.4
Models for Pooling Information Technology Research

Companies in the information technology (IT) industry have at times joined forces to fund research that will aid the entire industry. The examples below could serve as models for end-user organizations to pursue as they increase their participation in IT-related research.

- *Semiconductor manufacturing technology (SEMATECH)*—This consortium allies 13 leading manufacturers of semiconductor devices from seven countries to pursue advances in semiconductor fabrication equipment. Established in 1987, SEMATECH was originally supported by equal funding from its member companies and the Defense Advanced Research Projects Agency but ended its reliance on federal funding in 1997. It has funded research on advanced technologies for fabricating semiconductors, including lithography, packaging, testing, design, materials, and interconnect technologies.
- *Microelectronics and Computer Technology Corporation (MCC)*—This organization provides research and development (R&D) services in electronics and IT. Its fundamental business is consortia R&D, in which members define and participate in highly leveraged R&D projects that meet their strategic business requirements. MCC members are eligible to participate in the projects and fund only those projects of most interest to them. Each participant receives a royalty-free, unrestricted license to intellectual property resulting from a project, meaning that each can use new technologies internally and/or commercialize them. As of 1999, the MCC had 17 members and 4 foreign project participants.
- *Semiconductor Research Corporation (SRC)*—This organization sponsors basic, precompetitive university research related to integrated circuit technology. It pools funding from industrial members and leverages federal and state government support of key research programs. The funding terms for contracts vary; however, the trend is toward multiyear research efforts (typically 3 years) with an initial 12-month funding term. At the end of the multiyear period, the researchers may compete again for new support. The SRC supports two types of research— core and custom. Core research is funded from the pool of SRC member funds and constitutes most of the portfolio. Custom research is funded by a single company and represents 10 to 14 percent of the portfolio. As of April 2000, SRC had 40 members from industry and government and was funding work at 67 U.S. universities.

---

nal problems and challenges worthy of research, and also in identifying individuals who can convey those challenges to external researchers. In other words, they are matchmakers, putting together internal and external resources and facilitating access to internal facilities for empirical research activities. Such organizations can also be vehicles for ensuring that the research project is chosen in consultation with organizations well versed in this process. Government agencies, for example, could enlist the aid of federal agencies that are experienced in funding IT research, such as the NSF, DOE, NASA, and the Defense Advanced Research Projects Agency (DARPA).

The federal government is attempting to forge stronger links between the IT research community and end users in federal agencies. The Digital Government program, for example, uses the NSF as an intermediary to fund IT research addressing the medium- to long-term R&D and experimental deployment needs of federal agencies.[16] The program requires at least one government agency to be "significantly involved in defining and executing the research" and requires recipients of grants to integrate into their projects experts in domains that are primarily or exclusively associated with government. Agencies are encouraged to share facilities, data, or personnel with the researchers and/or to provide funding either directly or jointly with the NSF.[17] Although the program is new and small (approximately $3 million was allocated to it in FY00), it has succeeded in attracting a number of proposals that involve a range of federal agencies with little or no experience in funding IT research.[18] However, many projects reflect the agencies' interests in developing software and systems to meet particular near-term needs and their desire to examine different technological solutions to determine which offers the best combination of features. NSF program managers hope to create a research culture in federal agencies that will promote longer-term research and facilitate the agencies' adoption of new technologies once the research is completed, but this process will take time. Mechanisms may be needed to demonstrate the feasibility and applicability of new technologies to help agencies better evaluate their risks and benefits (Larry Brandt, NSF, "The NSF Digital Government Research Program," presentation to the committee, June 14, 1999).

Another attempt to strengthen linkages between researchers and end-user organizations is IBM Corporation's First-of-a-Kind (FOAK) program.[19] The FOAK program, initiated in 1995, links IBM's Research Division with its industry solution units (ISUs) to apply innovative technologies to real customer problems. The idea is to do research in the marketplace as well as in IBM's laboratories so that customers can gain access to innovative technologies, researchers can get early marketplace feedback and insight into the applications of new technologies, and the ISUs get solution assets that could be reused to solve other, similar customer problems. By choosing the appropriate customer problem to work on, researchers hope they can generate solutions that are general enough to solve other customer problems not only in the same industry segment but also in other segments.

The FOAK projects are jointly funded, implemented, and administered by IBM Research and the ISUs. Starting in 2000, IBM created a new review board for the program that draws members from the Research Division and IBM's Global Industries Division. Managers have also emphasized the need for a lead person who is responsible for driving the resulting innovations into the marketplace. Leaders in several divisions (e.g., Global Services, Lotus, and Sofware) have championed proposals and sponsored project teams in two of the divisions (Research and Global Industries). These teams work with ISUs and business partners, who bring domain expertise and marketing experience to the effort.

Roughly 25 percent of IBM's research budget is dedicated to the FOAK program. Since the program started in late 1995, more than 80 projects have been funded. Of these, more than half have been successfully completed and their outcomes deployed in the marketplace (either as a product or as part of a solution). About 15 percent of the projects were terminated, either because they could not get a customer commitment or failed to achieve key project milestones. As of April 2000, the program had about nine active projects and was driving considerable patent activity. Many researchers were skeptical in the beginning ("What do you mean, work on real customer problems?"), but most have come to view the program as valuable to their long-term research. By engaging early on with real customers in the marketplace, researchers have been able to gain early insight into the value and application of their technology and into future directions for their research. Successfully deployed systems include an Internet-based electronic ticketing system for Swiss Railway, a set of sophisticated pattern-matching algorithms used to discover molecular relationships in the process of new drug development, a continuous speech recognition system for radiological transcriptions at Massachusetts General Hospital and the Memorial Sloan-Kettering Cancer Institute, and a mail analyzer that allows customers to automatically queue problem reports.

Industry Internships and Sabbaticals

Another means of increasing the linkages between industry end users and academic researchers is industry internships and sabbaticals. Such programs can help ensure that academic researchers develop an understanding of the challenges faced by end-user organizations (and vendors) in designing, developing, deploying, and operating IT systems. Of course, many students who graduate with advanced degrees in IT go to work in industry or government IT settings; in that sense, the university perspective is introduced into industry every time a student is hired. Internships in industry *before* students graduate could add real value, particularly if students select thesis topics that focus on some aspect of a real-world IT problem or social application. Work in the social applications of IT, in particular, would benefit from greater cross-fertilization between industry and academia, because it could provide academic researchers with access to large-scale computing and communications artifacts (i.e., operating physical systems) and the individuals responsible for them.

Similarly, exchange programs in which faculty members work in industry or government for a year and industry or government IT professionals work at universities for a year would help build a cadre of experts who are comfortable in both worlds. Alumni of such exchange programs could go on to play a valuable role in both research centers and interdisciplinary IT research groups. Equally important, both they and the veterans of student internships would form a core of individuals who could apply new research findings by designing and operating improved large-scale systems and social applications.

A number of IT-related internship and exchange programs exist, but most place students and faculty members in vendor organizations. The expansion of such programs to include end-user organizations might be facilitated by federal incentives. Because few end-user organizations (or systems integrators) have large research operations, they do not have a tradition of supporting interns in IT, nor do students view internships with such organizations as furthering their research careers. Seed funding for such a program through a federal agency such as NSF could encourage such internships and, if the program is successful, could convince industry to contribute funding as well. Universities might need to be persuaded that there is value in such programs, which would take students away from their faculty advisors for some period of time and could be viewed as delaying the completion of their studies. At the same time, however, such internships could give students valuable research experience and help them to select dissertation projects (or thesis topics). If successful, such internships and sabbaticals could also serve to demonstrate the value of IT research to end-user organizations, prompting them to support additional university-based research, benefiting both communities.

Industry experts could also be brought into the university system. Many universities tap into the expertise in local industry by hiring industry employees as adjunct faculty. Although adjunct faculty members do not typically participate in research projects, they could introduce new ideas to students and other faculty members alike. The Massachusetts Institute of Technology (MIT) has begun to experiment with another type of program to bring industry expertise into academia. It has appointed a small number of "professors of the practice," who teach and conduct research full- or part-time. These individuals are not expected to have publication records as long as those of their academic counterparts but are instead expected to have a significant record of accomplishments. The program is still new, and MIT has only a small number of such professors, but they add breadth and experience to the school's engineering programs.

Interdisciplinary Research in Academia

If research on the social applications of IT is to advance, then interdisciplinary research will be needed that involves participants and expertise from a wide range of academic disciplines. The work needs to involve not only computer scientists, engineers, and software experts but also business professors and organizational theorists who understand the relationship between IT and the organizational structures within which it is embedded, the human side of complex technical systems, and the market aspects of different social applications. The research teams need to include social scientists who can evaluate the impact of IT on individuals, families, organizations, and society and who understand the human-centric nature of computing. They could include specialists in particular application areas such as health care, manufacturing, finance, and e-commerce.

Researchers in business, economics, and the social sciences have already made numerous advances in understanding IT as it is used in a range of social applications (Boxes 4.5 and 4.6). Several opportunities exist for stepping up the involvement of experts in business, economics, social science, and law in research pertaining to IT. Nontraditional research mechanisms may be needed that will encourage the participation of end-user organizations in research, broaden the outlook of IT researchers, and/or overcome disciplinary boundaries in universities. The management of interdisciplinary research collaborations generates its own set of issues: technologists and social scientists have different vocabularies, methodologies, time perspectives, standards of evidence, and so on. Such differences need to be bridged if collaborations are to be effective.

Interdisciplinary research can be conducted in one of three ways. Individuals can broaden their own expertise: technologists can become increasingly facile with the uses of the technologies and the larger system (including sociotechnical system) contexts within which they are embedded, and experts in sociotechnical system contexts become more facile with technology. Alternatively, experts in the system contexts can collaborate more extensively and effectively with technologists. Or, new professions can arise to mediate between IT and its uses: this occurred in health care when the field of medical informatics emerged to help bridge the gap between IT and medicine (Box 4.7) and, even earlier, in civil engineering when an entire profession (building and landscape architecture) was established to deal with application, societal, and aesthetic

---

BOX 4.5
Examples of Business Research Related to
Information Technology

• *Critical success factors*—Work by Rockhart identified factors critical to the success of information systems in business settings. What information is critical to the success of a business? What questions would you want a database to answer? How do you design information systems to support business objectives?

• *Decision support systems*—Work by Keane and Morton promulgated the idea of using information systems to support corporate decision making at a variety of levels.

• *Information technology and strategic advantage*—Work at the Harvard Business School recognized that information technology (IT) is not just for back-office operations but rather is an element of a firm's competitive advantage. Companies that deploy and employ IT systems more wisely than others can benefit in the marketplace.

• *Computer-supported cooperative work*—This research introduced the idea of using information technology to allow people to work cooperatively within and across organizations, to overcome differences in geography or time.

• *Productivity*— Productivity gains from IT investments have been difficult to measure, but Brynjolfsson's analysis of firm-level data (as opposed to industry-level data) indicates that there may be large payoffs, albeit with time lags. This work attempts to identify the factors that contribute to positive returns from IT investments within firms. What characteristics differentiate firms that do experience increased productivity from those that do not?

• *Software development methodologies*—Research by Cusumano provided guidance on software development methodologies from a management point of view.

• *Process handbook*—This repository of business process knowledge can facilitate further research and help determine best practices for deploying IT. The classification and structure of the database itself is a powerful tool.

SOURCE: Thomas Malone, Sloan School of Management, MIT, in a presentation at the National Academy of Engineering workshop "How Can Academic Research Best Contribute to Network Systems and Communications?" Washington, D.C., October 30, 1998.

---

issues. Each of these approaches has its strengths and weaknesses. The first approach, for example, effectively creates visionaries and leaders in a field but does not enable large-scale collaborations. The second enables a properly balanced team to be assembled but creates problems of coordination and management and makes it difficult to create a shared vision. The third approach can be effective in establishing a long-term capability

BOX 4.6
**Examples of Economics and Other Social Science Research
That Has Contributed to Information Technology Development**

• *Role of regulation*—Economics research by Alfred Kahn, Paul Joskow, Roger Noll, and Kip Viscusi redefined the role of regulations from one of protecting the public interest to one of stepping in when markets do not drive prices to marginal costs. This redefinition spurred deregulation in a number of industries, including communications.

• *Network externalities*—Work by Hal Varian, Paul David, Brian Arthur, Garth Saloner, Michael Katz, Carl Shapiro, and Nicholas Economides showed that the network industries and information industries are characterized by "network externalities," which make the value to a consumer of a particular product or service increase as more people use it. An example is an Internet connection, which is more valuable if more information is available and larger numbers of people are connected. This insight leads to an emphasis on getting products and services into the marketplace quickly, pricing them low at first to spur market growth and then raising prices as more units are sold and their value grows.

• *Internet economics*—Work in this area by Lee McKnight, Joseph Bailey, Hal Varian, and Jeffrey Mackie-Mason has implications for the pricing of Internet-based resources and services, such as concepts for allocating resources based on the willingness of users to pay.

• *Group dynamics and decision making*—Research by Sara Kiesler, Suzanne Iaconno, Wanda Orlikowski, and others (e.g., Siegel et al., 1986) on group dynamics and decision making in small electronic groups informed the design of systems that support group decisions.

• *Diffusion of applications*—Research by M. Lynne Markus (1987) and others on how critical mass predicts the diffusion of networked applications within organizations and informs the deployment decisions for information technology (IT) applications.

• *Distribution of the benefits of IT*—Research by Tora Bikson, Lee Sproull, and others demonstrating that peripheral members of social systems benefit more from use of electronic communication than do central members (e.g., Sproull and Kiesler, 1991) influenced policy decisions about subsidies for access to the Internet.

• *Information sharing*—Research by Paul Attewell, Tora Bikson, Sara Kiesler, Robert Kraut, Lee Sproull, and others demonstrated how personal attributes and organizational characteristics such as incentive systems influence peoples' use of IT for information sharing. Research by Julian Orr (1990) and others demonstrated that service technicians often have more useful technical expertise than do system designers and share their knowledge in a community of practice. This work influenced the design of a community-based troubleshooting database at Xerox Corporation that has resulted in significantly improved service performance (Bell et al., 1997).

SOURCES: Marvin Sirbu, Carnegie Mellon University, presentation at the National Academy of Engineering workshop "How Can Academic Research Best Contribute to Network Systems and Communications," Washington, D.C., October 30, 1998; Lee Sproull, New York University, personal communications dated August 22, 1999, and April 11, 2000.

BOX 4.7
Lessons from Medical Informatics

Insight into the challenges of interdisciplinary research related to information technology (IT) can be drawn from the field of medical informatics, which deals explicitly with linking the field of medicine and IT. A handful of universities and medical schools have established programs in medical informatics that combine training in both medicine and IT.[1] Graduates of these programs can be found in academic medical centers, health-related Internet start-ups, and other organizations. Some work in the IT departments of large health care centers. The number of health care organizations that have achieved a critical mass in this field is small.[2] All of these organizations employ physicians funded by IT payroll dollars who work with mainstream IT to improve its application to the core domain of the organization (medicine), with a heavy emphasis on the academic aspects of the intersection between IT and the user domain and an interest in experimentation, prototyping, and evaluation of impact. Results are published in academic journals and forums.

Several factors have contributed to the success of these programs. The first is that academic medical centers have a tradition and culture of research. The National Library of Medicine (NLM) funds training and research, and this funding continues over several years, leading to a measure of program stability. The programs funded by the NLM reside in the same organization as the IT function does (the university medical center), so there is organizational colocation. It is clear to the organizations that many complex initiatives require a deep knowledge of medicine to be solved correctly. The IT function (in particular, the chief information officer) must be comfortable with the academic component and the complex medical domain discussion that medical informatics brings to the table. Organizational mechanisms have been established to assimilate the research functions, such as new or revised pay grades, project approaches to involving researchers on teams, and tactics to develop budgets.

These factors are present in only one or two dozen out of a total of 5,000 health care organizations. At times, the linkage between medical informatics and the IT organization does not work very well. For instance, medical informatics programs do not solve all instances of IT staff failing to work well with end users. Medical informatics staff members are involved in a minority of a health care organization's projects; however, they are involved in the projects in which the domain (medicine) places the greatest design and operational stresses on implemented systems. One such system is computerized medical records, which are exceptionally complex to design and present numerous work-flow challenges.

---

[1] Examples of these programs can be found at Columbia University, Stanford University, and the University of Utah.

[2] In 2000, no more than two dozen health care organizations had significant medical informatics efforts. These included Partners Healthcare System in Boston, Children's Hospital in Boston, Vanderbilt University, Intermountain Healthcare in Salt Lake City, Columbia Presbyterian Medical Center in New York, and the University of Michigan.

SOURCE: John Glaser, chief information officer, Partners Healthcare System, Boston, Massachusetts, personal communication, July 13, 1999.

in an interdisciplinary area, but these areas can become somewhat separated from their parent disciplines. All three of these approaches combined can make a significant difference.

Interdisciplinary research related to IT is ramping up in universities, albeit slowly. An increasing number of active researchers in the information systems field list schools of management and business administration as their primary affiliation. Other important communities of researchers that are often overlooked are those in departments of communication and schools of education. All of these groups include individuals working on both fundamental and targeted research motivated by social applications of IT. In addition, an increasing number of faculty members with computer science degrees are appearing in other departments across campuses, particularly in information sciences and business. They are involving themselves in application areas such as digital libraries and e-commerce, focusing on both the social and technical aspects and collaborating with economists and legal specialists. A movement in human-centered computing, involving collaboration with disciplines such as sociology and psychology, is flowering in academia, albeit at a slower pace than similar efforts in the United Kingdom and Scandinavia.

A major obstacle to any increase in interdisciplinary work is the strong disciplinary orientation of many universities. Academic research is typically reviewed from the perspective of a particular discipline, similar to the way in which grant proposals are peer reviewed. The reviewers tend to be disciplinary experts and rarely reflect the interdisciplinary nature of the research. Efforts to establish interdisciplinary programs within disciplinary boundaries and to evaluate those programs often meet with criticism because they are viewed through the lens of a single discipline.[20] As a result, faculty members are often discouraged from pursuing interdisciplinary research. This is especially true early in a professional career, when gaining tenure is a major goal and a faculty member feels particularly vulnerable to peer pressure. Unfortunately, early habits often persist well into a career.

Traditional disciplinary work is reinforced by traditional disciplinary culture. Computer science, like any other field, has its own sets of terms, attitudes, norms, and customs with regard to what constitutes research and how to conduct it. Computer scientists have even found it difficult to collaborate with electrical engineers, although in general they collaborate more easily with researchers from engineering and the physical sciences than with those from the social and life sciences. Reasons for the difficulties in collaboration include factors such as project definition, laboratory orientation, availability of physical infrastructure and professional staff, teaching loads, amount of funding for a project, and so on. More subtle obstacles are attitudes about the relative merits of different fields, with each field manifesting its own flavor of chauvinism. These difficult-to-quantify realities complicate the establishment of collaborative relationships and projects.[21]

One solution to the problem has been the establishment of new schools, divisions, or departments (typically drawing on existing resources) within universities to encourage interdisciplinary research and education related to IT and its social, political, and economic contexts. For example, Carnegie Mellon University has long promoted interdisciplinary research by establishing separate departments and programs to pursue them. Its Department of Engineering and Public Policy—and others like it at MIT, Washington University, and elsewhere—have examined issues raised by the intersection of IT and public policy for several decades.[22] Many faculty members have joint appointments in these organizations and traditional academic departments. In recent years, a number of universities have transformed schools of library science into broader institutions that address issues linking IT and social applications (Table 4.1). These schools tend to draw faculty from a number of departments, including computer science, economics, social sciences, law, and business, but they can hire and promote faculty on the basis of their interdisciplinary work. In such an environment, a faculty can be built with backgrounds in a diversity of core disciplines, and the evaluation process can relatively easily be appreciative of contributions that cross disciplinary boundaries, in no small part because faculty who join such units have the appropriate vision and orientation. Many of these schools are as yet untested in terms of their abilities to sustain quality research of the type needed to make progress on social applications. They nevertheless exemplify the kinds of efforts that will be needed to make progress in this area. They also present more new opportunities for educating students in interdisciplinary research areas. By creating institutions with permanently assigned faculty, these schools and departments can develop curricula and teach classes more effectively than is generally possible if faculty are scattered throughout multiple academic departments.

Limited funding is another obstacle to greater interdisciplinary work at universities on the social applications of IT. Although there are many notable examples of university researchers who followed a vision and were able to sell their visions to potential funding sources, the much more common model is to shape the research in the directions favored by existing funding sources. Thus, as the funding goes, so (largely) goes the research agenda. The gross disparity between funding available for research in social science and that in computer science today does not bode well for prospects of new social-science-based activity.

Federal support for university research on the social and economic aspects of IT (one component of the larger research agenda motivated by

TABLE 4.1 Recently Established or Expanded University Programs on the Sociotechnical Aspects of Information Technology

University	School or Department	Research Emphases
Syracuse University	School of Information Studies	Information behavior, information retrieval, information policy, information and change, information management
University of California at Berkeley	School of Information Management and Systems	Information storage and retrieval, human factors, information policy (e.g., economics and intellectual property), management, networked information systems
University of California at Los Angeles	School of Education and Information Studies	Information technology and institutional change, technology and privacy, genre theory, linguistic aspects of computing, Internet culture, information search and retrieval, social effects of information technology, digital libraries, information policy, user-centered design
University of Illinois at Urbana-Champaign	School of Library and Information Science	Community architectures for networked information systems, information retrieval, computer-supported cooperative work, agents and multiagents, organization theory, information technology (e.g., artificial intelligence, distributed systems, groupware, human-computer interaction), information policy and public policy
University of Michigan	School of Information	Community technology, information economy, electronic work, digital libraries, archives and record management, human-computer interaction, information economics, management, and policy, library and information science

social applications) has come largely from NSF. The Computer and Information Science and Engineering (CISE) directorate's program in Computation and Social Systems (CSS; formerly the Information Technology and Organizations program) supports work in two related areas: (1) the integration, sustainable use, and impacts of IT in groups, organizations, communities, and societies and (2) theories and technologies for reasoning, decision making, interaction, and collaboration in groups, organizations, communities, and societies. For many years, this program has been the NSF's main source of support for truly interdisciplinary sociotechnical IT systems research.[23] Its awards have routinely gone to research groups that involve technical specialists from computer science or related science and engineering disciplines, as well as social scientists with deep interests in the technology and its social implications. When groups were made up solely of social scientists, the proposals still had to be reviewed by people with technical expertise.

For the most part, these awards tend to be small, providing support for one or two researchers over the course of 3 years or so (Table 4.2), and the total amount of annual funding has also been small, in the range of a few million dollars. As a result, only a small subset of the issues that need to be addressed is represented in ongoing research projects, and the technological aspects of the program are directed at component technologies (e.g., artificial intelligence and agents) rather than the large-scale social applications. More importantly, the smallness of the grants precludes the ability to bring together many experts from different disciplines (e.g., IT and the social sciences). The CSS program is expected to grow in the near future and fund a variety of work on social applications of IT (Box 4.8), but it is not clear how quickly this will occur or how large the projects will be or whether the program will begin to fund larger teams of researchers.[24]

TABLE 4.2 Recent Awards by the National Science Foundation's Computation and Social System Program

Project Title	Estimated Size of Grant ($)	Approximate Duration (years)
Studies of Decision Making in Complex, Dynamic Environments	75,000	3
Algorithmic Issues in Collaborative Filtering	326,260	4
Coordination: Integrating Organizational Style with Environmental Characteristics	441,170	4
Seeing Is Believing: The Value of Video for Remote Interpersonal Connections	499,400	3
The Design of Reputation Systems	362,300	3
Decision-Making in the Context of Commitments to Team Activity	250,500	3
Design of Time Cognizant Electronic Brokerages	295,440	4

SOURCE: National Science Foundation awards database. Available online at <www.nsf.gov>.

BOX 4.8
Representative Topics for Future Support by the
National Science Foundation's Computation and
Social Systems Program

• *The relationship between information technology (IT) and social transformations*—How can the relationship between IT and social transformation be best conceptualized? What new theories explain how information technologies diffuse and become well integrated into social contexts? How do social contexts influence the design and deployment of IT? What accounts for inequitable distributions of IT across groups and nations? What are the barriers to diffusion, acceptance, and transformation? What are the social and cultural divides that hinder access to, or acceptance of, new information technologies? How can these barriers and divides be overcome? How can human needs be best served?

• *Electronic interactions, relationships, and communities*—What are the communicative practices of electronic groups and communities? What are the sociotechnical foundations and implications of human interaction with intelligent agents? What are the theories that describe electronic interaction and what it means to the people who engage in it on a routine basis—for communicating across boundaries, working or learning at a distance, shopping, etc.? How can information and communications technologies be designed to enhance multiparty communications and the creation of knowledge? How are social relationships, trust, identity, commitment, and communities developed in electronic forums? What are the particular risks and social vulnerabilities that may emerge? How can conflict, crises, fragmentation, and other negative outcomes be managed? What is the relationship between electronic groups or communities and their larger social and cultural contexts? How are coordination, collaboration, interdependence, negotiation, learning, and knowledge creation achieved over distance and time?

• *Social ecology and social institutions*—How is the landscape of America changing (its communities, highways, shopping malls, public marketplaces, firm size and location, architecture, etc.)? What are the transformations of work, households, medical centers, educational establishments, communities, commerce, the military, etc., that matter? What new social and technical practices are emerging in these institutions? Who benefits and who loses through these processes? How do these changes affect family life, work opportunities, teaching and learning strategies and success, access to and quality of health care, and the distribution of wealth and resources for people in different economic strata, job status, geographic locations, etc.? How do these changes affect information and consumer privacy? How are digital or virtual enterprises developed in these contexts, and what do they mean for existing social institutions and the humans that participate in them?

SOURCE: National Science Foundation awards database. Available online at <www.nsf.gov>.

On a larger scale, the NSF has attempted to address the social applications of IT from an institutionwide (cross-directorate) perspective. In 1997, it launched the Knowledge and Distributed Intelligence (KDI) initiative (see Box 4.9), a bold experiment in fostering cross-disciplinary research inspired by social applications of IT that originated within the CISE directorate and the Social, Behavioral, and Economic Sciences (SBE) directorate. Its existence was brief, in part because of programmatic uncertainty both within NSF and externally in the research community. That uncertainty related to the goals and approaches associated with the initiative and the intellectual and practical challenges of pursuing cross-disciplinary research.

BOX 4.9
Knowledge and Distributed Intelligence

[Knowledge and distributed intelligence (KDI)] activities aim to improve our ability to discover, collect, represent, transmit, and apply information, thereby improving the way we conduct research and education in science and engineering. These efforts promise to change how we learn and create, how we work, and how we live. . . .The objective is to create networked systems that can make all kinds of knowledge available to anyone, located anywhere, anytime.

—*National Science Foundation KDI brochure*

The evolution of KDI as a broad theme within the National Science Foundation reflects the integration of multiple streams of research and development drawing on many scientific and engineering disciplines. The components are enormously varied, including, for example, research in computational biology, computer networks and communications, high-performance computing, database management and information retrieval, mathematical modeling and simulation, artificial intelligence, human learning and cognition, science, mathematics and engineering education, geospatial information systems, and science and engineering indicators. These components are combined into programs of varying scope and scale.

The KDI activity aims at a new level of intellectual coalescence. It recognizes the progress made to date in developing and deploying information technology across science and engineering research, and it recognizes that challenges for the future include assuring that such technological support can be used and is useful. It attempts to move beyond mere access to information and to develop methods to intelligently absorb, refine, and analyze information to glean useful knowledge. Organizationally, KDI is a cross-directorate, cross-disciplinary effort with three core components:

• *Knowledge Networking* is intended to advance understanding of the potential of new information technologies for communication, coordination, and collaboration in science, engineering, education, and other applications. The goals of

continued

BOX 4.9 Continued

knowledge networking are (1) to develop an understanding of the fundamental processes through which knowledge is created, communicated, validated, and valued in distributed systems of information, both natural and engineered, and (2) to improve the technical, social, educational, and economic performance of knowledge generation and use, collaborative computation, and remote interaction.

• *Learning and Intelligent Systems* is intended to advance understanding of learning in both natural and artificial systems and of how that learning can be supported, harnessed, and used in creative ways. This component also promotes the use and development of technologies that support enhanced learning for children, workers, and the general public across different disciplines and fields. The activity encompasses both basic research and applied efforts to transfer learning technologies to communities.

• *New Challenges in Computation* involves the development of methods and tools to discover, model, simulate, display, and understand complex systems and complicated phenomena and to manipulate large volumes of distributed data in real time.

In addition to the core components, there are currently six KDI-related initiatives in specific technological or content domains that are evolving in cooperation with other federal agencies and private-sector organizations: (1) universal access, (2) digital libraries initiative, (3) Next Generation Internet, (4) integrated spatial information systems, (5) functional genomics, and (6) digital government. These initiatives expressly address issues of how to design and develop technologies that can be used more effectively and by more people. They reflect experiences with early information technology in a variety of contexts as well as ambitious objectives for progress.

SOURCE: CSTB (1998b).

The NSF's support for work related to social applications of IT will probably expand in coming years as IT is deployed more ubiquitously in public life, as well as in homes and schools. The President's Information Technology Advisory Committee recommended increased federal funding for research on the social and economic impacts of IT (PITAC, 1999). The NSF's Information Technology Research (ITR) initiative calls for research in several areas of IT that could be relevant to the problems identified in this chapter, including human-computer interfaces, information management, and the social and economic implications of IT.[25] Its budget for the initiative was $90 million in FY00, to be used to support a mix of small (about $150,000 per year), medium (about $1 million per year), and large

($2 million to $4 million per year) projects. ITR could serve as a mechanism for supporting larger-scale efforts related to social applications of IT, perhaps even small centers. In addition, CISE expects to allocate $30 million to new information technology centers in FY00 to support fundamental research that spans the field of IT and encompasses scientific applications or addresses areas of social, ethical, and workforce issues (NSF, 2000). The challenge will be to find a suitable set of peers to review the proposals, drawing from the IT, social science, and domain-specific communities.

Interdisciplinary Research in Industry

Industry tends to be less wedded to a disciplinary research structure than universities are, and it has made a modest investment in interdisciplinary research motivated by the social applications of IT. Xerox Corporation, for example, has long kept social science researchers on the staff of its Palo Alto Research Center to help understand how people interact with IT systems in a variety of organizational settings. The work of the social scientists has been credited with improving the usability of Xerox copiers and streamlining internal processes for disseminating the knowledge of field service technicians (Bell et al., 1997). AT&T employs a number of economists to study the economics of the telecommunications industry, and several computer manufacturers, Apple Computer among them, have hired psychologists and cognitive scientists to inform their work on human-computer interfaces. In recent years, a number of Internet-based companies have recognized the need to make their Web sites more usable and have begun to hire employees with degrees in the social sciences and humanities.[26] These efforts tend to focus on issues closely associated with product design and implementation and are diminutive in comparison to research on the purely technical aspects of IT.

As the market for IT-related services continues to grow, a number of traditional vendors of IT products are becoming more deeply entwined in the provision of large-scale IT systems and services. This trend could lead to greater investment in research on the social applications of IT. AT&T Labs, for example, recently announced a plan to fund research in the computer science and business departments of universities participating in the Internet 2 initiative, as a means of developing public key infrastructure for improving security across the Internet. The collaboration will be managed by a board of experts from industry, government, and academia who will invite participation from other players in those domains. In addition, MIT and Microsoft Corporation announced a partnership to develop educational technologies. Microsoft is investing $25 million in the venture over 5 years to pursue a range of projects, from online learning to new models for academic publishing. The projects will be managed by a steering committee consisting of members of Microsoft Research and MIT (Robinson and Guernsey, 1999).

IBM took such efforts a step further by establishing an Institute for Advanced Commerce within its Research Division in January 1998. The institute is a forum for examining fundamental shifts in business and trade in an information economy, with the goal of developing long-term, replicable electronic commerce solutions to meet corporate needs. It explores emerging economic trends and technologies to better understand the technical, business, and social processes that are shaping the electronic marketplace, and it has a business research center that studies the changing nature of work, industry structure, commerce, and technology. The institute began with an initial funding commitment of more than $10 million and is home to more than 50 researchers with expertise in IT, economics, and social science. Its board of directors consists of recognized IT researchers as well as IT executives from end-user industries such as automobile manufacturing and retail trade. Work is under way in areas such as (1) the evolving marketplace, (2) privacy, (3) variable prices and negotiated dealings, (4) managing the end customer, (5) the impact of globalization, (6) high-performance computing for commerce, and (7) system foundations (see Box 4.10 for a listing of recent projects in the institute). As of early 2000, the institute had produced more than a dozen reports on topics such as analyzing clickstream data to understand Web-based merchandising, business-to-business e-commerce, Internet auctions, and pricing in a free-market economy that contains software agents. It also has hosted several conferences on issues such as privacy in a networked world, gathering data on the information economy, and Internet-based negotiation technologies.

Industry efforts to conduct interdisciplinary research on the social applications of IT will undoubtedly be linked to business interests. Indeed, IBM is establishing an internal organization to help move new technologies into the marketplace by engaging customers in research. Of course, a key issue will be the ability of these programs to maintain a long-term outlook while producing more immediate results to suit ongoing business development opportunities. Time must pass before the program's effectiveness can be more rigorously evaluated.

Multidisciplinary Research Centers

The notion of interdisciplinary academic departments is realistic in the sense that similar organizations already exist, in the form of multidisciplinary research centers that involve technologists, social scientists, and end users. These centers range from centralized research facilities

---

BOX 4.10
Examples of Projects Pursued by IBM Corporation's
Institute for Advanced Commerce

The IBM Corporation's Institute for Advanced Commerce has pursued projects in the following areas, among others:

- *Information economies*—the practice of analyzing and simulating the future to understand long-term directions when billions of sellers, buyers, and agents interact in the electronic marketplace;
- *Cyber auctions*—strategies to apply competitive bidding strategies for ordinary online business activity rather than as a special case;
- *Internet EDI*—electronic data interchange over the Internet to link suppliers, retailers, factories, warehouses, and assembly lines into one ring of networked systems;
- *Micropayments*—technologies to support very low cost purchases with low transaction costs and carefully controlled risks;
- *E-checks*—the equivalent of paper checks with the same financial properties as paper checks but with lower cost and greater ease of use; and
- *E-coupons*—the equivalent of paper coupons online, offering new possibilities for selective marketing and aggressive pricing.

SOURCE: IBM Corporation's Institute for Advanced Commerce home page at <http://www.ibm.com/iac/>.

---

that house researchers from many different disciplines under a single roof to virtual centers that enable interaction among researchers at different institutions. Their primary objective is to bring together researchers from the needed disciplines to jointly tackle a related set of problems, creating a critical mass of expertise to drive broad progress. A previous report by the National Academy of Sciences (1987) describes the benefits of the center mode of research as follows:

> Centers contribute to science by enabling researchers to accomplish challenging, longer term projects that they could not undertake at all or as efficiently as individual investigators because of the need for stable support, large facilities or support teams, or simply the need to bring together diverse experiences and expertise. By involving external parties as well as students in their research activities, centers contribute to the more rapid transfer of new knowledge and to the training of professionals with an awareness of potential applications.

Experience to date suggests several factors that are important to the success of such centers: (1) capable and enthusiastic center directors, (2) high-quality investigators, (3) a mix of university and industry researchers, (4) a research agenda approved by all of the main participants, (5) acceptable arrangements to handle intellectual property and protect proprietary information, and (6) stable funding for long enough (perhaps 10 years) to produce real results.

In addition to those factors, multidisciplinary research centers for the social applications of IT might want to consider the following:

- *Focus*—A center might need to focus on a particular application domain or a particular set of generic problems, such as e-commerce, medical informatics, or privacy.
- *Broad range of participants*—To ensure that the centers conduct research motivated by social and economic needs as well as a desire for fundamental advances, they may need to link researchers from universities with industry vendors and experts from user organizations, including both companies and government agencies.
- *Links to testbeds or operational facilities*—Each center would probably need to be linked to, and built on, large testbeds at one or more of the participants' sites so that researchers could have the sustained access to actual or near-operational systems or applications that is required to gain insight into real-world problems. The concern, of course, is that the individuals who manage major IT activities do not want researchers tinkering with their computers and software or taking up too much of their operators' time. One option is to give researchers access to these systems so they can observe but not alter them. Another option is to work with vendors and end-user organizations on new prototype systems and applications. A third option is to work on experimental testbeds that simulate real-world needs and operations.

Universities and industry have established a number of research centers to pursue multidisciplinary research on IT topics. The Information Networking Institute at Carnegie Mellon University, for example, was established in 1989 to examine the technologies, economics, and policies of global communication networks. The staff researchers have backgrounds in computer science, social science, cognitive science, and economics, and the institute has funding from both government and industry sources. The Media Lab at MIT, the Berkeley Wireless Research Center, and the Georgia Center for Advanced Telecommunications Technology (located at the Georgia Institute of Technology) also draw researchers from different academic disciplines and seek support from a number of industrial sponsors as well as from government. The main challenge for such centers—in addition to the challenges of peer review and promotion outlined above—is funding. To support a staff of, say, 30 researchers plus graduate students, a center needs several million dollars a year, which tends to come from industry memberships or from project funding by either government or industry. Sustaining such funding can be a challenging task—especially if funding is sought from organizations (such as end users of IT) without a tradition of funding IT research.

At times, the government has helped establish research centers, either by concentrating research funding at particular universities (as DARPA has done with MIT, Carnegie Mellon, Stanford, and the University of California at Berkeley) or by establishing more formal programs that accept competitive proposals for the establishment or sustenance of a larger research center. The NSF, for example, has established programs to support science and technology centers (STCs) and engineering research centers (ERCs), both of which have been extensively evaluated and provide valuable lessons that can inform the establishment of other types of centers, such as those being considered under the NSF's ITR initiative (described above). The STC program is described below. Information on the ERCs is contained in Box 4.11.

The STC program, initiated in 1989, funds 28 centers that conduct interdisciplinary research in various fields of science (five of the centers conduct research directly applicable to IT).[27] The STCs receive, on average, $2.3 million a year from NSF, plus funds from industry, the universities that host the centers, and other federal agencies.[28] External reviews of the STC program have been favorable and have recommended continuation of the program. An assessment by the Committee on Science, Engineering, and Public Policy (COSEPUP) found that "most of the centers have been conducting outstanding research" and that "the STCs as a whole have done an excellent job of disseminating their results whether they are applied to basic science . . . or more applied fields" (NAS-NAE-IOM, 1996).[29] Others have noted that the center mode of research is necessary to conduct large-scale, complex, interdisciplinary research such as that of an STC, and that the universities hosting STCs are removing traditional barriers between academic disciplines and are combating the biases against interdisciplinary work.

Some concerns have been raised about such centers: primarily the amount of time and energy dedicated to nonresearch missions. The NSF requires the STCs to engage in outreach activities, such as educational programs for grades K-12 in the communities in which they are located. The scale and type of the outreach programs vary from center to center, but their existence is a requirement for consideration for NSF funding (NSF, 1998). The COSEPUP report expressed concern that too much emphasis was being placed on community outreach and K-12 education at

BOX 4.11
The Engineering Research Center Program

The National Science Foundation (NSF) began funding engineering research centers (ERCs) in 1985 to create stronger links between industry and academic engineering programs and improve both the competitiveness of U.S. manufacturing industries and the quality of engineering education by making undergraduate and graduate training more relevant to industry needs. Thirty-four ERCs have been established. Each receives funding from NSF for 5 years, after which the funding can be renewed for another 5 years.[1] Industrial participation is required. Companies that participate in ERCs must do more than contribute money: They must contribute intellectually, as well, to encourage interaction between students and representatives of industry. The ERCs average more than 30 industrial partners apiece.

Both an internal NSF review of the ERC program in 1997 and an external review by the National Academy of Engineering (NAE) in 1989 reported that ERCs contributed significant benefits to the nation, both economically and educationally.[2] The NAE review concluded that the ERCs were responsible for novel research that was fundamentally important, making previously impossible interdisciplinary work feasible and providing experiences for students "that clearly excite them." The NSF assessment reported that the ERCs discover new industry-relevant knowledge at the intersections of the traditional disciplines and transfer that knowledge to industry, while preparing a new generation of engineering leaders capable of leading in industry by engaging successfully in team-based, cross-disciplinary engineering to advance technology.

More than half of the firms involved in the ERCs that responded to an NSF survey reported that participation influenced the firm's research agenda, and two-thirds reported that ERC participation increased the firm's competitiveness. A majority of firms were able to improve products or processes, and 25 percent were able to create new products or processes as a result of ERC research. In addition, firms that employed graduates of the ERCs reported that the employees were "more productive and effective engineers than peers in the same firms." More than 80 percent of ERC graduates' workforce supervisors reported that the graduates were more prepared overall than their peers, contributed more technically, demonstrated a deeper technical understanding, were better at working in interdisciplinary teams, and had a broader technical understanding.

The NAE review questioned several aspects of NSF management of the program. Primarily, it was concerned about the fact that the NSF had chosen to reduce promised funding levels at ERCs to reduce costs per center. The review also reported that the ERC application process was too time consuming and that the selection process had been inconsistent over the years. Concerns over community outreach were not a problem because ERCs are not expected to engage extensively in such activities.

---

[1]The NSF funding averages about $3 million per center, which represents approximately one-third of the total funding for the centers, the balance coming largely from industry.

[2]The NAE report concludes with the following comment: "If the federal government is to assist industry in its fight to remain competitive, this is precisely the kind of program that it should support. If universities are to help build a technology base on which industry can draw, this is precisely the kind of role that they should play. And if industry is to take a hand in shaping policies that influence its long-term well-being, then here is precisely the way to become engaged." See NAE (1989).

SOURCES: National Academy of Engineering (1989), National Science Foundation (1997).

the expense of research and recommended that the outreach continue but be given a lower priority (NAS-NAE-IOM, 1996).[30] Although they may spend considerable time on center activities such as these, the scientists involved report that they and their work benefit from the collegial interactions and exposure to the community and industry.[31] Also noted by COSEPUP was the importance of leadership to the success of an STC. If the center was to be more effective than just a group of individual researchers who happened to share a building and some equipment, its projects needed to be well integrated and effectively managed. Collaboration is an integral part of the center mode of research, but it must be nurtured, because most academic researchers are accustomed to working individually or in small teams.[32] Lack of suitable leadership can undermine the value of a center.

Embedding Information Technology Research in Other Disciplines

As computing and communications have become embedded in many social applications, the role of computing in some disciplines other than computer science and engineering has changed and expanded. Because researchers in other disciplines are faced with designing systems in which IT is an essential element, they need to understand basic IT in its modern form—software applications distributed over a heterogeneous computer and network infrastructure—much better than is typically the case. They need to appreciate both the opportunities and the limitations of IT. An important responsibility will be the conceptualization and analysis of distributed information system requirements and specifications and the acquisition of sophisticated software applications through internal development, outsourcing, or purchase.

Because IT is becoming such a fundamental and pervasive aspect of many fields, it is natural for many departments on a university campus to become involved in research on the application of IT to their respective fields. It is becoming increasingly common for faculty and students in these departments to be facile with IT, and not infrequently the departments hire faculty members with a computer science background or degrees who have experience in the appropriate application areas. This is not a new phenomenon—it has a long history in other core disciplines such as mathematics and economics.[33] Initially, collaboration with outside experts is a sufficient solution, but eventually the subject becomes important enough to deserve in-house expertise.

Accordingly, it can be expected that research related to the applications or implications of IT will be expanded in departments as diverse as engineering (and the subspecialties thereof), business, the social sciences, arts and performance, music, and others. One or more new disciplines may arise out of these opportunities, much as computer science itself arose out of the collaborative efforts of mathematicians, electrical engineers, and physicists. This is a natural process that needs to be encouraged. Most likely some portion of the additional IT research funding being made available under the IT^2 initiative will be devoted to cross-disciplinary research of this kind. Aside from setting up new programs (as outlined above), a number of other initiatives could help to establish interdisciplinary programs or to embed IT issues more firmly within other disciplines. For example,

- Joint degree programs could be established between computer science and engineering and other relevant disciplines, such as the sub-specialties of engineering or business.
- Restrictions on graduate programs in computer science could be relaxed to encourage students with backgrounds in other disciplines to pursue degrees. Conversely, students with undergraduate degrees in computer science and engineering could be recruited into the graduate programs of other disciplines.
- Just as they have added expertise in mathematics and economics to other disciplines, universities could hire faculty members with strong backgrounds in computing for other departments, in part so that they could develop discipline-specific courses and teaching materials in the application of IT. Initially, many of these faculty members would probably have computer science degrees and work experience in a particular application domain; typical combinations might include business and transportation IT, computing embedded in mechanical systems, and so on.
- Minors could be established in computer science and engineering programs and made available to students whose primary interests lie in other relevant disciplines.
- Computing courses could be established for the benefit of a broad cross-section of students again modeled after mathematics and economics. Such courses could provide a breadth of understanding not available from more specialized courses.
- Postdoctoral training programs could be established for social science or computer science Ph.D.s who wish to develop skills in research on IT in context.

In addition to promoting additional research on social applications, the expansion of interdisciplinary programs would help to redress the teaching and disciplinary imbalances that are likely to be created by increased student interest in IT. At the same time, this expansion would provide a badly needed influx of graduates with strong backgrounds in IT combined with domain-specific understanding. Many computer science departments are today experiencing an enrollment surge similar to that of the early 1980s. Given current trends in technology, the wealth of job opportunities, and the excitement surrounding IT, this enrollment surge may be more permanent this time. Unfortunately, such growth often comes at the expense of other engineering disciplines, even though many of those disciplines continue to be vibrant and challenging and offer excellent job opportunities.

EXPANDING THE SCOPE OF INFORMATION TECHNOLOGY RESEARCH

The research programs described in this chapter are initial forays into the social applications of IT. In the process, many different models are being created that will coexist and complement one another. These research efforts will have to be redoubled, always informed by an awareness that multiple, complementary models of research exist. Researchers in traditional IT must broaden their outlook to encompass the social context for the technology, thereby changing what is thought of as the core of IT research.[34] Conversely, researchers in other academic disciplines and end users of IT systems must become more actively engaged in IT research. To achieve the desired balance, new models for funding and conducting research must be explored. Only in this way will IT's potential to serve society be fully tapped.

BIBLIOGRAPHY

Abt Associates, Inc. 1996 *An Evaluation of the NSF Science and Technology Centers (STC) Program,* Vol. I. Abt Associates, Cambridge, Mass.

Association for Computing Machinery (ACM), Special Interest Group on Human-Computer Interaction. 1992. *Curricula for Human-Computer Interaction.* ACM Press. Available online at <http://www.acm.org/sigchi/cdg/cdg2.html>.

Bass, L., P. Clements, and R. Kazman. 1998. *Software Architecture in Practice.* Addison-Wesley, Reading, Mass.

Bell, D.G., D.G. Bobrow, O. Raiman, M.H. Shirley. 1997. "Dynamic Documents and Situated Processes: Building on Local Knowledge in Field Service," pp. 261-276 in *Information and Process Integration in Enterprises: Rethinking Documents.* T. Wakayama, S. Kannapan, C.M. Khoong, S. Navathe, and J. Yates, eds. Kluwer Academic Publishers, Norwell, Mass.

Benjamin, Matthew. 1999. "Clunky Internet Sites Get Social Science Treatment," *Investor's Business Daily,* October 15, p. A6.

Bennis, W., and P. Ward Biederman. 1998. "None of Us Is As Smart As All of Us," *IEEE Computer* 31(3):116-117.

Bernstein, P.A., and E. Newcomer. 1997. *Principles of Transaction Processing.* Morgan Kaufmann, San Francisco.

Bijker, W.E., T.P. Hughes, and T. Pinch, eds. 1987. *The Social Construction of Technological Systems.* MIT Press, Cambridge, Mass.

Brown, John Seely, and Paul Duguid. 2000. *The Social Life of Information.* Harvard Business School Press, Boston.

Cairncross, F. 1997. *The Death of Distance: How the Communications Revolution Will Change Our Lives.* Harvard Business School Press, Boston.

Clement, A. 1994. "Computing at Work: Empowering Action by Low-Level Users," *Communications of the ACM* 37:52-65.

Cohen, W.M., and D.A. Levinthal. 1990. "Absorptive Capacity: A New Perspective on Learning and Innovation," *Administrative Science Quarterly* 35:128-152.

Computer Science and Technology Board, National Research Council. 1989. *Scaling Up: A Research Agenda for Software Engineering.* National Academy Press, Washington, D.C.

Computer Science and Telecommunications Board (CSTB), National Research Council. 1992. *Computing the Future: A Broader Agenda for Computer Science and Engineering.* National Academy Press, Washington, D.C.

Computer Science and Telecommunications Board (CSTB), National Research Council. 1994. *Information Technology in the Service Society: A Twenty-First Century Lever.* National Academy Press, Washington, D.C.

Computer Science and Telecommunications Board (CSTB), National Research Council. 1996. *Computing and Communications in the Extreme.* National Academy Press, Washington, D.C.

Computer Science and Telecommunications Board (CSTB), National Research Council. 1997. *More Than Screen Deep: Toward Every-Citizen Interfaces to the Nation's Information Infrastructure.* National Academy Press, Washington, D.C.

Computer Science and Telecommunications Board (CSTB), National Research Council. 1998a. *Fostering Research on the Economic and Social Impacts of Information Technology: Report of a Workshop.* National Academy Press, Washington, D.C.

Computer Science and Telecommunications Board (CSTB), National Research Council. 1998b. "Advancing the Public Interest Through Knowledge and Distributed Intelligence," Computer Science and Telecommunications Board, Washington, D.C.

Computer Science and Telecommunications Board (CSTB), National Research Council. 1999. *Summary of a Workshop on Information Technology Research for Crisis Management.* National Academy Press, Washington, D.C.

Computer Science and Telecommunications Board (CSTB), National Research Council. 2000. *The Digital Dilemma: Intellectual Property in the Information Age.* National Academy Press, Washington, D.C.

Davenport, T.H. 1993. *Process Innovation: Reengineering Worth Through Information Technology.* Harvard Business School Press, Boston.

Deck, Stewart. 1999. "Human Side Key to Data Warehousing," *Computerworld* (February 15):14.

Diffie, W., and S. Landau. 1997. *Privacy on the Line: The Politics of Wiretapping and Encryption.* MIT Press, Cambridge, Mass.

Gibbs, W.W. 1994. "Software's Chronic Crisis," *Scientific American* (September):86-95.

Grenier, R., and G. Metes. 1996. *Going Virtual: Moving Your Organization into the 21st Century.* Prentice-Hall, Englewood Cliffs, N.J.

Grief, Irene, ed. 1988. *Computer-Supported Cooperative Work: A Book of Readings.* Morgan Kaufman, San Mateo, Calif.

Hutchins, E. 1991. "Organizing Work by Adaptation," *Organization Science* 2:14-39.

Iacono, S., and R. Kling. 1984. "Office Routine: The Automated Pink Collar," *IEEE Spectrum* (June):73-76.

Jones, C. 1996. *Applied Software Measurement.* McGraw-Hill, New York.

Keen, P.G.W., and C. Balance. 1997. *On-Line Profits: A Manager's Guide to Electronic Commerce.* Harvard Business School Press, Boston.

Kleinrock, L. 1974. "Research Areas in Computer Communication," *Computer Communication Review* 25(1):33-35, July.

Kling, R., and W. Scacchi. 1984. "The Web of Computing: Computer Technology as Social Organization," *Advances in Computers* 21:1-90.

Markus, M.L. 1987. "Toward a 'Critical Mass' Theory of Interactive Media: Universal Access, Interdependence, and Diffusion," *Communication Research* 14:491-511.

McKnight, L.W., and J.P. Bailey. 1997a. "Internet Economics: When Constituencies Collide in Cyberspace," *IEEE Internet Computing* 1(6):30-37, December.

McKnight, L.W., and J.P. Bailey. 1997b. *Internet Economics.* MIT Press, Cambridge, Mass.

Messerschmitt, David G. 1999. *Networked Applications: A Guide to the New Computing Infrastructure.* Morgan Kaufmann Publishers, San Francisco.

Mitchell, W.J. 1996. *City of Bits: Space, Place, and the Infobahn.* MIT Press, Cambridge, Mass.

National Academy of Engineering (NAE). 1989. *Assessment of the National Science Foundation's Engineering Research Centers Program.* National Academy Press, Washington, D.C.

National Academy of Public Administration (NAPA). 1995. *National Science Foundation's Science and Technology Centers: Building an Interdisciplinary Research Paradigm.* NAPA, Washington, D.C.

National Academy of Sciences (NAS), Panel on Science and Technology Centers. 1987. *Science and Technology Centers: Principles and Guidelines.* National Academy Press, Washington, D.C.

National Academy of Sciences-National Academy of Engineering-Institute of Medicine (NAS-NAE-IOM), Committee on Science, Engineering, and Public Policy. 1996. *An Assessment of the National Science Foundation's Science and Technology Centers Program.* National Academy Press, Washington, D.C.

National Science Foundation (NSF). 1997. *The Engineering Research Centers (ERC) Program: An Assessment of Benefits and Outcomes.* NSF, Arlington, Va.

National Science Foundation (NSF). 1998. *Science and Technology Centers (STC): Integrative Partnerships.* Program Solicitation NSF 98-13. Available online at <http://www.nsf.gov/od/oia/stc/nsf9813.html>.

National Science Foundation (NSF). 1999a. *Digital Government.* Program Announcement NSF 99-102, Computer and Information Science and Engineering Directorate. Arlington, Va.

National Science Foundation (NSF). 1999b. "National Science Board Approves Five New NSF Science and Technology Centers," Press Release, July 29. Available online at <http://www.nsf.gov/od/lpa/news/press/99/pr9945.htm>.

National Science Foundation (NSF). 2000. *FY2001 Budget Request to Congress.* Available online at <http://www.nsf.gov/home/budget/start.htm>.

O'Leary, D.E. 1998. "Enterprise Knowledge Management," *IEEE Computer* 31(3):54-61.

Orr, J. 1990. "Sharing Knowledge, Celebrating Identity: War Stories and Community Memory in a Service Culture," pp. 169-189 in *Collective Remembering: Memory in Society,* D.S. Middleton and D. Edwards, eds. Sage Publications, Beverly Hills, Calif.

President's Information Technology Advisory Committee (PITAC). 1999. *Information Technology Research: Investing in Our Future.* National Coordination Office for Computing, Information, and Communications, Arlington, Va., February. Available online at <http://www.ccic.gov/ac/report/>.

Resnick, P., and H. Varian, eds. 1997. "Special Section: Recommender Systems," *Communications of the ACM* 40(3):56-58.

Robinson, Sara, and Lisa Guernsey. 1999. "Microsoft and MIT to Develop Technologies Together," *New York Times Cybertimes,* October 5. Available online at <http://www.nytimes.com/library/tech/99/10/biztech/articles/05soft.html>.

Rosenberg, R.S. 1997. *The Social Impact of Computers*, 2nd ed. Academic Press, New York.

Schofield, J. W. 1995. *Computers, Classroom Culture, and Change*. Cambridge University Press, Cambridge, United Kingdom.

Shapiro, C., and H. Varian. 1998. *Information Rules: A Strategic Guide to the Network Economy*. Harvard Business School Press, Cambridge, Mass.

Siegel, J.L., V. Dubrovsky, S. Kiesler, and T. McGuire. 1986. "Group Processes in Computer-Mediated Communication," *Organizational Behavior and Human Decision Processes* 37:157-187.

Sproull, L.S., and S. Kiesler. 1991. *Connections: New Ways of Working in the Networked Organization*. MIT Press, Cambridge, Mass.

Stonebraker, Michael. 1998. "Are We Working on the Right Problems?" *SIGMOD Record* (ACM Special Interest Group on Management of Data) 27(2):496.

Stonebraker, M., P.M. Aoki, R. Devine, W. Litwin, and M. Olson. 1994. "Mariposa: A New Architecture for Distributed Data," pp. 54-67 in *Proceedings of the 10th International Conference on Data Engineering*, IEEE Computer Society Press, New York.

Wald, Matthew L. 2000. "New Systems for Controllers May Ease Air Traffic Woes," *New York Times*, March 23. Available online at <http://www.nytimes.com/library/tech/biztech/articles/23traffic.html>.

Walton, R.E. 1989. *Up and Running: Integrating Technology and the Organization*. Harvard Business School Press, Cambridge, Mass.

Washington Technology. 2000. "Federal Agency IT Expenditures," January 10, p. 6.

Wulf, William. 1999. "A Call for Technological Literacy," *IEEE Computer Applications in Power* 12(2):10.

NOTES

1. The President's Information Technology Advisory Committee (1999) identified nine major transformations that IT will bring to society.

2. Other examples can be found to further demonstrate the introduction of IT into an existing application. One example is remote conferencing, which is intended to reproduce and improve on face-to-face meetings or voice-only teleconferencing as a means for group interaction. In business, enterprise resource planning applications are intended to improve standard business processes such as human resources, finance, and sales, building on a history of more focused multifaceted systems for manufacturing resource planning.

3. This topic was the subject of an earlier CSTB study. See Chapter 4 of CSTB (1994).

4. For example, the acquisition and use of word-processing applications in organizations are affected by status hierarchies. At one point managers bought word-processing systems that were used by the word-processing pool. The users, lower status clerical personnel, had no control over what was used or its conditions of use (Iacono and Kling, 1984). Suggestions for improvements in the application or its conditions of use that were made by users were ignored because the users had low status (Clement, 1994). As the function of word-processing clerical personnel was taken over by white collar workers doing their own word processing, those white-collar workers encountered hidden interdependencies. For example, people could not exchange documents with others who were using incompatible software. Sociologists have been conducting analyses of the socially embedded nature of (apparently) stand-alone systems since the early 1980s (e.g., Kling and Scacchi, 1984). Also see Bijker et al. (1987) for a more general example of the social construction of technological systems.

5. The challenges and opportunities for designing systems that support a larger and

diverse population of users in a larger variety of applications, focusing on issues of usability, are outlined in CSTB (1997).

6. It is fairly easy to understand the capabilities needed by a word processing program or spreadsheet, although as collaborative authoring features have been added, these capabilities have become increasingly sophisticated and complex. A scientific computation has a relatively well-defined form and capability. Even a business application such as transaction support or management of accounts receivables or payroll records are reasonably well defined and understood from the outset. Broader application concepts, epitomized by the expansive term "e-commerce," inherently embrace numerous interactions among systems, organizations, and individuals at multiple levels.

7. As used here, the term "economic" refers to a broad range of purposeful activity, including not only activity associated with various goods- and services-producing industries but also that associated with research, learning, and government.

8. "Knowledge management" is a new term that has the disadvantage of being a management buzzword, with the attendant hype, but if the hype can be set aside, the concept can be leveraged to set ambitious objectives for making better use of information through technology.

9. See Stonebraker (1998) and Stonebraker et al. (1994).

10. For a detailed discussion of the complexities of intellectual property protection in a digital environment, see CSTB (2000).

11. The core role of governments is affected by IT, particularly by the global nature of networks. The concept of sovereignty rests largely on the geographical separation of jurisdictions, which is undermined on a global network. The trend toward more international governance mechanisms to deal with international issues is a natural response to globalization, but the trend is accelerated by global computer networking and the applications it supports. Issues such as privacy, restricted access for children, and taxation demand not only new governance mechanisms but also new technologies to support them.

12. Here again, networking is a driver, building on historical improvements in transportation and telecommunications and resulting shifts in markets, organizational scope and scale, and institutional relationships. Business processes and relationships associated with contemporary IT cannot be appreciated accurately without acknowledging that history.

13. The CSTB developed a powerful illustration of the value of systematic study of a specific application domain. Asked to look at crisis management, the board intrigued a group of computer scientists with no knowledge of that domain by exposing them to the problems of people whose jobs revolve around planning for, and responding to, civilian and military crises (CSTB, 1996). The communication about the problems inherent in crisis management, in turn, led to new computer science research. Some of the problems and solutions were common to those found elsewhere, but even some of those had domain-specific requirements, as evidenced by a project participant's observation that some of crisis management technology was like "digital libraries with deadlines."

14. It must be emphasized that social applications research is about technology as well as social, economic, and political systems. Its goal is to make technological progress more dependent on visionary attention to the uses and needs for that technology and not simply on a near-term, incremental commercial and technical research agenda. As IT is encumbered with few fundamental limits and is mostly what we make of it, the goal is to aim technological advances in directions that offer the most benefit to society. This research is not only about the impact of technology on society, as emphasized by the report of the President's Information Technology Advisory Committee (1999), but also about the impact of society and humanity on the requirements of future technologies, with the aim of maximizing the beneficial impact and minimizing the harmful ones.

15. These figures are from the Office of Management and Budget as cited in *Washington Technology* (2000).

16. The Digital Government program is administered by the Computer and Information Sciences and Engineering (CISE) directorate at NSF but grew out of an effort by the Federal Information Services and Applications Council (FISAC) of the Computing, Information, and Communications Research and Development (CIC R&D) Subcommittee of the National Science and Technology Council. FISAC was created to stimulate and foster the migration of technology from the IT community to government application missions and information services communities and to identify challenges from applications to the IT R&D community. It has participants from across the federal government (including the Department of Health and Human Services, the Department of Defense, the National Aeronautics and Space Administration, the Department of Agriculture, the Department of Transportation, and the Environmental Protection Agency). It (1) promotes the early application of advanced computing, information, and communications technologies and R&D capabilities to critical federal government missions, (2) supports multiagency leadership in efforts that demonstrate, deploy, and implement advanced computer and information technologies that have the potential to be widely applicable to federal agency missions, (3) encourages pilot projects to assess the critical computing, information, and communications technologies (e.g., security technologies) needed by applications, and (4) supports broad administration goals in the international arena that eliminate barriers to applications. It drew inspiration from CSTB (1996).

17. Additional information on requirements for the Digital Government program is available in the program solicitation. See NSF (1999a).

18. For example, the first solicitation, in September 1998, attracted 50 proposals (many of them for planning grants) that involved, among others, the Bureau of the Census, the Bureau of Labor Statistics, the Federal Emergency Management Agency, the Coast Guard, the National Cancer Institute, the Department of Justice, the National Oceanographic and Atmospheric Administration, the U.S. Geological Survey, the Department of Energy, the Department of Housing and Urban Development, the General Services Administration, the Federal Reserve Bank, the National Institute of Standards and Technology, the National Security Agency, the Office of Management and Budget, and the Environmental Protection Agency.

19. Information on IBM's FOAK program was provided by Armando Garcia, IBM Corporation, personal communication dated July 28, 1998, and by Carol Kovak, IBM Corporation, personal communication dated April 20, 2000.

20. As an example of this phenomenon, consider the case of the Computers, Organizations, Policy, and Society (CORPS) group within the Department of Information and Computer Science at the University of California at Irvine. CORPS concerns itself with studies of the organizational, economic, and social aspects of computing and has strengths in human-computer interaction, computer-supported cooperative work, and information retrieval. When the department was reviewed in 1997 as part of a mandatory 5-year external review of its research and graduate programs, the review committee (which consisted primarily of respected computer scientists) recommended that CORPS be removed from the department and placed somewhere else in the university, not because the research was weak (on the contrary, the review committee declared it to be excellent and important), but because the researchers used perspectives informed by the social sciences and therefore could not understand the engineering perspective at the heart of computer science. The department did not take the review committee's advice (on this subject at least), but the case demonstrates the challenges of rewarding interdisciplinary efforts in the framework of highly specialized disciplines.

21. These and other attitudes and perceptions about barriers to cross-disciplinary collaboration were elicited by CSTB Director Marjory Blumenthal through conversations with

MIT faculty members in computer science, electrical engineering, and social sciences, as well as administrators, in 1998.

22. Historically, most civil engineering departments have been, by necessity, sociotechnical systems departments. Similar divisions have been tried at many universities. In the 1960s and 1970s, the Sloan Foundation funded a number of universities to create divisions of this type. Other examples include MIT's Energy Laboratory and Carnegie Mellon University's Robotics Institute, which go back 25 years or more. Historically, these centers flourished for a number of years and then either atrophied or faded as funding shifted to different sociotechnical system areas or the faculty champions retired.

23. The NSF has also supported some work on sociotechnical systems through its Directorate on Social, Behavioral and Economic Sciences (SBE), but most of that work has focused on issues not directly associated with IT. Some researchers at the nexus of computing and the social sciences claim that SBE has not been supportive enough of the centrality of technology in such research, but in recent years, the directorate has cosponsored work (with the CSS program) on research challenges related to the social and economic impacts of IT on intellectual property protection in a digital environment. See CSTB (1998a) and CSTB (2000).

24. A "Dear Colleague" letter posted on the CISE Web site in 1999 noted that increased future funding was anticipated for the CSS program and called for proposals related to traditional CSS interests and the broader issues of social and economic implications of IT. Proposals could request up to $300,000 in funding for 36 months. The CSS expected to make about 10 awards in FY99. See National Science Foundation, Computing and Information Science and Engineering Directorate. Undated. "Dear Colleague" letter from Michael Lesk, division director, Information and Intelligent Systems Division. Available online at <http://www.interact.nsf.gov/cise/html.nsf/html/css_dcl?OpenDocument>.

25. Indeed, the purpose of NSF's ITR program is to "enhance the value of information technology for everyone." The complete list of areas in which NSF is soliciting proposals under the ITR program is as follows: software, IT education and workforce, human-computer interface, information management, advanced computational science, scalable information infrastructure, social and economic implications of IT, and revolutionary computing. Letters of intent for proposals exceeding $500,000 were due in November 1999; those for smaller projects were not due until January 2000. The NSF anticipated making awards under the ITR program in September 2000. See NSF (1999a).

26. Many Web designers do not understand user behavior, including why users often leave sites soon after going to them. In an attempt to understand a user's experience of a Web site, Modem Media uses the technique of role playing, in which employees pretend to be users that fit a certain profile. Modem Media intends to hire psychologists and anthropologists to expand its efforts to understand user behavior. Meanwhile, Sapient announced plans to buy E-Lab because of E-Lab's knowledge of "patterns of behavior that reveal and drive the nature of experience." However, Web site usability expert Jakob Nielsen says social scientists are not the answer, and that companies should focus instead on conducting usability tests with actual customers. See Benjamin (1999).

27. The STC program was initiated in response to President Ronald Reagan's 1987 State of the Union address, which proposed the establishment of federal centers to promote U.S. economic competitiveness. Of the original 25 centers funded from the first two program solicitations, 23 remain; 5 new centers were granted funding in July 1999. See NSF (1999b).

28. Industrial support is not a requirement for the centers, but the STCs average eight industrial partners per center. See National Academy of Public Administration (1995).

29. A bibliometric analysis conducted by Abt Associates, Inc., found that the journal publications of STC researchers were cited 1.69 times as often as the average U.S. academic paper published and that the journals in which STC scientists published had greater influence than the average scientific journal. In addition, papers from STC researchers are cited

two to four times as often in U.S. patents as the average academic research paper. See Abt Associates (1996).

30. In most cases, outreach did not significantly interfere with the conduct of research, but it did in the case of at least one STC. The center was told after one NSF site visit that it did not conduct enough outreach programs, so it began participating in so many outreach activities that after another NSF site visit, the center was told that it did not conduct enough research. In response to the first site-visit report, almost all of the time of the postdoctoral scientists and almost all the resources of the center in the summer months were devoted to K-12 outreach programs.

31. Most of the time is spent by a center's director and administration, and only a small proportion of the time is spent by the actual researchers.

32. The Abt Associates evaluation of the STC program was even more favorable than the COSEPUP report. Abt writes that "individual centers have produced significant research achievements in fundamental knowledge and the development of research tools, and have identified a range of downstream impacts of this work." Abt found the centers to be particularly flexible and effective in responding to scientific opportunities and reported that "industry partners consider their affiliations with the STCs to be immensely beneficial." In addition, the Abt report viewed the K-12 educational programs more favorably than did the COSEPUP report. See Abt Associates (1996).

33. As an analogy, consider the roles of mathematics and economics in other fields. As they became increasingly critical to a number of fields—mathematics to physics and economics to business or agriculture, for example—collaboration as a way of addressing the resulting challenges soon became inadequate. Rather, domain experts felt the need to become sufficiently adept at mathematics or economics to contribute directly in these areas. The situation is similar with IT, which is becoming an integral part of the sociotechnical applications within which it is embedded; that is, the artificial separation of application-specific and information technology expertise is no longer effective. A solid grounding in mathematics is considered essential to the natural sciences and engineering, and a solid grounding in economics is considered essential to business, agriculture, and a number of other fields. Similarly, modern forms of IT should be considered normal and essential parts of the background in a number of other fields. These fields include particularly the education of future engineers in fields as diverse as civil, mechanical, aerospace, electrical, and nuclear engineering, and also the education of future business managers (many of whom specialize in the social sciences and humanities as well as business). A broad cross-section of students in other natural and social science disciplines also need to take at least a foundation course in these technologies, analogous to a first course in economics.

34. This continual expansion of what is considered the core is healthy and needs to be strongly encouraged. Two fields that were once considered applications of computers are computer graphics and database storage systems. After computer science researchers began to make progress on these topics and publish papers and the capabilities became a normal part of many systems, they gradually came to be considered part of the core of the computer science research community. The technologies surrounding e-commerce are in the process of making this transition. Controversy surrounding the publication of the CSTB report *Computing the Future: A Broader Agenda for Computer Science and Engineering* in 1992 suggests that change is not always welcome or even understood. See CSTB (1992).

5

Expanding the Scale and Scope of Information Technology Research

The twenty-first century begins with unprecedented opportunities to use information technology (IT) to meet a growing number of societal needs. The payoff from investments in IT research initiatives launched a half a century ago have become manifest: IT has moved from the laboratory to the office, store, and home and has been incorporated into personal belongings of all types. It is also transforming countless aspects of business, government, and social interaction from education to health care to commerce, and as the potential of IT grows, so, too, do users' expectations for it. More people want IT to do more things, more easily, with more trustworthiness, and with more reach into society. The IT research community has many ideas about the ways in which computer science and engineering can be developed and applied to meet those expectations and new ones that will emerge as further progress is made. Paradoxically, however, it looks as if it will be more difficult to make practical progress. The potential of IT and the challenges that must be overcome to realize that potential are rising in tandem, boosting the level of required investments. Everyone can see the growth of markets for IT goods and services, but the need for more research is less obvious. Nevertheless, the range of emergent issues for IT research to address is increasing, calling for an expanded research agenda.

Many reports call for more funding for IT research. Such pleas come in the face of the misperception that companies that sell large amounts of IT products and services and that generate large revenues or market valuations are capable of the types of research needed. Many reports also point out that academic research, funded largely by the federal government, is essential for expanding the knowledge base.[1]   Building on that work, this report also advocates a large research effort that fosters advances in a number of important, specific areas of IT. At the same time, it goes beyond previous appeals by arguing that the metamorphosis of IT from distinct devices (both hardware and software) into complex, large-scale societal infrastructure calls for a shift in the emphases of IT research, which in turn requires different approaches to the organization and conduct of IT research. Traditional mechanisms for funding and conducting IT research are not necessarily attuned to today's research challenges, so new mechanisms must be developed. Attention to the ways in which research is supported and conducted is more important than ever, given the allure held by industry over the past few years for the talent that historically filled the ranks of graduate students and faculty. Today's reality is that research competes with other activities, and research programs must emphasize compelling and important problems that will attract and retain talented individuals.

This chapter summarizes the study committee's primary recommendations for ensuring the continued well-being of the nation's research base in IT. The premise, based on the arguments put forth in the preceding chapters, is that IT research can no longer focus almost exclusively on the IT components that have been the hallmark of past initiatives but must expand to include commensurate research efforts on the problems of large-scale systems and the social applications that they support. The chapter recommends the continuation of ongoing and substantial funding and support for traditional areas of IT research, but it also calls for new research that emphasizes large-scale systems and social applications. It recommends both meaningful efforts to promote something that has proven difficult to achieve—interdisciplinary research—and diversification in the modes of supporting and conducting such research. If successful, these research efforts could ultimately improve education in large-scale systems and social applications, helping to create a workforce better able to research, develop, and use IT systems.

Implicit in the recommendations is a recognition that the IT research community is stepping into uncharted territory in which many new research challenges are arising and even familiar problems can assume new forms. The recommendations therefore seek to foster experimentation with a variety of approaches to bringing together diverse communities with different sets of expertise and different perspectives on the issues of IT research—characteristics that have contributed to the nation's history of success in IT (CSTB, 1999a). They lay out the desired characteristics of research mechanisms but recognize that multiple approaches may need to be tried, evaluated, and fitted to the particular characteristics of the institutions involved.

The recommendations are organized according to the group of stakeholders, decision makers, and policy makers to which they are directed: those in government, universities, and industry. As the discussion notes, however, these groups will have to interact to ensure that the set of research programs put in place will meet society's growing needs for IT and assure that this and future generations can safely depend on IT systems.

RECOMMENDATIONS FOR GOVERNMENT

The federal government has an important role to play in helping to expand the IT research agenda. Government agencies have long been an important source of funding for the IT research community as well as for the other research communities that may need to become more closely integrated into IT activities. Although federal expenditures for IT research are dwarfed by those of industry, they constitute the overwhelming majority of research funds provided to universities and thus are critical in supporting long-term fundamental research that can benefit a wide range of companies, both established companies and start-ups. Moreover, because federal funding is so pervasive in academia, it can be used as a lever to help direct academic research toward needed areas. In doing so, it can lay the groundwork for more subtle transformations of research and development (R&D) in industry as well. The committee makes four recommendations to help guide this process.

Recommendation 1. **The federal government should continue to boost funding levels for fundamental information technology research, commensurate with the growing range of research challenges.**

The first step in expanding the scope of IT research is to ensure the availability of sufficient funding to address the growing range of research problems that must be tackled. The scope of inquiry for IT-related research is clearly growing (as is the need for more creativity and flexibility in how funds are allocated and spent). The unprecedented growth in the complexity, size, and social engagement of the IT systems now being deployed calls for fundamentally new concepts, abstractions, and methodologies to master and harness IT for the good of the society. Attaining those concepts, abstractions, and methodologies is the goal of fundamental research. Hence, increased funding is needed not only to support continued advances in the capabilities of IT components (e.g., increased processing power, storage capacities, and communications bandwidth) but also to develop solutions to the problems posed by large-scale systems and social applications of IT. The committee views components, systems, and applications as three equally important areas for research, noting that they play roles in IT analogous to the roles of biomedical research, physiology, and medicine in the health sciences. Each area informs work in the others, and fundamental scientific understanding is needed in all three areas to ensure a properly functioning system.

As noted above, the government is the primary vehicle for support of fundamental IT research. Although industry funds a considerable amount of research (some of which is fundamental research) in its own laboratories and in universities, intense competitive pressures and the need to generate positive returns for investors force companies to direct more of their R&D funding to projects with more certain results and more obvious applicability to market needs. The potential social return on investments in research is enormous, but these investments will not be made without the government's lead.

It is not feasible to specify a precise dollar amount by which IT research funding should increase, but the increases recommended by the President's Information Technology Advisory Committee (PITAC) and requested by the Clinton Administration for fiscal years 2000 and 2001 are representative of the magnitude of the annual increases needed for some time to come (PITAC, 1999). Government program managers report that they receive far more high-quality research proposals than they can fund (a situation that is common in other fields, too). How the money is spent is at least as important as the amount. Researchers in the field observed, in testimony to the committee and in other contexts, that the allocation of federal funding shows less vision and more emphasis on process than it did in the middle of the twentieth century. The historic comparison is important, because there is a correlation between the approach to funding management and the yield. Today's circumstances demand a more visionary, less process-bound approach, as will be discussed below, because the needs of large-scale systems and social applications can be met only with innovative, revolutionary work. The Defense Advanced Research Projects Agency (DARPA), in particular, has a history of supporting revolutionary work, and this orientation should be reinforced and encouraged.

Recommendation 2. **The National Science Foundation and the Defense Advanced Research Projects Agency should establish significant programs of fundamental research in large-scale information technology systems.**

Large-scale IT systems pose difficult technical (and nontechnical) problems that are manifested in a variety of ways: delays in designing and deploying new IT systems, failures of operational systems, inability to add new functionality to existing systems, and unexpected behavior. The direct cost of these failures is high.[2] By some estimates, between 70 and 80 percent of all major system development efforts are never finished, seriously overrun their cost and development time objectives, or fail to provide the desired functionality. Hundreds of millions—even billions— of dollars are spent on such failed efforts. The indirect costs of fragile systems are even greater because of the potential for widespread damage from failures of critical IT infrastructures used for controlling the electric power grid, communications systems, or financial transactions.

Problems with large-scale systems are not new, but the steady push to build and use such systems means there is an imperative to address those problems now. System failures are not only the stuff of daily news, they are also the stuff of congressional hearings and inquiries by regulatory agencies. Improved techniques for designing and implementing large-scale systems will require fundamental research to build a stronger scientific base for understanding such systems. A stepped-up research program should include not only case research that examines particular systems also methodology research that seeks common architectures, techniques, and tools that can influence a wide range of large-scale systems. Two elements are key to success: the enabling resources (i.e., funding and the talent it nurtures, infrastructure, access to appropriate artifacts) and the cultivation of a motivated community of researchers.

Although all federal agencies face problems with large-scale systems, DARPA and the National Science Foundation (NSF) are the best positioned to lead research efforts in this area because it needs fundamental science and engineering and because they have the longest history of managing related research and the closest contact with the appropriate research communities. Both DARPA and NSF have a number of programs in place that address elements of the large-scale systems problem, but their programs have not been linked to form the larger thrust that would give this problem area the high profile it deserves. A stepped-up program would help create the critical mass of researchers needed to address large-scale systems issues and help form a research community around this set of problems. Strong federal leadership of the sort that DARPA and—to a lesser, but growing, extent—NSF have demonstrated in the past could bring about a more comprehensive approach.

The development of the fundamental Internet technology provides a model: effective program management led a dispersed group of researchers to work on separate projects toward a shared goal. A dynamic mix of people and institutions participated in different ways and at different times according to their interests and capabilities and the needs of the project or program. Both DARPA and the NSF should experiment with program management to promote such leadership, creative research, and community efforts to tackle today's large-scale systems challenges—which are, of course, similar to some of the early Internet challenges. These agencies will need to ensure the quality of the research while allowing researchers sufficient freedom to pursue fundamental, visionary work.

The research conducted under a broad program on large-scale systems should pursue a diversity of problems and approaches. As described in greater detail in Chapter 3, it should do the following:

- Support both theoretical and experimental work;
- Provide small, medium-size, and large awards to support individual investigator research, small teams of researchers, and larger collaborative efforts;
- Pursue a range of approaches to large-scale systems problems, such as improved software design methodologies, system architecture, reusable code, and biological and economic models;
- Attempt to address the full scope of large-scale systems issues, including scalability, heterogeneity, trustworthiness, flexibility, and predictability;[3] and
- Provide academic researchers some form of access to large-scale systems.

Access to large-scale systems could be provided in any of the several forms: researchers could team with organizations that deploy or operate such infrastructures; they could create separate experimental testbeds that would allow them to develop, demonstrate, and test new techniques without worrying about interfering with operational systems; or existing systems (such as portions of the Internet) could be better instrumented to provide researchers with the kinds of data they need for analysis. Some combination of these approaches will undoubtedly be needed.

Given the broadening circle of agencies interested in and involved with IT research, DARPA and NSF should attempt to involve in this research program other federal agencies that operate large-scale IT systems and that would benefit from advances in their design. In other words, participants should include not only other agencies with a history of funding IT research (such as the Department of Energy, the National Aeronautics and Space Administration, and the National Institutes of Health) but also agencies that have not traditionally funded IT research but have large budgets for developing and procuring IT systems (such as the Internal Revenue Service, the Federal Aviation Administration, and the Social Security Administration). Doing so may help to ensure that researchers have access to research facilities that would allow them to better understand the problems faced in large-scale system design, development, and operation. Agencies such as the Deaprtment of Health and Human Services and the National Institute of Standards and Technology might be able to expand their support for fundamental research and system problems, too.

One approach for engaging a diverse set of agencies in an IT research effort would be to build a vigorous program within NSF to understand the Internet and make it more robust. This effort could build on ongoing activities, such as the Next Generation Internet program, which involves several federal agencies, including DARPA, NSF, NASA, DOE, and NIH (via the National Library of Medicine).[4] The idea would be to use the Internet as the experimental testbed and build an institutional structure that facilitates research on it. In addition to generating useful technical results, this Internet-as-testbed approach could evaluate whether the approaches the committee suggests are effective in practice.

Recommendation 3. **Federal agencies should increase support for interdisciplinary work on social applications of information technology that draws on the expertise of researchers from IT and other disciplines and includes end users of IT systems.**

People use IT. That has long been the case. What is different now and for the future is that, as more people use IT, and in more ways, they are less likely to be expert users or interested in how IT works (as opposed to how well it works); furthermore, they want to make more and better use of IT in ways that affect their lives more intimately and directly than the early systems did in scientific and back-office business applications. These are issues with which the traditional IT research community has little experience. Successful work on the social applications of IT will require new computer science and engineering as well as research that is coupled more extensively and effectively to other perspectives—perspectives from other intellectual disciplines and from the people who use the end results, that is, the goods, services, and systems that are deployed. For some time now, the Computer Science and Telecommunications Board (CSTB), echoed by PITAC and the Clinton Administration, has been calling for research on the societal impacts of IT; the present committee is emphasizing a complementary, technical sort of research that will result in IT with fewer adverse and more positive impacts.

The ongoing Information Technology for the Twenty-First Century (IT²) initiative, in particular the social, economic, and workforce component of the IT Research (ITR) program at the NSF, provides a basis for addressing both the impacts of the systems and new approaches to them; the committee, however, envisions a more substantial effort that interacts with the rest of the IT research effort. The bases for such work are already evident within programs supported by DARPA, NSF, and other agencies. The NSF's Computing and Social Sciences program and Digital Government program are important steps in the right direction, and they could serve as models or launching points for more expansive efforts if they prove successful in the long term, but at present, they are limited in size and scope. Broader programmatic support is needed, along with the attendant nurturing of a research community. The major expansion that is warranted should have the following characteristics, which are discussed below:

- Research support provided through a variety of mechanisms;
- Explicit participation of end users and systems integrators in the research process;
- Participation of federal agencies that are major users of IT systems, not just the traditional funders of IT research;
- Access to operational systems and support for testbeds;
- Management and oversight provided by traditional funders of IT research; and
- Pursuit of fundamental knowledge of the interaction between IT and the context in which it is deployed.

Research support mechanisms should range from small, single-investigator grants to medium-size collaborations among researchers from different disciplines, to activities characteristic of research centers that enable large numbers of researchers to interact for extended periods of time and across multiple projects. Significant progress will not be made on social applications through single-investigator research alone; efforts will be needed across the full range of program scales and scopes. The NSF has recognized this need in its solicitation for the ITR program, which calls for grants of many sizes, including for the establishment of centers to focus on social, economic, and workforce issues. The Computing and Information Science and Engineering (CISE) directorate has limited experience in managing such efforts, but it can build on NSF's experience with science and technology centers, engineering technology centers, and supercomputing centers. It will need to ensure that centers maintain a strong focus on research and produce high-quality results through periodic evaluations.

Another way to organize larger research programs would be to cluster activities around a project rather than around a center per se, as DARPA and, to a lesser extent, NSF have done in the past. Program managers could pick specific problems to work on (e.g., a design project, such as air traffic control, control of the electric grid, or payment for health care services), establish research goals to be pursued, facilitate the relationship between the research community and the system to be studied, and issue a call for proposals to participate—much as has been done with the Digital Libraries Initiative.[5] The life of such projects, unlike that of the center, would not be fixed at 5 or 10 years but would be linked to the natural cycle of study implied by the testbed artifact. Such a project would be more dynamic than a center, allowing a changing mix of researchers and institutions to participate in different phases of the project as their interests and the needs of the project suggest as opposed to binding them together for a set period of time. Program managers at DARPA and NSF would exercise leadership by establishing a common direction for all the researchers, even if they were not all working under the same contract. A process of this kind would draw on a set of programmatic goals to motivate research rather than emphasize a particular form of organizing researchers. It would more closely resemble the organization of early research on the Internet rather than the organization of NSF's Science and Technology Center program.

Research programs motivated by social applications must engage end users and system integrators in order to better understand the problems that people and organizations are confronting with IT systems and the range of potential solutions and to gain the inspiration for research. It may be unrealistic to expect end users and systems integrators to actually conduct research, at least initially, but they should at least participate on advisory boards or otherwise contribute actively to the research process. Over time, they should play a more active role in funding research and perhaps even in conducting it. The differences between them and the research community in culture and approach to the use of time and resources may make it difficult to engage them, but once the benefits are demonstrated, the committee expects that end users and system integrators will become more supportive of such work.

The participation of federal agencies that are major users of IT systems is also important. Government systems are, by definition, large-scale artifacts of public interest; they are, by observation, artifacts that present problems and opportunities that challenge the state of the art.[6] The difficulties experienced in getting these systems right show the limitations of current technology and of the skill base in industry. Government agencies would save money and improve their productivity and service quality if there were a better understanding of ways to reliably and efficiently design, operate, maintain, and upgrade large-scale systems and social applications of IT. Research based on government systems would undoubtedly improve the knowledge base for private-sector systems as well. Designing a program for agencies that lack the funding, personnel, and orientation to research will be more difficult than designing conventional research programs, but again, the Digital Government program, which has forged links between many agencies, should be leveraged, at least to explore what is possible and to initiate experiments. The coordinating structure of Digital Government, the Federal Information Systems Advisory Committee (FISAC), is charged with building bridges between the IT research community and government agencies, and its activities should be encouraged and strengthened. Experimentation will be necessary, because differences among agencies will demand different mechanisms for research linkages. Some activities under FISAC's purview (e.g., those associated with universal access) hold great potential for social applications research.

An important element of efforts to better understand the social applications of IT—which are based on large-scale systems—is researcher access to operational IT systems for purposes of observation, data collection, and analysis. Many research proposals should include plans for gaining such access, which could come through the participation of end-user organizations, as described above. Access to operational systems for testing and demonstrating proposed solutions would also be desirable but may not be feasible because of the need to keep many operational systems running almost continuously and the uncertainties inherent in introducing new elements into an existing system. Accordingly, researchers will need to develop plans for testing new research results in more limited testbed systems, in which outcomes can be evaluated before the solutions are deployed in operational systems.

Although end users and systems integrators must be encouraged to participate in research on social applications, organizations more experienced in managing IT research (such as DARPA and NSF within the federal government) will need to oversee such programs, as is being done in the Digital Government initiative. In the committee's judgment, these organizations are the best qualified to ensure that the research maintains a focus on long-term, fundamental results rather than devolving into applied research and development and targeting the needs of specific end users. Early experience with the Digital Government program demonstrates that what end users perceive as research is often seen by the IT research community as development. A strong focus on fundamental research is necessary if leading IT researchers are expected to participate in the research program and if meaningful, broadly applicable insight is to be gained.

Finally, the work funded in this area should pursue a fundamental knowledge of the interaction between IT and the context in which it is deployed. A central element of the overall program must be to inform IT research as well as understand the social and economic implications of IT applications. One challenge will be to establish effective peer review mechanisms to ensure the quality of the research. Because reviewers will need to be drawn from the range of disciplines encompassed by an individual proposal, programs in specific areas need to be announced beforehand (such as digital libraries) so that appropriate sets of reviewers can be assembled to evaluate groups of related proposals.

Recommendation 4. **The Bureau of the Census should work with the National Science Foundation to develop more effective procedures for classifying data on federal and industry investments in information technology R&D that better account for the dynamic nature of the industry.**

Better data on industry investments in R&D would allow for better-informed policymaking about research support, especially levels of funding. Such data are currently gathered for the NSF by the Census Bureau, but they are highly inconsistent from one year to the next, owing largely to frequent reclassifications of companies into, out of, and among the industry sectors most closely allied with IT.[7] Significant improvements could probably made without increasing the cost of data collection by simply aggregating the data in a more consistent way from one year to the next. Admittedly, the dynamic nature of the IT industry and waves of mergers and acquisitions among major players can make company classification difficult, yet existing procedures for classification appear to give priority to accurate reporting for a given year rather than across years. Moreover, they tend to categorize a firm according to the industry classification that best describes the composition of its domestic payroll rather than its main source of revenues. As firms move production overseas or change the workforce mix through mergers, acquisitions, spin-offs, and outsourcing, their industry classifications can change dramatically, producing equally dramatic changes in reported research.[8] Large, diversified IT companies would appear to be most prone to reclassification because their lines of business span several industry sectors. They also tend to have the largest R&D budgets, so reclassifications can have a large effect on the reported, aggregate statistics.

Efforts are under way to replace the Standard Industrial Classification codes with a set of North American Industrial Classification System codes that will provide better coverage of the information and information technology industries.[9] This change is unlikely to have a significant effect on the quality of industrial R&D data in the IT industries unless improved methods are developed for classifying firms into the new categories and ensuring greater consistency in such classifications over time. Attempts to improve the collection and reporting of IT R&D in industry should include efforts to develop more robust procedures for classification that are less sensitive to small changes in company structure. The goal should be to facilitate the compilation and reporting of more consistent sets of data series describing past, present, and future investments in IT R&D. These issues will become even more important as the nation continues its course toward an information economy and IT becomes more pervasive.

RECOMMENDATIONS FOR UNIVERSITIES

Whereas government and industry will be the primary sources of funding for an expanded IT research agenda, universities will be primary sites for conducting that research. They will also be the primary institutions for educating the next generation of researchers, developers, and users of large-scale systems and social applications. Research is closely tied to education, forming part of the educational process of graduate and some undergraduate students and generating additional knowledge that cannot be conveyed through more conventional course work. Universities have a long tradition of conducting fundamental research on IT that has contributed to innovation in industry. This tradition must be extended to the problems of large-scale systems and social applications. This will not be an easy task in today's environment. Universities are not presently set up to address these important areas, and they will need to change if they are to help make IT better. Many computer science and engineering departments are caught up in Internet-related technologies, which will make it hard to shift attention to issues of large-scale systems and social applications when so much can be done using a traditional component-oriented approach. Nevertheless, there may be pockets of interest that can be motivated in the near term. In the longer term it may become more apparent that many of the most successful Internet-based innovations are those that pursue social applications—which face the challenges of large-scale IT systems. Several steps can be taken to shift attention to large-scale systems and social applications.

Recommendation 5. **Universities should take steps to increase the ability of faculty members and students to participate in interdisciplinary research related to information technology and research on large-scale systems.**

Given the tendency of faculty members and other researchers to orient their research to conventional disciplinary pursuits, they will not be able to pursue interdisciplinary research focused on social applications of IT without additional incentives and the removal—or relaxation—of existing barriers to interdepartmental collaboration. Increases in the amount of research funding available for interdisciplinary work (as recommended above) would be an important means of achieving both objectives, but universities should also implement changes that will enable their faculties to work at the intersection of multiple disciplines and help research staffs to win interdisciplinary research funding. The steps they take will vary from one university to another, reflecting the relative strengths and weakness of different departments and the relationships among them, but several areas are ripe for examination and should be addressed, as noted below. Efforts to enable university research in large-scale systems and the social applications of IT will also enrich educational opportunities in these areas, enhancing the nation's ability to conduct research on IT and make better use of it.

Recommendation 5.1. **Universities should ensure that their hiring, review, and tenure processes are aligned with the interdisciplinary nature of the research that this report recommends.**

As noted in Chapter 4, one barrier to interdisciplinary research in universities is the difficulty of hiring, promoting, and granting tenure to faculty members who pursue interdisciplinary work. Their work is often viewed through a disciplinary lens that does not properly appreciate work that crosses disciplinary boundaries. Within the computer science community, work on applications is seldom seen as a valuable or respectable target of research. Any of a number of mechanisms could be used to address this problem, depending on the university. Some universities have established interdisciplinary schools, divisions, or departments that can hire and promote faculty members who specialize in multiple interdisciplinary areas, but this is not necessarily the only solution. These formalized structures also contribute to the university's educational missions that help train future generations of students and IT-related workers. Other universities have found ways to establish tenure committees and review processes that more accurately assess interdisciplinary research, even if that research takes place within a traditional academic department. Computer science departments or university administrators could also promulgate policies stating that research in interdisciplinary or applications-oriented areas will be given full consideration in the promotion and tenure process.[10] Any one of these approaches—or a combination of them— could be appropriate. The key is to ensure that disciplinary-based review procedures do not disfavor work at the intersection of disciplines while simultaneously ensuring the quality of research. All interdisciplinary research cannot be of high quality, and quality control is especially important in fields with growing budgets.

Recommendation 5.2. **Universities should encourage closer ties between faculty and student researchers and their counterparts in industry, especially in companies with pressing needs to resolve problems of large-scale systems and social applications of information technology.**

The forging of stronger ties between universities and companies engaged in building or operating large-scale systems or social applications of IT could help university researchers to gain (1) greater exposure to, and insight into, the challenges faced by these types of organizations and (2) access to some elements of the research infrastructure. One way to strengthen such ties is to appoint representatives from such companies to departmental review committees and advisory boards. Another mechanism, which should be strongly encouraged, is to promote sabbaticals and internships to facilitate direct interaction between university researchers and industry.

One of the most effective mechanisms for transferring knowledge and expertise is to have people work together. Indeed, a number of leading researchers require all their Ph.D. students without industrial experience to spend one summer or semester in industry to gain what they consider invaluable experience.[11] The problem with pursuing such an approach in the areas of large-scale systems and social applications is that few IT end-user companies have internship programs for IT researchers (most IT companies with research labs have such programs). University administrators should work with such companies to establish trial internship programs that could be expanded if they prove successful. Officials will need to work with funding agencies and foundations to secure funds for such programs, at least until the end-user organizations become convinced of their value and provide additional support themselves. University administrators should also promote interest in these programs among faculty and students. Some faculty members may be hesitant to encourage students to take time away from their university laboratory, especially if their absence would create staffing problems for critical research projects. But if the internship programs are designed to benefit the students, and spending time in industry is important for students, then such issues as time away from professors and staffing research projects should be planned for in advance. If the internships are as successful as this committee envisions, their contribution to the quality and effectiveness of IT research will quickly become apparent.

Recommendation 6. **Senior faculty members should take the lead in pioneering research on large-scale systems and social applications of information technology.**

Universities need to find ways in which junior faculty can work on important, interesting problems. In most cases, junior faculty members are at a disadvantage in pioneering new research in interdisciplinary areas. Concerns about gaining tenure within the existing disciplinary structure of most universities can dissuade them from proposing revolutionary research ideas early in their careers, as can the difficulties inherent in securing federal funding for interdisciplinary research. The recommendations above are intended to alleviate some of these problems, but they do not address them all. The trend away from large grants to university research labs and toward smaller grants to individual investigators has further limited the ability of senior faculty to support innovative work by junior faculty. The expanded research programs outlined above on large-scale IT systems and social applications of IT could address part of this problem by making additional funding available, but the leadership of senior faculty members will also be important in legitimizing new research areas. By building on the vision of research in large-scale systems and social applications that is laid out in this report and communicating that vision to the research community and to funding agencies and universities, senior faculty will help create more opportunities for junior faculty to strike out in these new directions.

RECOMMENDATIONS FOR INDUSTRY

Industry is an important partner in any attempt to expand the scale and scope of IT research. It both funds and conducts IT research, and, ultimately, it must harvest the fruits of research to develop new products, processes, and services for clients. In the eyes of some, industry is already the leader in work on large-scale systems and social applications because it is intimately involved in developing systems to support innovative applications in commerce, publishing, health care, education, and many other fields. Yet, industry's development activities may have exceeded its research capacity, contributing to the deployment of systems that are not well understood. As noted in Chapter 2, most industry research is concentrated in the vendor community—the companies that produce IT components (e.g., hardware, software, and devices). These companies must continue to invest in research that enables continued progress in IT, but they and other organizations that use IT need to become more involved in research that addresses large-scale systems and social applications.

Recommendation 7. **Organizations that are significant end users of information technology systems should actively seek opportunities to engage in IT research.**

As IT becomes increasingly intertwined in the operations of end-user organizations in the public and private sectors, there is an increased need to bring such organizations into the research process. These organizations can contribute to the IT research base through any of a variety of mechanisms, some of which were outlined above: by funding research in other organizations (such as universities), by conducting research themselves (although most end users currently lack this capability), by forming industry consortia, or by providing input into ongoing research initiatives to ensure that the right problems are being addressed and that the solutions are viable. Participation in the IT research process will make them better-informed consumers of IT goods and services and will help guide IT research into areas that are well matched to particular end-user needs and problems. Incentives for such organizations to invest in IT research are growing as they become increasingly dependent on IT systems to carry out their missions, yet most such organizations lack the resources and expertise needed to manage IT research programs conducted either internally or externally.

The committee recognizes the difficulty of engaging end-user organizations in a productive way but believes that greater collaboration between them and IT researchers is critical to ensuring that IT evolves in a way that will meet real-world needs and address the problems faced by organizations reliant on such systems. The federally sponsored programs recommended above are intended to help bridge the gap and introduce end users to the processes of IT research, but these programs should not be the only mechanisms through which end users engage IT researchers. End users should consider other activities, such as supporting university research that is applicable to their needs, serving on the advisory boards of IT research groups in universities and industry, supporting internships for students in IT-related academic programs, and forming external research groups that monitor work in the IT research community and serve as liaisons between companies and IT researchers.

This process needs to be viewed as a long-term, evolutionary one that can grow into more active participation in research over time. Eventually, end-user organizations may fund research or engage in research programs with vendors and academic research groups. Before this can happen, end users need to become more familiar with the IT research community. Although the incentives for such activities may not be immediately obvious, the committee believes that such engagement will ultimately prove beneficial to end-user organizations in terms of an improved ability to make IT systems perform the needed functions on time, within budget, and with high reliability.

Recommendation 8. **Information technology companies with established R&D organizations should develop mechanisms for engaging end users more actively in the research process.**

Vendors need to be involved in any effort to expand the scale and scope of IT research. They have an established tradition of conducting problem-oriented research and have a better understanding of customer needs than do most university researchers or government program managers. For the foreseeable future, vendors will remain the main funders of IT-related R&D. In recent years, industry research has become more applied as companies attempt to link research efforts to more clearly defined areas of corporate interest. Work on large-scale systems and social applications may give them an opportunity to increase the amount of fundamental research conducted while maintaining—or even increasing—the applicability of their research to user needs. The better their understanding of the fundamentals of large-scale IT systems and social applications, the better they should be able to develop systems and applications for their clients.

IT companies should explore a range of options for pursuing more interdisciplinary and systems-related research while continuing their research on IT components. Several mechanisms could be used. Companies could establish programs similar to IBM Corporation's First-of-a Kind program to link their researchers more closely to cutting-edge end users with interesting problems that call for research. Doing so will not only align research more closely with customer needs, making it more valuable in the long term, but will also create better-educated customers who can interact more effectively with researchers. Or they could fund joint research with end users in universities or industry, as Microsoft Corporation is doing in its educational venture with the Massachusetts Institute of Technology (MIT).[12] Another approach is to increase company contacts with, and support for, university researchers by allocating more resources for students and faculty to spend time in industrial facilities and for industrial researchers to visit university laboratories. Money is a significant obstacle to such interactions, as is the argument that staff members have more compelling things to do. Research managers and corporate executives must also provide leadership to ensure that these relationships are established and to maintain a commitment to making them work.

CONCLUSION

Expanding IT research in scale and scope will be essential to ensuring that society captures the full benefits of the investments it has already made in IT. Continued progress is needed in the areas of research that enabled the IT revolution unfolding today and that are the foundation for the nation's transition to an information economy. Additional work on large-scale systems and the social applications of IT will allow society to transform a range of interactions in all walks of life. The recommendations in this report emphasize putting in place the processes that will expand the research agenda and bring the needed range of expertise to bear on problems that have plagued large-scale systems and social applications. They reflect the uncertainties surrounding the course that future IT development and deployment will take, as well as the differences in the abilities of the various stakeholders to participate productively in the process. These initial, if tentative, steps need to be taken so that IT can better serve society's growing range of needs as it enters the twenty-first century.

BIBLIOGRAPHY

Committee for Economic Development (CED). 1998. *America's Basic Research: Prosperity Through Discovery*. Committee for Economic Development, New York.

Computer Science and Technology Board (CSTB), National Research Council. 1989. *Scaling Up: A Research Agenda for Software Engineering*. National Academy Press, Washington, D.C.

Computer Science and Telecommunications Board (CSTB), National Research Council. 1992. *Computing the Future: A Broader Agenda for Computer Science and Engineering*. National Academy Press, Washington, D.C.

Computer Science and Telecommunications Board (CSTB), National Research Council. 1995. *Evolving the High-Performance Computing and Communications Initiative to Support the Nation's Information Infrastructure*. National Academy Press, Washington, D.C.

Computer Science and Telecommunications Board (CSTB), National Research Council. 1996a. *Continued Review of the Tax Systems Modernization of the Internal Revenue Service. Final Report*. National Academy Press, Washington, D.C.

Computer Science and Telecommunications Board (CSTB), National Research Council. 1996b. *Computing and Communications in the Extreme: Research for Crisis Management and Other Applications*. National Academy Press, Washington, D.C.

Computer Science and Telecommunications Board (CSTB), National Research Council. 1999a. *Funding a Revolution: Government Support for Computing Research*. National Academy Press, Washington, D.C.

Computer Science and Telecommunications Board (CSTB), National Research Council. 1999b. *Trust in Cyberspace*. National Academy Press, Washington, D.C.

Council on Competitiveness. 1996. *Endless Frontier, Limited Resources: U.S. R&D Policy for Competitiveness*. Council on Competitiveness, Washington, D.C., April.

President's Information Technology Advisory Committee (PITAC). 1999. *Information Technology Research: Investing in Our Future*. National Coordination Office for Computing, Information, and Communications, Arlington, Va., February. Available online at <http://www.ccic.gov/ac/report/>.

NOTES

1. See, for example CSTB (1992, 1995, 1999a), Council on Competitiveness (1996), and CED (1998).

2. Several of the more high-profile failures have resulted in hundreds of millions of dollars being spent over several years. For instance, the Federal Aviation Administration has spent $42 billion to modernize the air traffic control system over the past two decades, and the system has still not been completed (see Chapter 3).

3. See Chapter 3 for a more in-depth discussion of these topics.

4. The Next Generation Internet program encompasses three related efforts: research on, and development of, new networking technologies; development of revolutionary applications that take advantage of enhanced networking capabilities; and deployment of several testbed networks across which new technologies can be deployed and revolutionary applications can be run. Additional information is available online at <www.ngi.gov>.

5. The Digital Libraries Initiative is a multiagency initiative that, in its second phase, will pursue research related to the development of the next generation of digital libraries, both to advance the use and usability of globally distributed, networked information resources and to encourage existing and new communities to focus on innovative applications areas. The initiative attempts to stimulate the partnering arrangements needed to create next-generation operational systems in areas such as education, engineering and design, Earth and space sciences, biosciences, geography, economics, and the arts and humanities. Its sponsors include the NSF, DARPA, the National Library of Medicine, the Library of Congress, the National Endowment for the Humanities, the National Aeronautics and Space Administration, and the Federal Bureau of Investigation. The research centers on topics such as human-centered computing, content, and systems, as well as on testbeds and applications. Support is provided for both individual investigator grants and multidisciplinary research groups. Additional information about the program is available online at <www.dli2.nsf.gov>.

6. It is also true that federal agencies have had many successes in creating new computer systems, successes that do not get as much publicity as the problems. But these successes are more a testimonial to the skill and perseverance of federal IT managers than a reason to praise the available knowledge base.

7. These sectors include those defined by the following Standard Industrial Classification (SIC) codes: 357, office, computing, and accounting machines; 366, communications equipment; 367, electronic components (including semiconductor devices); 737, computer and data processing services; and 48, communications (e.g., telephone and other communications services).

8. Linda Cohen, a member of the study committee, and Jerry Sheehan, a member of the CSTB staff, are examining this issue in greater detail. They will produce a summary paper on their findings late in the year 2000.

9. On April 9, 1997, the North American Industry Classification System (NAICS) became the new standard code system to describe business establishments and industries, replacing the Standard Industrial Classification (SIC) codes. This new system will be used by the U.S., Mexican, and Canadian governments to collect and distribute statistical information.

10. Recommendation 5.1 echoes a recommendation from an earlier CSTB report that also called for an expanded research agenda for computer science. See CSTB (1992).

11. David Patterson, University of California at Berkeley, personal communication, April 6, 2000.

12. As noted in Chapter 4, Microsoft announced a partnership with MIT in 1999 to pursue educational technologies. Microsoft is investing $25 million in the effort, and projects will be managed by a steering committee consisting of equal numbers of members from Microsoft Research and MIT.

Appendixes

Appendix A

Two Research Topics Involving Social Applications

To illustrate the kinds of research it envisions on the social applications of information technology (IT), the committee looks briefly at two research topics. The first, deconstructing wireless, is the subject of an ongoing collaborative effort to analyze the wireless communications industry. The second, network security, is well known and is being pursued by researchers around the world. It is touched on here to demonstrate its interdisciplinary aspects.

DECONSTRUCTING WIRELESS

One actual research project on the social applications of IT is "deconstructing wireless," which is being conducted by researchers at the University of California at Berkeley, Princeton University, and the Swiss Federal Institute of Technology at Lausanne.[1] This collaboration of engineers and economists is taking a fresh look at the wireless communication industry. The researchers define deconstruction as a research paradigm that takes a top-down, interdisciplinary view of a large-scale global system, in this case wireless networking. Deconstruction is necessitated by the confluence of technology and economic, business, and policy considerations in such systems.

A system and market like wireless networking is heavily influenced by the rapid pace of technological advance as well as by policy (e.g., telecommunications regulation, privacy concerns, and universal service requirements), law (e.g., intellectual property protection and competitive constraints), economics (e.g., investments, network externalities, lock-in), business considerations (e.g., complementors and competitors, standardization), and the needs and wishes of users (both individuals and organizations). In the past, researchers have addressed these influences one by one. This project recognizes that there are strong relationships between these influences that can be exploited to create new opportunities. Although wireless technology can be shaped in many ways, the most effective design for the technology needs to take into account economics, industry, and policy issues.

The methodology of deconstruction differs from standard systems analysis (see Figure A.1). The first step is to decide which specific business and societal goals will be the central focus. For their work on wireless networking, the researchers chose two:

• Achieving a level of flexibility in the system architecture such that new terminal software can be quickly deployed and the barriers to entry for new services and business models can be lowered and
• Maximizing the effectiveness of competition in the industry by removing technological and other impediments to competitive offerings and market entry.

Once these goals had been set, the next step was to postulate an architecture for the system that seemed best able to achieve the goals. Postulating an architecture is part of a "divide and conquer" strategy to

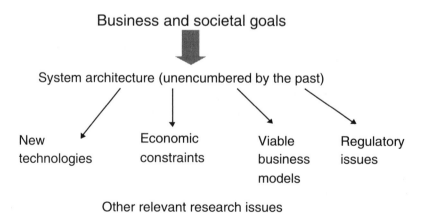

FIGURE A.1 Deconstruction starts with identifying business and societal goals and then postulating a system architecture.

break the research challenges into manageable pieces. Of course, the elements of the overall architecture are critically important in their own right because they not only influence much of the research that will follow but also ultimately determine the model that will be used for industry structure and competition.

Deconstruction deliberately ignores issues like legacy systems and the practical need for incremental advances in the technology. It does so in order to create a mental experiment that, because it takes nothing for granted, can yield real breakthroughs in insight. If important opportunities are identified in this way, they can later influence real-world systems, or perhaps even result in entirely new networks (just as the Internet once did).

Finally, many individual research issues must be addressed to realize the business and societal goals in the context of the postulated architecture. In this project, the issues have been technological, economic, and policy-related. Two of the collaborators (Katz and Farrell) are economists with experience in telecommunications regulation at the Federal Communications Commission and can address economic and policy issues. The other three researchers are technologists who can address technical issues.

One way to better understand the deconstruction process used in the wireless networking project is to examine the classification of interdisciplinary work shown in Figure A.2. It divides disciplines into three categories: (1) those that emphasize the foundations of knowledge (e.g., the

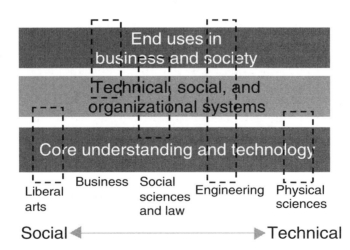

FIGURE A.2 A classification of interdisciplinary work into three categories of learning.

humanities, physical and biological sciences, communications devices, and electronics); (2) those that emphasize *systems*, which are assemblages of elements that perform higher-level functions (e.g., chemistry and cosmology in the physical sciences, physiology and ecology in the biological sciences, sociology, economics, and law in the social sciences, and power, computing, and communications in engineering); and (3) those that interact directly with people, organizations, and society (e.g., business, music, and the arts). Of course, some disciplines incorporate work that would fall into two or three of these categories, examples being engineering and the health sciences.

Deconstruction focuses on the systems level. It recognizes that many real-world systems, like wireless networks, are actually mixes of different types of systems, especially technical and social, and it brings together perspectives from different disciplines to address common challenges. The deconstruction of wireless networks that is being performed must have, at a minimum, contributions from engineering (communications and computing), social sciences (economics and law), and business.

The confluence and interdependence of technical and nontechnical factors become evident in this research. There are many new technologies (known or unknown but motivated by this application) that could be applied to wireless networks. With existing or new technologies, the architecture of the network itself and the structure of the industries that support it could be shaped in many ways. The question becomes, What way will come closest to achieving the business and societal goals set forth at the beginning? How can investment in new networking concepts be stimulated, and how can users be induced to actually adopt the new technologies? Will new networking concepts (better ideas) automatically be adopted by a free marketplace, or is regulatory intervention required? These questions can only be answered satisfactorily by considering a host of economic and policy questions. In turn, the forces at play in the marketplace and in the regulatory arena directly affect how the technology is molded and positioned.

A simple example will serve to illustrate this last point. Mobile code is a promising technology for dynamically downloading software to processors internal to the network and to terminals. Such processing has been proposed, for example, for converting between different data representations or for accommodating parts of a network with widely different capabilities (like wireless access and fiber backbone). This should contribute to competition by allowing new application functionality to be transparently deployed long after the infrastructure supporting it is provisioned. However, it raises a host of questions: How is that software licensed and paid for? Who provides the necessary processing cycles, and how are they paid for? How is the allocation of these processing resources determined, since they are shared over multiple applications and users, coordinated in a way that achieves end-to-end objectives? In the presence of virulent competition, they are likely owed by different economic entities, which raises questions that go beyond coordination to include pricing and settlements of revenues. These questions have stimulated new research on the coordination of multiple resource allocations using e-commerce mechanisms (such as some sort of auction). This suggests that existing e-commerce mechanisms such as credit card clearinghouses, might be employed. Because the revenues for each usage are likely to be small, however, the technology has to be conceptualized to result in very small transactions costs, which affects both the technology design and the viable economic mechanisms it implements. The best combination of effectiveness and cost will be obtained by considering mechanism and technology design as a whole.

NETWORK SECURITY

Large public networks such as the Internet and the public switched telephone network represent a formidable management challenge. Not only are they large and complex systems, but they display the characteristics of sociotechnical systems. They must meet the needs of their subscribers, and they involve many people in their operation and maintenance. Their ownership is fragmented, so that operation and maintenance must be effected across different service providers who often simultaneously complement one another (they provide end-to-end service) and compete with one another (for customers). Hands-off business relationships must be maintained in negotiating arrangements for interconnection, for determining pricing to customers, and for settlement of revenues.

Generally three levels of management are recognized for such networks. Network management encompasses provisioning the network's facilities and operating them, including detection of and recovery from faults. Service management enables the opportunistic establishment of end-to-end services in response to customer requests. Business management ensures that customers are monitored and billed for services and that the resulting revenue is passed back to constituent service providers.

It can be presumed that such a network is under continual assault from many directions, from hackers and even terrorist organizations. These assaults may be directed at users of the network or at the network itself. The perpetrators may have monetary gain, terrorist disruption, or simple vandalism in mind. Most existing approaches to security focus on the users and uses directly, attempting to make them secure individually under the assumption that the network environment itself is not secure.

In addition, the network operator will take measures to protect the network itself.

Efforts to monitor the Internet in an attempt to detect and foil criminal or terrorist attempts will involve the network infrastructure taking a much greater responsibility than heretofore for the security of users, on a massive scale, and suggests an important, supplementary role for the network and service management functions. While it appears to be a promising direction for research into what is undoubtedly a serious problem, many approaches could be taken. Thus, it would be interesting to mount an effort on greatly expanded security measures in networks, with the goal of identifying approaches that are on the one hand affordable and, on the other, effective at identifying and foiling attacks and protecting sensitive data and bringing the perpetrators to justice.

To a large extent, security is a technical challenge, as the questions raised have significant technical components. How can malicious behavior be distinguished from normal innocuous network usage (the answer may involve a kind of pattern matching at both micro and macro levels)? How can security mechanisms be made scalable and affordable? Once such behavior is identified, how can it be verified with sufficient reliability to allow corrective action, and what sorts of action might be mounted? How can technical measures be put in place that will allow the perpetrators to be identified and their behavior proven to the satisfaction of a court? Which aspects can be automated, and which necessarily involve human intervention and judgment?

Taken as a whole, the network, its legitimate users, its operators, and the malicious agents constitute a sociotechnical system. That is, many issues of a nontechnical or only partly technical nature arise and must be considered before a reasonable conclusion can be reached. How can legitimate users' rights to privacy be preserved, and what are those rights? What is the likely nature of attacks that may be mounted, and for what purpose are they mounted? What characteristics of such attacks may allow them to be identified? What are the range of potential security breaches of the network and its users, and what would be their impact? Considering these impacts, how much can be spent on countermeasures, and how can the costs and risks to a business be analyzed?

The proposed approaches would have to deal with some practical realities. Network operators are businesses that must have revenue to compensate for costs. The willingness of users to pay for measures to counter somewhat speculative or unknown risks must be assessed. There must be some viable economic model to determine who pays for and who benefits from these measures. That such networks often have multiple ownership, which means fragmented operational responsibility, must be taken into account.

Experts and researchers in several disciplines could contribute to this research, in addition to computer scientists on the technical aspects. Risk analysis and cost/benefit analysis would fall to economists, who would set the parameters on the acceptable costs and cost recovery mechanisms. The organizational structures that would most effectively realize the security functions—including, for example, human interventions—could be studied by business. Motivations and scenarios for attack could be provided by political scientists, allowing the range of possibilities to be narrowed. In the case of individual vandals and hackers, psychological profiles and likely behavior patterns would be very useful input.

NOTE

1. The researchers are David Messerschmitt, Michael Katz, and Joseph Farrell from the University of California at Berkeley, Sergio Verdu from Princeton, and Jean-Pierre Hubaux from the Swiss Federal Institute of Technology.

Appendix B

Biographies of Committee Members

SAMUEL H. FULLER, *Co-chair*, is vice president for research and development at Analog Devices Corporation. He was formerly vice president for technical strategy and chief scientist at Digital Equipment Corporation, where he led the creation of the research laboratories for Digital focused on distributed computing, high-performance computing, Internetworking, and human-computer interfaces. He also initiated work that led to Digital's Ethernet, workstations, Unix, and Internet products. Before joining Digital in 1978, Dr. Fuller was an associate professor of computer science and electrical engineering at Carnegie Mellon University, where he was involved in the performance evaluation and design of several influential experimental multiprocessor computer systems. Dr. Fuller received his B.S. from the University of Michigan in 1968 and his M.S. (1969) and Ph.D. (1972) from Stanford University. He is a member of the National Academy of Engineering, the Institute of Electrical and Electronics Engineers, and the Association for Computing Machinery. Dr. Fuller is a member of the National Research Council's Commission on Physical Sciences, Mathematics, and Applications and was a founding member of the Computer Science and Telecommunications Board (1986-1992). He served on the steering committee for CSTB's Competitiveness Colloquium on Systems Integration (1989-1991) and on the committee that wrote the CSTB report *Cryptography's Role in Securing the Information Society*.

DAVID G. MESSERSCHMITT, *Co-chair,* is the Roger A. Strauch Professor of Electrical Engineering and Computer Sciences at the University of California at Berkeley and from 1993 to 1996 was department chair. Before 1977 Dr. Messerschmitt was at AT&T Bell Laboratories in Holmdel, New Jersey. His current research interests include issues overlapping signal processing (especially video and graphics coding) and transport in broadband networks with wireless access, network services and protocols for multimedia, wireless multimedia computing, and the economics of networks. Dr. Messerschmitt has served as a consultant to a number of companies and is a cofounder and director of TCSI Inc. He is a fellow of the Institute of Electrical and Electronics Engineers, Inc., a member of the National Academy of Engineering, a member of the advisory committee for the National Science Foundation's Computer and Information Science and Engineering directorate. From 1993 to 1998, Dr. Messerschmitt was a member of the Computer Science and Telecommunications Board of the National Research Council. He won the 1999 Alexander Graham Bell medal for exceptional contributions to the advancement of communication sciences and engineering. He received a B.S. degree from the University of Colorado and an M.S. and Ph.D. from the University of Michigan.

PAUL BARAN is generally regarded as the inventor of packet switching, based on his work at RAND in the 1960s. He is a founder of several Silicon Valley companies, including Com21, Inc., a provider of broadband cable modem technology for high-speed modem and data services, where he is chairman of the board. He also serves on the advisory board of Geocast, a digital data broadcasting company. Mr. Baran received the B.S. degree in electrical engineering from Drexel University in 1949 and the M.S. degree in engineering from UCLA in 1959. He was awarded an honorary Doctor of Science in Engineering degree by Drexel University in 1997. He is a member of the National Academy of Engineering, a life fellow of the Institute of Electrical and Electronics Engineers, Inc. (IEEE), an International Marconi Fellow, an American Association for the Advancement of Science fellow, and a trustee of the IEEE History Center.

LINDA COHEN is professor of economics and chair of the Department of Economics at the University of California at Irvine. Her research interests concern political economy, government regulation, government policy for research and development, positive political theory, and law. Dr. Cohen previously worked as a research associate at the Brookings Institution in Washington, D.C. She was a member of the Department of Energy Program Review Committee on Airborne Nuclear Waste Management, a member of the advisory panel in support of the congressional Office of Technology Assessment's study of magnetic fusion research and development, and a member of the Panel on the Study of Human Factors Research Needs in Nuclear Regulatory Research for the National Research Council. She is currently a member of the Public Interest Energy Research Advisory Panel for the California Energy Commission. Dr. Cohen is coauthor of *The Technology Pork Barrel* (Brookings Institution, 1991) and is a fellow of the California Council for Science and Technology.

JOHN A. COPELAND is a professor in the school of electrical and computer engineering at the Georgia Institute of Technology. He holds the John H. Weitnauer Chair and is currently director of the Communications Systems Center. He was director of the Georgia Center for Advanced Telecommunications Technology from June 1993 to November 1996. Before joining Georgia Tech in March 1993, Dr. Copeland was vice president of technology at Hayes Microcomputer Products (1985-1993), vice president of engineering technology at Sangamo Weston, Inc. (1982-1985), and a researcher at Bell Labs (1965-1982). He began his career at Bell Labs conducting research on semiconductor microwave and millimeter-wave devices. Later, he supervised a group that developed magnetic bubble computer memories. In 1974, he led a team that designed CMOS integrated circuits, including Bell Labs' first microprocessor, the BELLMAC-8. His last contributions at Bell Labs were in the area of lightwave communications and optical logic. At Sangamo Weston he was responsible for R&D groups at 10 divisions. At Hayes he was responsible for the development of modems with data compression and error control and for Hayes' representation on CCITT and ANSI standards committees. Dr. Copeland received his B.S., M.S., and Ph.D. degrees in physics from the Georgia Institute of Technology. He has been awarded 37 patents and has published over 50 technical articles. In 1970 he was awarded IEEE's Morris N. Liebmann Award for his work on gallium arsenide microwave devices. He is a fellow of the IEEE and has served as editor of the *IEEE Transactions on Electron Devices*. He also served on the Board of Trustees for the Georgia Tech Research Corporation (1983-1993).

ALBERT M. ERISMAN is director of Mathematics and Computing Technology for the Phantom Works within the Boeing Company. He leads a staff of 250 computer scientists, mathematicians, statisticians, and engineers who provide leadership for Boeing in all areas of information technology and mathematics. Dr. Erisman has been with Boeing since 1969. His work has been in mathematical algorithms, mathematical software, and the application of these technical areas to the improvement of Boeing engineering and analysis codes. More recently he addressed the broader area of the application of advanced information technology to the transformation of business processes. Management focus has included the linking of research and development with business requirements, the delivery of technology for business benefit, and the management of an innovative environment. Dr. Erisman has published two books and more than 20 technical papers. In December 1989, he was named one of 11 inaugural technical fellows of the Boeing Company. The technical fellowship was established to recognize professional excellence among engineers and scientists who have made significant technical contributions to Boeing. He was a member of the National Research Council's Committee on Supercomputing, a member of a National Science Foundation panel to assess the state of mathematics education and research, and has held various offices in the Society for Industrial and Applied Mathematics. Dr. Erisman earned a B.A. in mathematics from Northern Illinois University in 1962 and both his M.S. and Ph.D. degrees in applied mathematics from Iowa State University in 1967 and 1969, respectively.

DANIEL T. LING is vice president of Microsoft Research, Redmond. He joined Microsoft Research in March 1992 as a senior researcher in the area of user interfaces and computer graphics. He has been particularly interested in the design of agent-based user interfaces, user interface architectures, intelligent and adaptive interfaces, and virtual worlds. He was later named director of research. Before to joining Microsoft, Dr. Ling was a senior manager at the IBM Thomas J. Watson Research Center. He initially worked on special-purpose VLSI chips for displays and was a coinventor of the video-RAM dynamic memory. He subsequently managed departments that conducted research on advanced microsystems based on 370 and RISC architectures and the associated systems and VLSI design tools. One of these departments initiated work on a novel machine architecture, organization, and design known as America, which led to the IBM RS/6000 workstations. He subsequently managed the Veridical User Environments department that engaged in research into innovative user interfaces including multimodal interfaces, virtual worlds technology, and 3D visualization. Dr. Ling also served on the staff of the director of development in the General Technology Division overseeing the development of CMOS chip technologies and on special assignment to the vice president of systems research. He received his B.S., M.S., and Ph.D. degrees in electrical engineering from Stanford University. He was also a Fannie and John Hertz Foundation fellow. Dr. Ling holds seven patents and is the author of a variety of publications in solid state physics, systems, user interfaces, and holography. He was awarded an IBM Outstanding Innovation Award in 1986 for his coinvention of the video-RAM. He is a member of the Institute of Electrical and Electronics Engineers, the American Physical Society, and the Association for Computing Machinery. He also serves on advisory committees for the University of Washington and the University of California at Berkeley.

ROBERT L. MARTIN is the chief technology officer for Lucent Technologies. His expertise has been at Bell Laboratories and Bellcore, where he held a variety of positions related to systems development. He has been responsible for Unix, network management systems, intelligent network systems, packet switching, and broadband access systems developments. Dr. Martin received his B.S. in electrical engineering from Brown University in 1964 and his M.S. and Ph.D. degrees in electrical engineering and computer science from Massachusetts Institute of Technology (MIT) in 1965 and 1967, respectively. In 1985, he attended the MIT Alfred P. Sloan School Senior Executive Program. A fellow of the Institute of Electrical and Electronics Engineers, Inc., Dr. Martin was a member and the first chair of the IEEE's Software Industrial Advisory Board. He has served on the National Research Council's Computer Science and Telecommunications Board and is now a member of the Federal Communication Commission's Technological Advisory Board.

JOEL MOSES is institute professor, professor of engineering systems, and professor of computer science and engineering at Massachusetts Institute of Technology (MIT). He was previously head of the Electrical Engineering and Computer Science Department, dean of engineering, and provost of MIT. He led the development of the MACSYMA system, a forerunner of the major formula manipulation systems available today. He is a co-originator of the concept of knowledge-based systems. His current interests include the organization of large complex systems. Dr. Moses is a fellow of the Institute of Electrical and Electronics Engineers, Inc., and of the American Association for the Advancement of Science and is a member of the National Academy of Engineering (NAE) and the American Academy of Arts and Sciences. He is a former member of the academic advisory committee for SEMATECH, a former member of the White House Office of Science and Technology Policy's committee on High Performance Computing and Communications, a member of NAE's Committee on Engineering Education, a member of the National Research Council's Committee on Workforce Needs in Information Technology, and a former member of its Manufacturing Studies Board and its Board on Telecommunications and Computer Applications. He is a member of the advisory boards of the engineering schools at Columbia University and the University of Michigan. He received a B.A. (1962) and an M.A. (1963) from Columbia University and a Ph.D. (mathematics, 1967) from MIT.

NORINE E. NOONAN is assistant administrator for research and development at the Environmental Protection Agency. She was formerly vice president for research and dean of the graduate school at Florida Institute of Technology and, before that, branch chief for science and space at the Office of Management and Budget. Dr. Noonan also held faculty appointments at the University of Florida and Georgetown University. From 1982 to 1983, she served as an American Chemical Society Congressional Science Fellow. Her areas of expertise are in research management, federal budgetary processes, and science and technology policy. She is a member of Phi Beta Kappa and Sigma Xi, a fellow of the American Association for the Advancement of Science, and a member of the American Society for Cell Biology. She has served on several other National Research Council committees, notably the Committee on Antarctic Policy and Science, the Task Force on Alternative Organizations for the Future of Space Science, and the Committee on Building an Environmental Management Science Program. Dr. Noonan received her B.A. in zoology summa cum laude from the University of Vermont and her M.A. and Ph.D. in cell biology from Princeton University.

DAVID A. PATTERSON holds the E.H. and M.E. Pardee Chair of Computer Science at the University of California at Berkeley and has taught computer architecture since joining the university's faculty in 1977. At Berkeley, he led the design and implementation of RISC I, probably the first VLSI Reduced Instruction Set Computer. This research became the foundation of the SPARC architecture currently used by Fujitsu and Sun Microsystems. As part of the celebration of the twenty-fifth anniversary of the microprocessor in 1996, *Microprocessor Report* and COMDEX named SPARC one of the most significant microprocessors. Professor Patterson was also a leader of the Redundant Arrays of Inexpensive Disks project, which led to high-performance storage systems from many companies. He was also involved in the Network of Workstations project, which led to cluster technology used by Internet companies such as Inktomi. These projects led to three distinguished dissertation awards from the Association for Computing Machinery (ACM). His current research interests are in building novel microprocessors using intelligent DRAM (IRAM) for use in portable multimedia devices and in creating intelligent storage (ISTORE) to provide computers for Internet services that are highly available and easily maintained and that can be gracefully evolved. Dr. Patterson was a chair of the computer science division in the Electrical Engineering and Computer Science Department at the University of California at Berkeley, the ACM Special Interest Group in Computer Architecture, and the Computing Research Association. He has consulted for many companies, including Digital Equipment Corporation, Hewlett Packard, Intel, and

Sun Microsystems, and is also the coauthor of five books. He is a member of the National Academy of Engineering, a fellow of the Computer Society of the Institute of Electrical and Electronics Engineers (IEEE), and a fellow of the ACM. He is also a member of the Computer Science and Telecommunications Board of the National Research Council. His teaching has been honored by the ACM with the Karl V. Karlstrom Outstanding Educator Award, by IEEE with the Undergraduate Teaching Award and the James H. Mulligan, Jr., Education Medal, and by the University of California with the Distinguished Teaching Award and the Diane S. McEntyre Award for Excellence in Teaching. He received the inaugural Outstanding Alumnus Award of the UCLA Computer Science Department as part of its twenty-fifth anniversary and has received the IEEE Technical Achievement Award, the IEEE Reynold B. Johnson Information Storage Award, and the IEEE John von Neumann Medal.

STEWART PERSONICK is the E. Warren Colehower Chair Professor of Telecommunications at Drexel University and director of the Center for Telecommunications and Information Networking, also at Drexel. Until 1998, he was vice president of information networking at Bellcore. He began his career at Bell Laboratories in 1967 and spent 18 years as an individual researcher and an R&D manager focusing on fiber-optics technology and applications. Between 1985 and 1998, he managed organizations focusing on emerging telecommunications technology, systems, services, and applications and was heavily involved in industry and government activities related to the emerging national information infrastructure. Dr. Personick received his B.S. from City College of New York and his Sc.D. degree from MIT. He is a fellow of the Institute of Electrical and Electronics Engineers, Inc., a fellow of the Optical Society of America, and a member of the National Academy of Engineering. He was a member and former chair of the U.S. Federal Networking Council Advisory Committee, is a frequent lecturer on the national information infrastructure and related telecommunications subjects, and is the author of several books and numerous articles on telecommunications technology and applications.

ROBERT SPROULL is vice president and fellow at Sun Microsystems Laboratories and leads its Application Technologies Center. Since his undergraduate days, he has been building hardware and software for computer graphics, such as clipping hardware, an early device-independent graphics package, page description languages, laser printing software, and window systems. He has also been involved in VLSI design, especially of asynchronous circuits and systems. Before joining Sun, he was a principal with Sutherland, Sproull & Associates, an associate professor at

Carnegie Mellon University, and a member of the Xerox Palo Alto Research Center. He is a coauthor with William Newman of the early textbook *Principles of Interactive Computer Graphics* and author of the book *Logical Effort*, which deals with designing fast CMOS circuits. He is a member of the National Academy of Engineering and the U.S. Air Force Scientific Advisory Board.

MARK WEISER (deceased) was the chief technologist at the Xerox Palo Alto Research Center (PARC). He joined Xerox PARC as a member of the technical staff in 1987 and later headed the Computer Science Laboratory. From 1979 to 1987, Dr. Weiser was assistant and associate professor and associate chair in the Computer Science Department at the University of Maryland. He started three companies, and his 75 plus technical publications are in such areas as the psychology of programming, program slicing, operating systems, programming environments, garbage collection, and technological ethics. Dr. Weiser's work since 1988 focused on ubiquitous computing, a program he initiated that envisions personal computers being replaced with invisible computers embedded in everyday objects. He believed that this would lead to an era of calm technology in which technology, rather than causing users to panic, would help them focus on what is really important. Weiser was also the drummer with the rock band Severe Tire Damage, the first live band on the Internet. Dr. Weiser had no bachelor's degree; his Ph.D. was in Computer and Communications Sciences from the University of Michigan (1979).

PATRICK WINDHAM is a consultant on science and technology policy issues. He operates his own firm, Windham Consulting, and also serves as a senior associate with R. Wayne Sayer and Associates, a government relations company. In addition, he is a lecturer in the public policy program at Stanford University. From 1984 until 1997, Mr. Windham served as a senior professional staff member for the Subcommittee on Science, Technology, and Space of the Committee on Commerce, Science, and Transportation of the U.S. Senate. He helped senators oversee and draft legislation for several large civilian science and technology agencies and focused on issues of science, technology, and U.S. industrial competitiveness. From 1976 to 1978 he worked as a congressional fellow with the Senate Commerce Committee, and from 1982 to 1984 he served as a legislative aide in the personal office of Sen. Ernest Hollings. Mr. Windham received an A.B. from Stanford University and a Master's of Public Policy from the University of California at Berkeley.

IRVING WLADAWSKY-BERGER is vice president of technology and strategy for the IBM enterprise systems group. He was formerly general manager of the Internet Division at IBM, where he was responsible for IBM's Internet and e-business strategy and for coordinating its implementation across the company. He joined IBM's Thomas J. Watson Research Center in 1970, where he focused on organizing technology transfer programs to move the innovations of computer science from IBM's research labs into its product divisions. After joining IBM's product development organization in 1985, Dr. Wladawsky-Berger continued his efforts to bring advanced technologies to the marketplace, leading IBM's initiatives in supercomputing and parallel computing, including the transformation of its large systems through the incorporation of parallel computing architectures. He has managed a number of IBM's businesses, including the UNIX-based RS/6000 Division. Dr. Wladawsky-Berger is co-chair of the President's Information Technology Advisory Committee. He was a founding member of the Computer Science and Telecommunications Board of the National Research Council and a member of the NRC's Commission on Physical Sciences, Mathematics, and Applications. Dr. Wladawsky-Berger received his M.S. and Ph.D. degrees in physics from the University of Chicago.

Index